AN INTRODUCTION TO
ECONOMIC REASONING

MARSHALL A. ROBINSON is president of the Russell Sage Foundation. Formerly, he was vice-president of the Ford Foundation, and before that dean of the Graduate School of Business at the University of Pittsburgh and a member of the senior staff of the Brookings Institution.

HERBERT C. MORTON is a senior fellow and director of public affairs at Resources for the Future, in Washington, D.C. He was formerly associate commissioner of the U. S. Bureau of Labor Statistics, director of publications at the Brookings Institution, and assistant professor at the Amos Tuck School of Business Administration at Dartmouth College.

JAMES D. CALDERWOOD is Joseph A. DeBell professor of business economics and international trade in the School of Business Administration at the University of Southern California. In addition to serving as a consultant on economic and educational affairs in a score of countries, he is deeply involved in the economic education movement in the United States and serves as western representative of the Joint Council on Economic Education.

An Introduction to
ECONOMIC REASONING

BY

MARSHALL A. ROBINSON
HERBERT C. MORTON
and
JAMES D. CALDERWOOD

FIFTH REVISED EDITION

Anchor Books
Anchor Press/Doubleday
Garden City, New York
1980

The first, second, third, and fourth editions of *An Introduction to Economic Reasoning* were originally published in hardcover by The Brookings Institution.

The Anchor Books edition is the first publication of the fifth edition.

Anchor Books edition: 1980

ISBN: 0-385-12867-3
Library of Congress Catalog Card Number: 77-82963

FROM THE FOREWORD
TO THE FIRST EDITION

This book on economic reasoning is an introduction to economics for laymen. It is for adults who have a fragmentary knowledge of economic affairs and who seek a framework for more systematic thinking about economic issues. Its purpose is to help the reader explore the meaning of economic events and acquire skills for thinking economic issues through to some conclusion. It is hoped that this treatment will show that economic analysis can assist those who wish to reason for themselves and can help them reach independent judgments respecting economic matters.

The book was originally prepared for the use of adult discussion groups. The topics covered and the length of the volume were dictated by the needs of these groups. In an effort to help them, the authors have attempted to strip economic analysis to its bare essentials. They do not wish to make economic analysis appear easier than it is. But they do believe that laymen with varied backgrounds and experience, who are far removed from college courses and have many demands on their time, need a way to get started on the subject —a way to get into it. They hope that this book will serve to encourage further study.

It is a *way of thinking* about economic issues rather than a full review of economics that is introduced here. The purpose is to show how to examine an economic question, rather than to display the warehouse of economic knowledge that experts might apply. Thus the approach is to present the essentials of fact and formal definition, and to hurry the reader on to a consideration of selected problems on which he may exercise his powers of analysis.

With each chapter there are suggestions for additional reading. The materials selected have been chosen for the purpose of helping the reader expand his general background. Therefore those interested in detailed analysis of specific problems will want to look beyond the selections listed. In the belief that an extensive bibliography frequently tends to discourage beginners by forcing them to make premature choices of what to read, these lists have been kept to a minimum. It is hoped, however, that with this beginning, readers will obtain the skill needed to select and read additional economic literature.

The authors and the Brookings Institution are grateful to many members of the economics profession and to the leaders and participants of test groups who generously provided suggestions for the improvement of the book. A special debt is owed to the following people who read and criticized an early draft of the volume: Sumner H. Slichter, G. L. Bach, Horace Taylor, R. A. Gordon, Arthur Upgren, Walter Salant, John G. Gurley, L. H. Kimmel, and Sylvia Stone. The authors' view of the requirements of this type of book prevented them from accepting some of the suggestions that were offered; thus the authors alone are responsible for the final result. . . .

The suggestion that a volume of this sort be written came originally from Mr. C. Scott Fletcher of the Fund for Adult Education. The President of the Brookings Institution proposed the approach followed in this treatment. The Institution is indebted to the Fund for Adult Education for providing financial support for this project. To the authors who have labored to prepare this introduction to economic reasoning, the Institution is especially grateful.

Robert D. Calkins
President, Brookings Institution

January 1, 1956

PREFACE TO THE FIFTH EDITION

Nearly twenty-five years have passed since the first edition of this book was published. During its first dozen years, the book went through four editions and was translated into thirteen languages (Arabic, Spanish, French, Swedish, Dutch, Portuguese, Farsi, Japanese, Korean, and four languages of India: Marathi, Hindi, Bengali, and Gujarati; another foreign edition, with a special supplement on the Australian economy, was published in Australia. About two hundred thousand copies of the American edition were sold, and the book continued to be used in college and high school courses long after many parts of it were out of date, because it offered a distinctive approach that appealed to teachers and students.

What encouraged us to undertake this revision after such a long lapse was the recent publication by the Joint Council on Economic Education of *A Framework for Teaching Economics: Basic Concepts.* This report builds on the approach set forth in *An Introduction to Economic Reasoning* and develops it into a very useful teaching tool. Because of the widespread attention given to the Joint Council's report, the case for updating the book seemed persuasive.

In preparing the fifth edition, we have stuck to the basic notion of the earlier editions: to present "a way of thinking about economic issues rather than a full review of economics," and we have also retained the original chapter structure. Some chapters, such as the Introduction, are virtually unchanged, except for the problem. Others, like the chapter on "Economic Growth," which was revised to explore the interrelationships of economic growth, energy, and the environment, have been substantially reshaped. Inflation gets considerably more attention in the chapter formerly titled "Prosperity and Depression," now retitled "Inflation and Recession."

The Brookings Institution, which sponsored and published the first edition of this book, is in no way responsible for the fifth edition. Though much of the original volume has been retained, the extensive revisions contained in this new edition have been neither planned nor reviewed with the Brookings staff.

In presenting this new edition, we acknowledge our great debt to the Brookings Institution's former president, Robert D. Calkins. He designed the basic approach, offered encouragement, and kept us on track with wise and rigorous reviews of the manuscript for the first edition.

Marshall A. Robinson, who assumed principal responsibility for the first edition, served as reader and critic for this revision. Enough remains of his original contribution to warrant retention of his name at the head of the list of authors, though we absolve him of blame for any errors that we have unwittingly introduced.

Finally, we want to thank the editors at Anchor Books for their patience and support.

James D. Calderwood
Herbert C. Morton

March 1979

CONTENTS

Chapter 1

PROBLEMS AND GOALS

Economic problems are everybody's business because they are part of everybody's life. We read in our newspapers about taxes, foreign aid, strikes, welfare programs, poverty and unemployment, inflation, urban renewal, energy, Medicare, the environment, the balance of payments, the national debt, and many other things. We read of economic problems confronting the community, the state, the nation, and the world. We are urged to vote, to serve on committees, and to be for or against particular proposals that affect economic life. In fact, we are overwhelmed by information, interpretations, appeals, arguments, and advice.

To form opinions on current issues and to make judgments on public problems under these conditions, we all need the help of economic analysis. We need methods by which explanations may be found and alternative courses of action may be evaluated. This is what a study of economics can provide. Economics does not offer ready-made explanations and solutions. Instead, it offers tools and methods for the analysis of economic problems. It leaves to the individual the task of applying these tools and methods to the problems he or she wishes to solve.

This book presents a method of analyzing economic problems. It does not cover the entire subject of economics, but deals only with certain aspects of our own economy. It stresses problems of economic policy and explores them in terms of their effects on the growth and stability of our economy and their effects on the structure of our economic system. It concentrates on such problems and their background in order to show how economic analysis can help the citizen.

WHAT IS ECONOMICS ABOUT?

Economics is generally described as the study of how society produces and distributes the goods and services it wants. More specifically, it examines the activities that people carry on—producing, saving, spending, paying taxes, and so on—for the purpose of satisfying their basic wants for food and shelter, their added wants for modern conveniences and comforts, and their collective wants for such things as national defense and education.

Economics also includes the study of the various ways in which people organize economic life in order to satisfy their wants. These economic systems include not only the American one but also communism, socialism, and such tradition-oriented societies as the peasant villages of rural India and the tribal arrangements of the Amazonian Indians. An economic system can be described as a collection of institutions (such as banks or labor unions), laws, activities, social values, and personal motivations which together govern economic decision-making.

Every society needs an economic system, because the things people want are not provided free by nature. Goods and services must be produced, and the means of production —natural resources, human labor, machines, and other forms of capital—are scarce in relation to the demand for them. Therefore, people cannot have everything they want. They have to make *choices.* They have to decide what to produce now and what to produce later, how to use their scarce resources most efficiently, and how to distribute goods and services among the people. They must also consider whether these choices are to be made by the government, by the free price system, or by a mixture of both.

As a first step to understanding how these choices are made in our society, let us look at our objectives. What do we want our economy to do? What do we want it to be?

THE GOALS OF OUR ECONOMY

The goals of a free society are determined by its people.
American citizens are free, within wide limits, to direct their
economic affairs so as to serve their personal and social interests. They may save, join a union, buy a car, run a store, and
make a variety of other voluntary decisions. Political democracy also gives them a voice in determining the role that
government shall play. They may vote for or against a school
bond issue. Indirectly, they may influence governmental policies by electing representatives who pass legislation on taxes,
foreign aid, control of utilities, the size of the public debt,
and other governmental activities. Thus a predominantly free
economy and a democratic government give American citizens freedom to determine their personal economic goals and
the broader goals that society shall pursue.

Some of these goals are objectives of particular groups;
some are objectives for the whole society; and some are objectives that conflict with others. Some are transitory objectives designed to deal with particular problems without reference to the long-run goals of the public.

A few of the more familiar economic objectives are shown
in the following list.

Stable prices
Full employment
Market freedom

Freer trade among nations
Protection from the competition of foreign producers
Closer economic ties with our allies

Protection of the environment
Increased energy supplies
Freedom from government restrictions

More aid to the poor, the sick, and the aged
Lower taxes
Increased business investment

Co-operation among economic groups
Increased competition

The full meaning of all these objectives may not be clear at this point, but the list will give an indication of the diverse and often conflicting objectives of the American people. How do we go about reconciling such divergent interests? Are there trade-off points among them on which most people can agree? We shall offer only a tentative answer to these questions at this point. We may begin by looking for a common goal that seems to underlie all the individual and group objectives stated above. What is the broadest economic goal on which we can all agree?

Traditionally, the broad economic objective of the American people has been the achievement of high and rising levels of income and consumption under conditions that afford opportunity for individual advancement and free choice. Of course, we could debate whether having more goods and services will bring greater happiness or greater welfare, but in economics the amount of goods and services produced and consumed has generally been regarded as one suitable measure of economic welfare. This does not mean that economists believe that material goals are more important than other—moral, spiritual, or cultural—goals. But they usually proceed on the assumption that each of us is the best judge of what will best serve his or her own welfare. They assume that our actions indicate how we seek our goals.

In general, therefore, the economist assumes that income and consumption can be used as the principal measure of economic welfare because people have shown that they are willing to use their effort and ingenuity to produce things for their material satisfaction. But in every society there are economic, cultural, and moral limits to people's desires for more income and consumption.

In recent years an increasing number of people have come to believe that economic growth must be consistent with other, more "social" goals, such as an improved quality of life, a cleaner environment, safer working conditions, and equal employment opportunities for women and minorities. These "new priorities" are having a significant effect on the functioning of our economic system and on the achievement of our goals. In addition, what we do to achieve today's economic goals—more wealth for those now living, for example—must be consistent with the preservation of resources for the use of future generations. In this book, however, we shall concentrate on the economic conditions of welfare, leaving to others the larger task of defining what constitutes "the good life."

Greater income and consumption are only the first ingredients of "economic welfare." A number of other requirements must eventually be added to arrive at a full definition of this goal.

How are goods and services to be shared by the people of a society? Is an equitable distribution of income (however that may be defined) a goal of our society?

A complete definition of economic welfare must also include some concept of how much people should work. Should people have to work six or eight or fourteen hours a day? How important is leisure? Should everyone, including children and the aged, have to work, or should certain groups receive income without working?

The definition of economic welfare must also include some notion of what kinds of goods and services should be produced. Are some goods and services better than others? If so, which? Should the production of some goods (for example, saccharin) be prohibited? If so, which? The pattern of production will also be influenced by the relative importance of other goals, such as better health or a cleaner environment.

The decisions involved in defining "economic welfare" are the basic economic decisions confronting every society. What goods and services should we produce and how should we produce and distribute them so that we will get the maximum yield from our efforts? In the Soviet Union or in Italy (or in any other country) these decisions are made differently than in the United States. And in the United States they are made differently today than they were a century ago or even thirty years ago. The reasons for these differences will be explored in subsequent chapters. Now, however, it will be useful to obtain a general idea of how these decisions are made in the United States at the present time.

HOW DOES OUR ECONOMY PURSUE ITS GOALS?

One of the important characteristics of the American economy is its strong reliance on individual economic decisions. For this reason it is frequently given the name "private enterprise system." This term implies that individuals can usually choose their way of earning a living; they can save or consume as they see fit; and they can pursue their personal goals even when they do not conform with those of society as a whole, as long as they do not unduly hinder important social goals or the freedom of others.

How this unplanned and unregulated economy might function successfully was first explored systematically more than 200 years ago by a Scottish philosopher, Adam Smith. In his *Wealth of Nations,* Smith argued that most people are primarily concerned with their own interests (that is, they want things for themselves, their families, or their communities). He also noted that if people will specialize in their work and exchange the fruits of their labor with one another, everyone will be better off. He argued that the individual could best help himself by producing the things that other people want. Thus with individuals free to show what they want by the prices they are willing to pay, producers would tend to supply the things demanded by the public. Free competition, together with a price system that reflected the desires of consumers and the capabilities of producers, would, he argued, bring order and efficiency to an economic system.

Smith recognized that a free economy needs "rules of the game"—and the government must be the umpire. When individuals combine forces to get the better of someone else, or when other private restraints are put on individual competition, the self-interest of one individual may actually harm the rest of society. Hence he argued that one of the necessary functions of the government in a private enterprise system is to control restraints on competition. With the passage of time, these and other "rules" have multiplied; they have multiplied because the economy today is much more complicated than it was in the time of Adam Smith.

As the American economy has grown, each part has become more dependent on the functioning of the other parts. Consider, for instance, the number of people and the variety of occupations that are required to keep the average city worker on the job. City workers are far more dependent than their forefathers on a smoothly functioning economic system; indeed, their lives depend on it.

Understandably, then, additional "rules" have been developed to meet the needs of this interdependent society. For example, government now attempts to moderate the business cycles that throw men and women out of work in depressions or destroy their savings during periods of inflation. It also tries to reduce the insecurity of individuals by such devices as insuring depositors against bank failures, providing unemployment benefits for jobless workers, and paying old-age pensions to retired workers. In all these activities the American people have used the government as a means of improving the performance of their economic system.

Governmental intervention is also frequently necessary because certain types of economic activity cannot be carried out by individuals operating on their own initiative. The armed forces, for example, cannot be operated as a private business. Highways, water supplies, sanitation, police protection, and many other economic services require government action. All of these services reflect essential collective wants that for one reason or another cannot readily be satisfied by "private enterprise."

The powers of the government are used to modify the workings of a private enterprise system in many ways. By tariffs the government tries to protect certain producers and workers from the effects of competition from abroad; by subsidies it encourages the production of a variety of minerals and farm and industrial products. It taxes the rich more heavily than the poor; and it even passes laws that help prevent one firm from selling a product at a lower price than another.

In view of all this governmental activity, the American

economy can hardly be called a wholly "private enterprise system." Perhaps a better term is a "mixed economy"—a system based on a combination of private and governmental economic decisions. Individual decisions in the free market still play a major role in determining what things will be produced and how they will be produced and distributed, but the effects of individual actions are modified in a number of ways by the government.

Thus the American people pursue their economic goals by both individual and collective action. Their personal decisions, the decisions of "special interest" groups, and the decisions of their government have an impact on the welfare of everyone. To prepare the way for increased understanding of the importance of these economic decisions, the rest of this chapter will explore some of the problems involved in economic reasoning.

REQUIREMENTS IN ECONOMIC REASONING

In analyzing economic problems, we need to keep three basic requirements in mind. It is important (1) to use language carefully; (2) to abide by the ordinary rules of logic; and (3) to understand the tools of the economist and to use them as they are intended to be used.

Effective communication requires that words should convey the meaning intended. They should mean the same thing to the speaker and to the listener, to the writer and to the reader. Such abstractions as democracy, capitalism, and welfare are especially open to misinterpretation. Obviously, such abstractions are occasionally necessary (this chapter, for instance, has many more than the others), but they should be discussed and defined when they are used.

In economics a good deal of confusion also arises because many everyday terms are used in a technical sense. Thus in common usage, "production" means growing or making something tangible, such as potatoes or automobiles. But to the economist, production has a broader meaning. It means satisfying the wants of others. The manager of an automobile factory, the assembly-line worker, the writer of automobile advertisements, the salesman—all are producers. Those who provide a service that commands a price and fulfills a need, such as the physician and the teacher, are also engaged in production.

Two other terms that cause confusion are "capital" and "investment." To the layman, "capital" usually means the funds awaiting investment or the stocks, bonds, and real estate a person owns. But to the economist, "capital" also denotes the tools, machines, factories, and other goods used to produce commodities. "Investment" is popularly used to mean the purchase of stocks, bonds, and real estate or other property yielding an income. But to the economist, it generally means the expenditure of funds on new equipment and other goods used in production. It is, in other words, part of the process of creating "capital."

Other economic terms have several meanings. For instance, it is unusual to find a group of people (even economists) who define "money" in the same manner. All of them may offer reasonable definitions but, because each is stressing certain aspects, the definitions differ. "Competition," "depression," "demand," and "income" are additional words that will need to be defined when they are to be used in careful analysis.

The solution of economic problems requires adherence to principles of logical thinking. These rules cannot be reviewed here in detail as they would be in a book on logic. But warnings can be stated against several types of error that frequently creep into ordinary discussion.

First is the fallacy that if one thing precedes another (even if the first thing always precedes the second) that the first is the cause of the second. The error is clearly illustrated in the sequence of day following night. Day does not cause night, or vice versa. Both result from the workings of the solar system.

Second is the error of thinking that a single factor causes a given result, when, in fact, a combination of factors may be responsible. For example, many people have had the mistaken idea that wage increases are the sole cause of inflation. In fact, a variety of influences may be involved, including the easy availability of bank credit, increased government spending, and shortages of important commodities, to mention a few.

Third is the fallacy of supposing the whole to be like the parts with which one is familiar. For example, it is a common error to suppose that government finance operates on the same principles as household finance, whereas government finance is really quite different. The government, with its power to tax and its power to borrow, can increase its income more easily than individuals or businesses.

Fourth is the fallacy that if things have happened in a given sequence in the past, they will happen that way again. This notion led many people to expect a collapse in prices shortly after the Second World War.

Fifth is the error of wishful thinking—seeing what one wants to see and believing what one wants to believe. This was the prevailing mood before the great stock market crash of 1929.

Another fallacy, which is not limited to discussions of economics by any means, may be called "personification" of a problem; that is, identifying a very complicated situation with a prominent person. The identification of President Herbert Hoover with the depression of the 1930s, as though he caused it, is a famous historical example of personification. This form of oversimplifying complex economic and political forces is a way of expressing emotions, but it adds little to the understanding of the issues involved.

A reasoned solution of problems also requires an attitude of detachment and objectivity. We must be able to accept logical results and not blind ourselves to them because we dislike them. "The first active deed of thinking," said Albert Schweitzer, "is resignation—acquiescence in what happens."[1] Objectivity, of course, is a term that is universally approved but only rarely defined. It implies that we are able to free ourselves from preconceptions that would otherwise prejudice our analysis and our conclusions. It is important that we understand the nature of some of the most common types of preconceptions.

[1] "Religion and Modern Civilization," *The Christian Century*, Vol. 51 (1934), p. 1520.

Many preconceptions stem from one's personal interests and from one's environment. For example, business executives who fear foreign competition naturally find it difficult to think objectively about tariff reduction. They may have to struggle to be objective about a revision of trade regulations and to view the problem in terms of larger foreign policy objectives. Similarly, workers who want higher wages find it difficult to be objective about the possible inflationary consequences of a wage increase.

Other preconceptions arise out of past experience. Once we have adjusted our thinking to the times, we are inclined to continue thinking the same way long after the circumstances have changed and new patterns of thought are required. For example, we can neither understand nor deal with government today by employing the accepted views of a generation ago. Instead of bringing our ideas up to date, too often we attempt to escape from the problems of the present by seeking refuge in an idealized past.

Reasoning about economic problems frequently requires the use and understanding of statistics. Many problems can be more accurately appraised by reference to figures on wages, prices, employment, production, and a host of other economic factors. But statistical evidence must be used with care. It is useful only if we know what the statistics measure. For instance, what does it mean to say that the "average" gross national product of the thirteen countries of South America in 1976 was $20.8 billion? It certainly means something different from the "median" gross national product, which was $5.1 billion. The "average" is obtained by adding up the gross national products of all thirteen countries and dividing this total by thirteen. Thus a few large gross national products (Brazil with $143 billion, Argentina with $40.7 billion, and Venezuela with $31.3 billion) pull up the average quite a bit. The median (or halfway) figure shows that half the countries had larger and half had smaller gross national products than Ecuador's gross national product of $5.1 billion. The difference is important and must be understood if the figures are to be used correctly.

This book cannot examine all the danger points in statistics, nor can it provide a list of "acceptable" sources of statistics. It can only urge beginning students to make sure they know what their statistics mean. If they do not, they would do better to avoid them.

Another tool of economic analysis is sometimes called "model building." It involves the use of assumptions to simplify the analysis of a complicated situation. Rather than attempting to consider all factors at once, analysts may set up a hypothetical "model" that enables them to consider various possibilities, one at a time. To take a simple model, let us consider the question: Will the sales of a particular make of new car increase if its price is reduced by five hundred dollars?

Offhand, most people would say yes; but their answer is based on a "model"—even though they do not say so explicitly. In other words, their conclusion probably rests on the assumption that other things do not offset the effect of the price cut. It assumes, for example, that the incomes of potential buyers do not decline. If wages and salaries fall, sales may stay the same or even decline. It also assumes that sellers of other automobiles do not reduce the prices of their cars. Again it assumes that tastes do not change. If tastes change, consumers may prefer to use a different kind of car.

In other words, in order to state the effect of a price cut on sales, we have to consider the possible changes in various other factors that can influence sales. "Model building" is simply the procedure of thinking through the effects of such influences in various combinations.

Some of the more intricate forms of model building depend on a number of assumptions. These assumptions are chosen either to approximate the conditions actually expected in a given problem, or to see what the consequences might be in a special situation. As a great deal of economic analysis utilizes such models, let us attempt to clarify the procedure.

The use of models in economic analysis is similar to the sort of thinking we do all the time. For example, a man may decide to go to the beach on Sunday *assuming* four things work out the way he expects: (1) the weather is sunny; (2) the car is running properly; (3) his wife wants to go; and (4) he does not have to work at home over the weekend.

There are other assumptions he has not put into his model because they seem less likely or less important; however, he is aware of them. For example, on the chance that his relatives may come for a visit that day, he tells his wife to have refreshments on hand. Thus he prepares for other possibilities, including the possibility that his assumptions will not be borne out.

It is also worth noting that in this illustration the man will probably not only announce the conclusion of his theoretical analysis ("we go to the beach Sunday") but he will also *state his assumptions*. If he fails to do so, he may be misunderstood. In other words, the "model builder" must explain both his conclusions and his assumptions.

The dangers in using models as aids to thinking are that some important conditions may be left out, or that a simplified "model" may be inappropriately applied to a complex situation. There is a familiar comment that "it is all right in theory but it won't work in practice." Yet if the theory follows sound logic and is applied where the model fits, it *will* work in practice. If it is logical, but is misapplied and therefore does not work in practice, the theory can still be valid for other occasions.

When economic theory is used in a changing world, a number of alternative "models" must be considered to fit the conditions that may occur. If, for example, we want to estimate the consequence of an increase in income taxes, it will be advisable to explore the results under several possible conditions. Such conditions might include: (1) gradual economic growth with falling unemployment and price stability (as in 1961–65); (2) gradual economic growth with falling unemployment and inflation (as in 1975–78); (3) a recession with high unemployment and price stability (as in 1960–61); (4) a recession with high unemployment and high inflation (as in 1974–75); and (5) prosperity with full employment and inflation (as in 1966–69).

Each condition, or assumption, will lead to different results because the effects of a tax increase are contingent on whether economic stability, depression, or inflation actually prevails. The analyst, therefore, justifiably says that the result will be one thing if one condition prevails and another if another condition prevails. His answers specify that *if* so and so occurs, *then* such and such will probably result.

Allowance must also be made for different results at different times. Because there are several stages of action and reaction in economic conditions, the economist must reckon with time in his analysis. A decline in milk production may lead first to higher prices for dairy products, then to higher prices for substitute products, later to an increase in milk production, and perhaps ultimately to a return of prices to their earlier level. Thus we must distinguish between the immediate—the "short-run"—and the "long-run" consequences of an event.

Clear and logical thinking helps us to make better decisions. The ability to apply the rules for clear thinking and the ability to use relevant information are basic requirements. Only if we master the use of simplified assumptions and learn to follow economic changes through to their many possible consequences can we arrive at useful conclusions for the conduct of economic affairs.

One of the major obstacles to economic understanding is the difficulty of sifting the volume of economic facts for those that will aid in the solution of a problem. It is important, therefore, to develop a systematic approach to the analysis of problems. Accordingly, the following sections illustrate an approach that may be used to analyze the two principal types of problems that confront the economist. The first is a problem that requires explanation, and the second is a problem that requires a decision.

EXPLAINING AN ECONOMIC EVENT

To explain an economic event is to answer the questions: What is it? Why is it? What of it? Suppose we try to explain a 5 per cent rise in prices as shown by the consumer price index. We want to know what happened, why, and what consequences may be expected.[2]

---

[2] This price index is an average of the prices of many items, expressed as a percentage of some "base period." For instance, if we decide that the average of the prices consumers paid in the

First, we try to *identify* the type of price increase that has occurred. Have all prices risen or only a few? Was the rise rapid or gradual? Did wages also rise? In other words, we try to determine the distinguishing characteristics of the price increase.

Second, we *look for causes,* by drawing on available information and economic theory for clues. If we observe that only the price of foodstuffs has increased, we look for changes in conditions that may have influenced the supply and demand for foodstuffs. We do so because experience tells us that a decrease in supply or an increase in demand, or both, tends to increase prices. Thus we might look for the causes in a possible crop failure, bad weather, strikes in food processing industries, changes in consumer demand, or comparable factors.

If, however, we observe that prices of clothing, furniture, and most consumer goods are also rising, we look for changes in conditions that affect the whole price structure: an increase in government spending or an increase in the money supply, for example. We do so because economic analysis tells us that an increase in total spending in the economy without a comparable increase in the supply of goods tends to increase prices. These, of course, are but a few of the possible causal factors. Many alternatives must be examined to attempt to discover why the event occurred.

Third, we *explore the possible implications* of the event. Although we can never know definitely what will occur in the future, it is important to figure out what is possible, and what is probable; a bare description of an economic event is seldom useful. Are prices likely to continue rising, to level off, or to decline? Will the price increase result in fewer sales and decreased production? The implications for future prices, production, and employment are what give the price increase its greatest significance. We try to determine the implications or potentialities of an event by reasoning out what could follow from it under various conditions. We look for historical precedents. Does past experience with inflation suggest any

"base period" 1967 will be labeled 100, then a 5 per cent rise from that period will cause the index to rise to 105.

clues? We also make assumptions for purposes of analysis that certain conditions may or may not prevail—that the economy will be in a boom or a depression, that war or peace will prevail, that production will expand or shrink with rising prices. Under each of these sets of assumptions about future conditions, we reason through the possible consequences of the price rise under study.

There are therefore three steps in explaining an economic event:

1. *Identify the event by describing it and by comparing it with other events that are similar and familiar.*

2. *Explore the factors that may have caused the event.*

3. *Try to discover the implications of the event by considering what the consequences might be under various circumstances.*

MAKING ECONOMIC DECISIONS

Decision-making requires the consideration of alternatives. Personal decision-making (such as buying a car or home), business decision-making (such as setting production levels or sales policies), and public policy decision-making (such as raising taxes) all require the same basic method of analysis. They require an examination of alternative policies or courses of action for achieving goals. They require the making of choices. And they require an evaluation of the trade-offs that are necessary when goals conflict.

We can illustrate in simplified form the main steps in the analysis of an economic problem by considering the current energy situation, including the higher prices resulting from actions taken in recent years both within the United States and by a foreign oil cartel.

1. Identify the Problem and Define the Issues.

The use of oil in the world has been increasing rapidly over the years. Its supply is limited and it is likely to become increasingly expensive in the years ahead. The main oil-producing countries have formed a cartel (the Organization of Petroleum Exporting Countries, or OPEC) so that they can act together to control production and prices. Since

1973, OPEC has raised crude oil prices more than eightfold.

The consequences for the United States (and for many other countries) have been as follows. First, the oil price rise contributed to a deepening of the recession of 1974–75. It did this by transferring income from Americans to foreign oil producers, who did not spend all of it within the United States. Second, the rise in oil prices contributed to the sharply higher inflation experienced in 1974 by exerting an upward pressure on costs of production. Third, the oil price rise helped produce a deficit in the nation's foreign trade balance—an excess of imports over exports.

2. Identify the Objectives.

The over-all objective of national policy is to have an adequate supply of energy at reasonable prices so that our economy may continue to grow and we will not be at the mercy of foreign producers. More specifically, our *short-run* objective is to economize in the consumption of scarce oil and gas, while our *long-run* objective is to develop new energy technologies, such as coal gasification and solar energy, which can eventually take the place of oil and natural gas when our supply of these is exhausted.

At the same time, however, the nation has certain other objectives which tend to conflict with the ones just mentioned. People want to preserve the environment, for example, and this may be hard to reconcile with increased offshore oil drilling and with increased strip-mining of coal, both of which may help alleviate the oil shortage. Also, many feel that oil and gas prices should be prevented from rising further in order to protect the interests of consumers, particularly those with low incomes. But protecting consumers may conflict with the desire to have higher prices to discourage consumption and encourage production. Finally, freedom from government controls is highly prized by many persons, particularly those in business. But more government action may conceivably be necessary to solve the energy problem.

Clearly, the nation has multiple goals, and the problem of reconciling conflicts among them in order to arrive at acceptable trade-off points is a difficult one.

3. Pose and Analyze the Alternative Courses of Action.

Seldom is there only one way of dealing with a problem. It is important, therefore, to identify a number of alternative approaches and to consider the possible consequences of each one. In the case of energy, as we have seen, two major issues face the nation, with each one embracing a series of subissues. The two major issues are (1) how should the scarce supply of oil and natural gas be divided among the consumers and industries that want it and (2) what can be done in the long run to develop new supplies of energy, make the nation less dependent on the foreign cartel, and eventually give us a replacement for oil and gas when supplies of these are exhausted?

Several alternatives present themselves. We could allocate the scarce supply by removing the price controls that now keep down the price of oil and natural gas in the United States and letting the forces of supply and demand in the market place push the price up even further. Higher prices would persuade people to consume less—for example, to drive less and keep their thermostats down.

A second approach would be for the government to raise prices by imposing higher taxes on gasoline and other oil products. Gasoline in Europe, for example, costs two or three times what it does in the United States, because of higher taxes. This curbs use.

A third approach would be for the government to reduce imports from abroad—perhaps by a quota system—and institute formal rationing in the United States, with consumers receiving ration stamps or allotments that would entitle them to a certain number of gallons of gasoline per week or month.

A fourth approach would be for the government to cut energy consumption by requiring better insulation of houses and the manufacture of lighter cars with better mileage, and by other energy-saving measures.

As for developing new energy supplies, one way would be to let the price of oil and natural gas rise. If these products were deregulated, their price would rise and presumably this would encourage producers to explore for and develop new sources of supply. A second approach would be to relax environmental controls, which at present restrict strip-mining, offshore oil drilling, and the building of new nuclear power stations. A third approach would be for the government to subsidize private business, either through direct money payments or through tax concessions or by restricting imports from abroad, to get them to develop new technologies such as shale oil or solar energy. A fourth approach would be for the government to go into the energy business itself and use tax money to build solar energy installations, nuclear reactors, and coal gasification plants.

4. Appraise the Alternatives and Decide.

All these alternative approaches need to be evaluated against the various economic goals of our society. Fundamental here is a recognition of the fact that each alternative involves costs as well as benefits, that we cannot achieve 100 per cent of all our goals simultaneously, and that trade-offs must be made. For example, allowing oil prices to rise raises questions of fairness. Would not the oil go to the rich, who could afford to pay the higher price, and be denied to the poor, who could not?

If the price of gasoline were raised by the imposition of a tax of, say, 50 cents per gallon, would not the removal of billions of dollars of purchasing power from the economy so depress aggregate demand that a recession might occur? This consequence might be avoided by cuts in other kinds of taxes or by a system of rebates to the public. But this could have a significant influence on the distribution of income in the nation.

The imposition of coupon rationing would raise questions of administrative efficiency. Experiences with coupon rationing in the past—during World War II, for example—suggest that it often leads to the creation of a large and inefficient government bureaucracy and also to illegal black markets.

Stimulating the development of new energy supplies by allowing oil and natural gas prices to rise also raises difficult questions. Would not the producers make excess profits? Would they invest these profits in new production, or possibly in more profitable non-energy enterprises? Would the government tax such profits? If on the other hand we try to encourage new energy production by relaxing environmental controls, will not society pay a high price through increased air and water pollution? But if we allow environmental considerations to obstruct energy production, will we not pay a high price through slower economic growth and lost jobs?

Even a brief look at the complex energy issue shows the importance of identifying the problem and our objectives, of posing the alternatives, and of evaluating each alternative carefully in the light of one's personal values and of society's goals. It is impossible to achieve all the varied goals of American society. Thus trade-offs must be made—something has to be given up here in order to gain more there. The essence of economic reasoning is thinking one's way through an issue in the way just described, so as to reach a rational conclusion that on balance is satisfactory.

To summarize, the foregoing steps are:

1. *Identify the problem and clarify the issues by studying their background and origin.*

2. *Identify the objectives and requirements that must be met in treating the problem.*

3. *Pose the alternative courses of action and analyze their consequences.*

4. *Appraise the alternatives and decide by determining how well each alternative fulfills the objectives and requirements.*

This chapter has stressed the following ideas:

1. Every society contains a variety of individuals and groups with divergent goals. Because economic resources are scarce in relation to wants, each society must, therefore, devise a way to select the goals it will pursue. In the American economy this selection is made by a combination of individual and group decisions. The study of economics is largely devoted to the implications of these decisions.

2. The beginning study of economics does not require an extensive vocabulary as long as students will make sure the terms they are using are clear to them and to others. Poor use of logic and the careless use of assumptions are by far the greatest handicaps to an understanding of economic affairs. Because our economy is a complex, interdependent system, it

is important to go beyond superficial or fragmentary information to get a complete answer to an economic question.

3. In dealing with questions of economic policy (deciding what to do) it is important to take the time to decide what we *want* to accomplish. Then, by analyzing the consequences of various plans of action, we can make a reasoned decision on what we should do. Skill in "analyzing the consequences" is, for the most part, the major benefit of studying economics.

Suggested Reading

Paul A. Samuelson, *Economics*, 10th ed. (New York: McGraw-Hill, 1976), Chap. 1, pp. 1–16. George Leland Bach, *Economics: An Introduction to Analysis and Policy*, 9th ed. (Englewood Cliffs, N.J.: Prentice-Hall, 1977), Chap. 1 and 3. These readings discuss what economics is all about and some of the problems in thinking about economic affairs. Further references to these two standard textbooks appear at the end of most of the chapters that follow. A third book is also frequently cited: *Readings in Economics*, by Paul A. Samuelson, 7th ed. (New York: McGraw-Hill, 1973).

G. L. Bach, James D. Calderwood, W. Lee Hansen, and Phillip Saunders, *A Framework for Teaching Economics: Basic Concepts* (New York: Joint Council on Economic Education, 1977). This booklet spells out what it means to be economically literate today. It analyzes the structure of the discipline of economics, identifying the basic concepts that people should understand if they are to think about economic issues in a reasoned way and showing how they can be used as an aid to decision-making. The booklet presents in summary form the approach that *Introduction to Economic Reasoning* previously spelled out in more detail.

Chapter 2

THE ECONOMY AND ITS INCOME

No Jack-of-all-trades could possibly produce for himself the extraordinary assortment of goods and services that a modern industrial economy puts within his reach. We know this well enough from our own experience. Virtually no one today is entirely self-sufficient. Division of labor and technological progress have made all of us dependent on the energy, skill, and creativity of others.

What may be less apparent is the way all the specialized tasks and diverse economic institutions are co-ordinated. If we have thought about the matter at all, we have probably been puzzled about how things get done in a predominantly free economy. For example, about 100 million Americans are at work producing goods and services for the nation. They are operating over 2.8 million farms, over 8 million business establishments, and about 80,000 governmental units that have an economic as well as governmental role to fulfill. At the beginning of 1979 they were producing goods and services at the rate of $2 trillion per year.

But if we look to see who is calling signals, or who has the master plan, we look in vain. No central authority has told workers where to work or what occupations to choose. No blueprint decreed that movies should be made in Hollywood and steel in Pittsburgh, or that many people should start to consume oleomargarine instead of butter. The millions of cars and trucks that roll off the assembly lines every year are not produced as part of any grand national design. Nevertheless, these things have happened.

How, then, are things co-ordinated in the American economy? This is one of the first questions we must explore if we are to prepare ourselves for analyzing economic problems and policies. Therefore, in this chapter we shall try to see how the economy manages to get things produced and distributed. Then we shall look at the national income statistics that help keep us informed about how the economy is working. Finally, we shall examine the way in which income is distributed, and the controversial and troublesome problems associated with this distribution.

THE "MARKET SYSTEM"

Chapter 1 stated that every economic system must answer three basic questions: What will be produced? How will things be produced? Who will receive what is produced? In the United States, the "market system" provides most of the answers to these basic questions.

A *"market" permits goods and services to be bought and sold.* Some markets are geographically small, covering only one town or a few city blocks; others are national or international in scope. For instance, a local restaurant typically draws its customers from a limited area, while a leading chemical manufacturing concern may draw its customers from all over the world. Some markets have a large number of buyers and sellers, and some have only a few. Some markets are tightly controlled by the government, and some are wholly private. Some involve transactions in only one specified product, and others include a wide assortment of products. Buyers and sellers in some markets make careful and rational decisions, and in others they act on the basis of habit, custom, or spur-of-the-moment impulses. In spite of these differences, all markets have certain common characteristics—they provide a link between consumers and producers, and they permit the exchange of goods and services.

The term "market system" has a more explicit meaning than mere exchange. Generally, it refers to the economic relationships in a society in which the physical means of production are privately owned and in which private individuals respond to opportunities for greater income. In a market system, prices for goods and services are the basic signals that direct production and distribution. Prices in a market system are determined largely by impersonal relations between buyers and sellers rather than by government order.

Deciding What Will Be Produced

In a sense, consumers "vote" for what they want by spending their incomes on the things they most desire. Producers tend to respond to these "votes" in order to earn income. Producers try, by advertising and other means, to make consumers want their products, but in the last analysis, output reflects "the election returns." When consumers are willing to pay enough to cover the costs of production and a profit to the producer, a commodity will tend to be produced. If consumers will not pay enough for a commodity, that item will generally be dropped and other commodities will be produced.

The market system also helps indicate how much to provide for investment in the improvement of our productive capacity. When people save, they reduce the number of votes cast for consumption goods. By making their savings available to business firms, they enable business to "vote" for the production of tools, machines, and other capital goods. Thus if producers are willing to pay an adequate reward to lenders, they may induce people to use their income for investment rather than consumption.

The market system is impersonal; it does not supply a moral judgment of the pattern of consumer demand. If the pattern of consumer demand were to give preference to submachine guns or opium instead of typewriters and flowers, the market system would tend to deliver a corresponding pattern of production. Since producers in a market system respond only to consumer desires that are backed up with money, the system will supply second homes for the wealthy even though some poor families lack adequate shelter.

The market mechanism does not have complete control over what is produced. Some goods and services, such as national defense, roads, the court system, are provided collectively, through the political process and administrative action. Individual decision-making in these areas either is not feasible or is not likely to be effective. Moreover, taxation is a logical way to finance such activities, because they cannot be provided for some people without being available to all. The protection afforded by military forces covers the entire nation; it cannot be limited to taxpayers, to rich or to poor, to men or to women. Some goods, such as education, are provided both in the market and by government. Unlike national defense, it is feasible to offer schooling in the private market, but most nations provide some free schooling (that is, education financed by government) for social or political reasons. Government also intervenes to help provide food, medical care, housing, and so on to those who cannot provide it for themselves. It also regulates the production and sale of guns, drugs, and toxic substances that may be a hazard to health. Thus government plays a role in the economy either because private markets cannot handle certain public goods or because social and political considerations have persuaded the nation that the market should be supplemented by governmental services or controls.

Deciding How Things Are to Be Produced

Once the market has indicated what to produce, a choice must be made of the mode of production. Should a product be produced with many workers and little capital equipment, or should it be produced with a lot of equipment and few workers? What firms should produce what items? What persons should work on what jobs? Broadly speaking, the market tends to indicate the method, the firm, or the person that can produce things most efficiently. Because consumers generally attempt to get the most for their money, they tend to purchase from producers who give them more per dollar. As long as businessmen and workers are interested in greater earnings from their effort, they tend to move into the forms of production that consumers prefer.

The market system does not always establish the most efficient mode of production. Supposedly, the market can show producers or workers whether they are producing the right thing in the right way. If they are not, profits and wages may fall. If the people involved have a strong income motive, they will move to another business where they can earn a better return for their efforts—where they are more efficient. But often other motives are more important than the desire for income. Farmers may enjoy being "close to the soil." Teachers may receive personal satisfaction from working with young people. Older people may be unwilling to leave their neighborhood and move on to other jobs. Thus people may not respond to the main driving force in the market system.

People may also remain in low-production jobs because they are unaware of better opportunities elsewhere. Or, if society discriminates against them for noneconomic reasons, they may remain in inefficient types of production.

Deciding Who Is to Receive the Goods and Services

The diagram on page 27 shows that the public receives income for selling productive services to producers in the market for productive factors. Workers get wages for their labor, the landlord gets rent, the writer receives royalties, and the owners of business receive profits. All use their income to pay for the goods they buy. The money income circulates, and, on each turnover, more is produced and purchased.

As shown in the diagram, goods and services are obtained by the public in return for money spent in the market for goods and services (upper half). And the amount that buyers can spend is determined by what they receive in the market for productive factors. In general, producers pay the sellers of productive services about what their services contribute to the dollar value of the product—competition among producers tends to force them to do so. Thus those whose services contribute the most receive the greatest incomes and obtain the greatest share of the goods produced. Those who produce little receive little. We should keep in mind that this measure of "value" and "contribution to production" is made by the market. People may feel that they have a valuable skill but, if they cannot sell it, it is valueless in the market sense. On the other hand, the market may set a high price on a skill they feel is worthless. In a market system, it is the price that counts.

In the American economy, the market does not have sole control over the distribution of income. People are free to give a portion of their income to relatives or friends, and charities are supported by private donations. Furthermore, society as a whole has decided to compensate some groups beyond their reward from the market. Veterans are given bonuses and pensions; old people receive medical care and other assistance; schools are provided for children, and many other governmental services are provided for people without regard to their ability to pay. The American people, in other words, feel that the market method of deciding who will receive the things produced is not always adequate.

The Circular Flow of Economic Activity

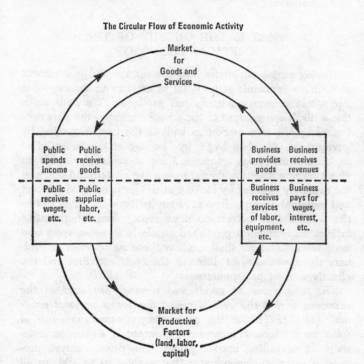

This diagram illustrates the circular flow of money payments (in a clockwise direction) and the flow of goods and productive services (counterclockwise) which are exchanged for money in the markets. The diagram also illustrates the basis for national income and product accounting described in the section that follows. The spending for goods and services (top half of the diagram) equals the spending for costs of producing the output (bottom half).

The government also changes the distribution of income by measures that work within the price system. It supports the price of certain agricultural commodities so that farmers will be able to receive a higher income. It provides subsidies for some businesses. It imposes regulations that boost prices of some products above the competitive level. By a variety of such policies, the government affects the prices of goods and services and therefore influences the distribution of income and production.

WHAT IS THE OUTPUT OF THE AMERICAN ECONOMY?

Having examined briefly how the market and government co-ordinate economic activity, let us now try to observe what our whole economy actually has produced. We shall make this a bird's-eye glimpse of the whole economy—the part controlled by the free market as well as the part controlled by government. We shall begin by "looking at the books." Just as businessmen may examine their accounting records to check on how they are doing, so can the citizen find out how the economy is doing by looking at the gross national product and national income figures. Familiarity with these statistics will help us understand news reports and interpretative articles on economics published regularly in newspapers and magazines. Later we shall see how these figures help us evaluate the desirability of different economic activities and the effectiveness of past policies.

The total value of goods and services produced in the economy during the year is called the "gross national product" (GNP). This is the most comprehensive measure of *what* we produce. It measures the output of all economic activity at prevailing market prices. The price measure provides a common denominator that enables us to add up all the dissimilar things we produce. Movies, dishwashers, wheat combines, ditch digging, police protection, toys, airplanes, and thousands of other goods and services can all be added by using their prices as a measure. However, as we shall see later, we must be sure we understand what these prices mean.

The goods and services included in the gross national product are sold to four major groups: consumers, producers, governments, and foreign buyers. In 1977, these groups purchased the following amounts of goods and services:[1]

Consumers	$1,206 billion
Producers	298 billion
Governments	394 billion
Foreign buyers (net)[2]	− 11 billion
Gross national product	$1,887 billion

• Purchases by consumers—officially labeled *personal consumption expenditures*—include three types of goods and services: *durables* (such as automobiles and television sets), *nondurables* (such as food and clothing), and *services* (such as house rent, movies, and medical and legal advice). Consumer spending for these purposes in 1977 was as follows:

Durables	$178 billion
Nondurables	479 billion
Services	549 billion
Total for 1977	$1,206 billion

• Purchases by producers—labeled *gross private domestic investment*—are subdivided into *fixed investment* and *change*

[1] These figures are based on statistics compiled by the U. S. Department of Commerce. For simplicity, the figures in this chapter have been rounded and some categories have been combined with others. The basic source of these and the other figures used in this section of the chapter is *Survey of Current Business,* a monthly publication of the U. S. Department of Commerce. The same figures may also be found in the *Federal Reserve Bulletin,* a monthly publication of the Board of Governors of the Federal Reserve System, and the Appendix to the *Economic Report of the President,* transmitted to the Congress annually in January.

[2] Usually labeled "net exports of goods and services," this item involves some accounting complexities that will not be discussed here. An explanation is provided in U. S. Department of Commerce, *The National Income and Product Accounts of the United States, 1929–74,* a supplement to the *Survey of Current Business.* Chapter 9 (below) contains an extensive discussion of the foreign trade of the United States.

in business inventories. Fixed investment includes *nonresidential construction,* such as offices, plants, warehouses, pipelines, and gas and oil wells; it also includes the machines, tools, and other equipment used in business enterprises, as well as the tractors and machinery purchased for use on farms. (Purchases to replace "worn out" equipment as well as expenditures for additional equipment are included.) Residential structures and equipment, including farm structures, whether for rental or personal use, are also treated as fixed investment.

The other type of investment—*change in business inventories*—measures the increase or decrease in the stocks of goods and materials held by business. An increase in inventories is considered to be a form of investment because it represents goods being processed or awaiting sale for *future* demand. For accounting purposes, these "unsold" goods are considered to be purchased by producers. In 1977, as in most years, business inventories increased. Sometimes, as happened in 1975, the change in business inventories will be negative. This means that by the end of 1975 businesses had sold more goods than they produced during the year. That is, they sold some of the goods that were produced in an earlier period. Thus, in order to determine what was actually produced during 1975 we have to *subtract* the inventory sales from the total sales. If we did not subtract them, the GNP—total spending on goods and services in 1975—would not be an accurate measure of production in that year.

In 1977, expenditures for these components of *gross private domestic investment* were as follows:

Fixed investment		$282 billion
Nonresidential structures and equipment	$190 billion	
Residential structures and equipment	92 billion	
Change in business inventories		16 billion
Total for 1977		$298 billion

• The third major type of purchases—*government purchases of goods and services*—includes expenditures by state and local governments throughout the country as well as those by the federal government. Federal expenditures are broken down into two main categories:

National defense, which includes purchases of munitions and payments to members of the armed services, and *other,* which covers all additional outlays for such things as the services of government employees and the purchases of goods from business. State and local expenditures involve outlays for roads, schools, public works, and all the other services provided by city, county, and state governments. These governmental expenditures, totaling $394 billion in 1977, may be broken down as follows:

Federal		$145 billion
National defense	$94 billion	
Other	51 billion	
State and local		249 billion
Total for 1977		$394 billion

A breakdown of GNP according to expenditures by the major groups of buyers helps us to see how people choose to spend their incomes. For instance, in 1977, consumers spent their income for the·purposes shown (in billions) in the following table:[3]

Food, beverages, and tobacco	$261.7
Clothing, accessories, jewelry	95.6
Personal care	16.7
Housing	184.6
Household operation	176.9
Medical and death expenses	117.9
Personal business (legal and financial service)	60.4
Transportation	172.1
Recreation	81.2
Private education and research	18.8
Religious and welfare activities	15.4
Foreign travel and payments abroad	5.1
Total personal consumption expenditures	$1,206.4

[3] *Survey of Current Business* (July 1978), p. 37. The figures have been rounded.

To be even more specific, the *Survey of Current Business* shows that in 1977 consumers spent $16.5 billion for tobacco; $5.3 billion for haircuts and beauty parlor services; $29 billion for physicians; $3.5 billion for funeral and burial expenses; $4.3 billion for books, and $1.7 billion for radio and television repairs. People spent more money for toilet articles ($11.5 billion) than they spent for dentists ($11.3 billion). But the most significant aspect of this breakdown is that it shows that our economic system responds to a wide variety of consumer interests.

The figures for gross national product also give some indication of how fully the nation is using its economic resources. For example, a decline of $20 billion in GNP generally indicates a slowdown in economic activity; it suggests that some workers or firms are idle or for some reason are producing less. As we shall see in Chapter 7, the policies the government adopts to combat such a decline will depend partly on whether the decline has occurred in investment spending, consumer purchases, or government spending, or some combination of all three. In other words, the figures for gross national product can help show when trouble is developing, and they can also give some clues for dealing with the problem. However, as we shall see, such changes in GNP must be examined carefully.

The dollar measure of the gross national product may rise or fall without a change in physical production. An increase may only mean, for example, that prices have risen. Because GNP figures are based on market prices, an increase in the price level may result in a higher gross national product even though real production of goods and services has remained the same or has fallen. Thus if we want to use GNP figures for comparative purposes or as a measure of *real* production, we must adjust the figures for changing prices. The table of GNP in current and constant prices on the next page shows how much difference changes in the price level can make over a period of a few years.[4]

---

[4] *Economic Report of the President* (January 1977), p. 188, and *Survey*, June 1979. The estimate for 1979 is based on data for the first three months of that year.

Year	GNP in prices prevailing at the time (in billions)	GNP in prices prevailing in 1972 (in billions)
1929	$103	$315
1933	56	221
1940	100	344
1950	282	534
1960	506	737
1970	982	1,075
1977	1,887	1,337
1979 (estimate)	2,267	1,418

Without the correction for falling prices, the first column indicates about a 50 per cent decline in production between 1929 and 1933; the second column, in which GNP is expressed in constant prices, indicates a decline of 30 per cent. The same type of contrast is shown for the period 1950–77; the increase in production looks much greater until we take the price changes out of it. The increase, expressed in market prices, is sixfold; in constant prices it is less than threefold. This price adjustment is important if we want to use GNP figures to compare output for two different periods; if we do not take it into account, we are measuring both production changes and price changes.

Figures for gross national product tell us *what* we produce, but they do not tell us *how* we produce it. We can get some idea about this by looking at our national income.

NATIONAL INCOME

The national income is the total income earned by those contributing to current production. The United States Department of Commerce has developed a method for counting the incomes of laborers, executives, firefighters, artists, and everyone else engaged in production, and it provides us with official estimates of the total.

National income figures exclude payments that do not arise from productive effort. They exclude, for example, the allowances that parents pay their children, the pensions or bonuses paid to veterans, and the interest on the public debt. Regard-

less of how essential these payments are, they are excluded
from the national income, because they are not payments for
"current production." Interestingly, compensation for housework by members of a family is also excluded. Few people
would deny that housework constitutes a large volume of
useful service—cleaning, washing, baby-tending, and so on—
but this contribution is not included in GNP or in national
income. If someone has a servant do all the housework, the
servant's income is included, but if that person marries the
housekeeper (and provides an allowance equal to the former
wages), the payment is no longer a part of the national income figures. Why? Primarily because it would be too
difficult for the Department of Commerce to make an accurate estimate of the value of household services.[5]

In 1977, the national income was $1,515 billion and the
gross national product was $1,887 billion. How do we ac-
count for the difference in totals? National income is the total
income received by those contributing to current production,
and gross national product is the total amount spent for
goods and services currently produced—and both are stated
in terms of current prices. But GNP is bigger because it includes some spending that is not considered income. The Department of Commerce can check its figure for national income by subtracting these non-income items from GNP.

The first deduction is an allowance for using of capital
equipment. This deduction is necessary so as not to overstate
the income produced during a calendar year. The example
given below illustrates the role of capital in the economic
process and shows why the allowance for the cost of replacing plant and machinery is not considered a part of national
income.

[5] It may come as a shock to some men to find out that the market
value of all the services their wives perform may exceed the income
of their husbands. A discussion of the many problems of measuring
national income can be found in U. S. Department of Commerce,
National Income 1954, a supplement to the *Survey of Current
Business*. Revised estimates of the national income and product
accounts (NIPA) are published annually in the July issue of the
Survey. For a discussion of the revision process, including changes
in some definitions, see the *Survey of Current Business*, National
Income Issue, January 1976, Part 1.

Suppose Mr. A agrees to dig a ditch for $200. To dig the ditch he must supply the labor and the capital equipment—in this case a new shovel, which he buys for $10. By the time the job is completed, the shovel is worn out. Thus his product (the $200 ditch) is produced by combining $190 worth of labor and $10 worth of capital. Mr. A's net income is $190 and the other $10 represents expenditure of capital. If Mr. A treats the whole $200 as income and spends it—without making an allowance of $10 to replace his shovel—he will reduce his ability to produce as efficiently in the future. In other words, in order to determine what he produces by his own labor he has to deduct the cost of his worn-out ("depreciated") capital. Similar allowances are made in calculating the income of a whole society.

In national income accounting, the term *net national product* (NNP) is given to the remainder of national output after the deduction for depreciation. NNP is generally nearly 10 per cent smaller than GNP.

GNP also includes another cost that is not considered income—the cost of some business taxes. These taxes, such as manufacturers' sales or excise taxes, are added to the cost of the product before it is sold. They increase the market price (the basis for measuring GNP) but do not represent a reward to one of the productive units. They are a transfer of funds from consumers to the tax collector and are not a payment for current production. Thus a package of cigarettes costing fifty cents may include only about thirty cents for the services of the grower, manufacturer, and dealer; all the rest goes to the federal and state tax collectors. Of course, the other twenty or twenty-one cents will eventually be used by the government to pay for "current production"—but it is counted when the government spends it, not when it is collected.

To summarize, the gross national product less capital consumption and business taxes equals national income. This relationship is shown by the following diagram. Together national income and gross national product measure the flow of income and the flow of goods and services. By looking at how the national income was earned, we can get some idea of how the goods and services were produced.

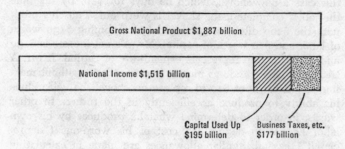

Gross National Product and National Income, 1977

Gross National Product $1,887 billion

National Income $1,515 billion

Capital Used Up $195 billion — Business Taxes, etc. $177 billion

The table below, showing which industries produced the National Income in 1977, gives some indication of how we produce our goods and services.[6]

Industries	Persons engaged in production (in millions)	Income produced[7] (in billions)
Private industries		
Agriculture, forestry, and fisheries	1.7	44.6
Mining	.8	23.2
Construction	3.9	77.2
Manufacturing	19.7	408.9
Transportation, communication, public utilities	4.7	119.9
Wholesale and retail trade	18.7	237.0
Finance, insurance, real estate	4.5	177.9
Services and other	17.2	213.1
Government		
Federal	5.8	81.2
State and local	12.6	151.5
Rest of the world	—	17.3
Total for 1977	89.6	1,551.8

[6] Survey of Current Business (July 1978), pp. 53 and 54.
[7] The figures in this column do not add up to the national income total cited previously because they are based on a different statis-

Manufacturing clearly accounts for more employment and income than any other activity. A century ago this was the position held by agriculture. Retail and wholesale trade is our second largest source of income, producing more income than finance, insurance, real estate, and mining combined; and the construction industry produced about two thirds more income than agriculture—with double the number of workers.

We can gain additional insight into the question of *how* we produce our national income from the following table, which shows the sectors, or types, of organizations producing the national income.[8]

Corporations	$921.5 billion
Partnerships and proprietorships	191.2 billion
Other private business	114.7 billion
Government	208.0 billion
Households and institutions	62.7 billion
Rest of the world	17.2 billion
National income in 1977	$1,515.3 billion

Corporations are clearly the dominating form of economic enterprise in our society; they permit the development of large pools of capital, and for a variety of reasons, they seem to be popular among investors and workers. Although the table does not show a separate classification for the single-owner form of business, it does indicate that the so-called "individual enterprise" is not nearly as important to total national income as it once was. Corporations and government are both "collective enterprise" so, even if all the rest were single-owner firms (which they are not), "individual enterprise" would account for only one third of national income.

Further information on *how* we produce our national income can be obtained from the following table showing the manner in which the national income is distributed

tical measure of depreciation. For a discussion of the "capital consumption adjustment," introduced in 1976, see *Survey of Current Business* (January 1976), Part 1, pp. 3 and 6.

[8] *Survey of Current Business* (July 1978), p. 31.

among what might be called "the services of labor and property."[9]

Compensation of employees	$1,153.4 billion
Proprietors' income (business, farm, professional)	99.8 billion
Corporate profits	144.2 billion
Rental income	22.5 billion
Interest income	95.4 billion
National income in 1977	$1,515.3 billion

Let us further examine the components of this breakdown of national income.

Compensation of employees is income earned by hired labor. It includes the wages paid to workers in all types of productive activity, the salaries paid to white collar workers and the executives of businesses. It includes the payments made by employers for pensions and welfare programs for employees.

Business, farm, and professional income (or proprietors' income) includes the income (or profit) of unincorporated businesses and farms, and of doctors, lawyers, and other professional people. It is therefore a mixture of independent labor income (about two thirds) and property income (about one third).

Corporate profits includes all the profits of the corporate businesses in the country. As such, it is the income earned by corporate property. When combined with the payments to businesses, farms, and professional people, it includes all the earnings of owners and operators of producing organizations.

Rental and interest income includes housing and commercial rents and interest payments on bonds, savings accounts, and insurance policies. These are payments made to persons for the use of their real or financial property.

Thus the national income is earned by working, operating a business, and owning or renting productive property. Inasmuch as operating a business is considered a form of labor, about three fourths of our national income may be said to be earned by labor services and one fourth by the services of property.

[9] *Survey of Current Business* (July 1978), p. 31.

The above figures showing the industries, the types of producing units, and the types of services involved in creating our national income help us to see how the national income is produced, and they also give us some clues regarding how the national income is distributed. In order to obtain a clearer idea of *who* receives the goods and services produced, we must examine the figures more closely.

Not all of the national income is distributed to individuals. Some of it is held by business, and some is transferred to the government. Thus national income is not the same as the total of all individual incomes—or what is called *personal income.*

Some examples will help show why personal income is less than national income. Corporations pay about 40 per cent of their income in corporation income taxes, and they retain more than half of what is left to plow back into investment. So only about one fourth of pretax corporate profits is actually paid to people.

Moreover, not all of the payments for wages and salaries were actually received by employees. Business pays part of it directly to the government for social security programs. Thus retained earnings of corporations, the corporation income tax, and the payments for social welfare programs are all parts of national income that are not included in personal income.

The fact, shown graphically in the accompanying chart, that not all national income is available to individuals is sometimes interpreted to mean that some income is "taken out of the economy" by corporations or government. But this is like saying that corporations and the government are not a part of our economy. Actually, the funds retained by business are used to purchase capital equipment and inventory, and the funds taken by government are used to purchase the wide variety of goods and services needed for governmental operations.

But there are also some payments to persons that were not included in national income. National income, it will be recalled, is the total of payments for productive services in our society. Some individuals, however, receive income payments that do not result from their current production. These payments are called *transfer payments.* A large volume of

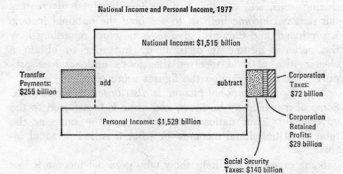

National Income and Personal Income, 1977

National Income: $1,515 billion

Transfer Payments: $255 billion

add

subtract

Corporation Taxes: $72 billion

Personal Income: $1,529 billion

Corporation Retained Profits: $29 billion

Social Security Taxes: $140 billion

transfer payments arise from government and are included in personal income. Government transfer payments are of the three broad types: (1) payments to recipients of various relief and social programs; (2) payments to veterans; (3) payments of interest on the national debt.

Finally, we should note that not all of the income paid to individuals (personal income) is available for personal use. There is a difference between what we quote as our wage or salary and what we get "after taxes." Income taxes, property taxes, and other taxes on individuals reduce the income we have for our own use. The deduction of these taxes from personal income leaves what is called *disposable personal income*—the income that individuals may use as they wish. In 1977, the figures were as follows:

Personal income	$1,529 billion
Less personal taxes	226 billion
Disposable personal income	$1,303 billion

Of this sum, people saved $67 billion and spent the rest.

Before inquiring how this personal income was divided among our population, let us bring all these parts of the flow of income and production together. The diagram on page 41 shows how all these concepts are related. Because the concepts used in this diagram will be used later in this volume,

The Flow of Spending and Income (in billions of dollars)

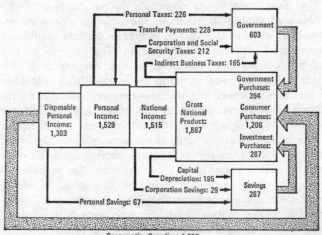

Consumption Spending: 1,206

The three gray channels represent the flow of the major types of expenditures that add up to the GNP for 1977. The solid arrows show the flow of income. Foreign buyers are included with investment purchases. Some other items have also been combined for simplicity, and thus the flows do not always add up to the totals that are shown. The most important omissions and adjustments are listed below:

1. An additional $12 billion in transfer payments to business must be deducted from GNP to arrive at the total for National Income.
2. Personal Income includes $27 billion in interest income and transfer payments not shown here.
3. Consumption spending is $30 billion less than disposable personal income because of interest paid to business by consumers and personal transfer payments paid to foreigners.
4. Government receipts are $19 billion less than government purchases and transfer payments—which is the amount of the federal deficit for 1977.
5. The figure for savings includes not only the flows shown but statistical discrepancies and other adjustments.

Data are from the *Survey of Current Business* (July 1978).

it will be helpful to study this picture of the flow of income carefully.[10]

One final topic merits discussion before we turn to the problem of income distribution: the difference between income and welfare. Changes in output or income should not be confused with changes in welfare. The national income and product accounts described in this chapter deal with goods and services exchanged in the market. Thus a number of factors that affect our welfare—ranging from the contributions of work performed in the home that increase our well-being to the pollution of the environment that decreases it—are omitted from the national accounts entirely. Moreover, an increase in leisure resulting from a shortening of the work week would be regarded as an improvement in welfare, although it would lead to a reduction in output. In recent years, some economists have attempted to estimate a "measure of economic welfare" by taking into account the costs of some of the side effects of modern industrial production. The Department of Commerce, however, has not been persuaded that such an effort at estimation is proper for the official economic accounts and has offered a number of arguments against changing its historic approach.

Closely related to this concern about measuring welfare has been the effort of social scientists to develop a set of "social indicators" that would supplement the economic accounts so as to provide a broader indication of changes in our well-being. In 1973, the federal government issued the first of what was intended to be a series of reports entitled *Social Indicators.* It provided eight measures of social concern: health, public safety, education, employment, income, housing, leisure and recreation, and population—a much broader array of statistics than are presented by economic data, but still including a great deal of economic data. Publication of the second edition, *Social Indicators 1976,* followed. Meanwhile, in Britain and other industrialized nations, the publi-

---

[10] Note that government receipts total only $603 billion, while expenditures and transfers total $622 billion. The government ran a deficit of $19 billion.

cation of social statistics on an annual or biennial basis has become as accepted as the publication of economic statistics.

HOW IS PERSONAL INCOME DISTRIBUTED?

In general, the income of our economy is distributed according to the market value of the individual's contribution to production. The determination of the individual's contribution is made, in principle, in the market where the actions of buyers and sellers rule. The linkage of income with productive contributions of individuals supplies much of our incentive to produce.

But productivity is not the only factor in our scheme of income distribution. Under a market system, it is possible for some persons to get a larger share by controlling the supply of things being sold, as price reflects not only the usefulness of a good but also its scarcity. Thus a variety of restrictive practices can be used to influence the distribution of income. Also the government can subsidize certain people. It can do so by direct payments or by laws that enable certain groups to bargain for a larger share of the total income of society.

Every system that has been devised for distributing income has involved some degree of inequality among individuals. In the United States, variations in income have always existed—largely because the services of different persons have been evaluated differently by the market and because the services of property have been valued very highly. But even if property incomes were distributed equally, there would still tend to be inequalities. Trained persons, and those with unusual skills and aptitudes, are considered more productive than those who are inexperienced, untrained, or lacking in special abilities. For their services, society is generally willing to pay more than for the more easily available services of unskilled workers.

The inequalities in distribution of money income were reduced during the first half of this century but have been substantially the same since that time. Early data are not wholly reliable, but it appears that near the turn of the century, about half of our income receivers had near-subsistence incomes. Fifty years later only a quarter of our income re-

ceivers were in this category. A more specific indication of
the change is given by the declining share of personal income after taxes going to the top income bracket.[11] The top
5 per cent of the income receivers obtained about:

> 34 per cent of the total disposable personal income in 1929
> 27 per cent of the total disposable personal income in 1939
> 18 per cent of the total disposable personal income in 1946

Recent data indicate that the share of the top 5 per cent has
changed little since 1946, hovering just below 16 per cent.

*Regardless of the changes that have occurred in the distri-
bution of income, there is still an observable concentration in
income payments.* Looking at the following chart, we see
that in 1977 the fifth of the nation's families with the lowest
incomes received only 5.4 per cent of the personal income of
the nation. At the upper end of the scale, the top fifth of the
spending units earned 41 per cent of the personal income.
This picture of the distribution of income is changed only
slightly by the federal income tax.

Distribution of Family Personal Income

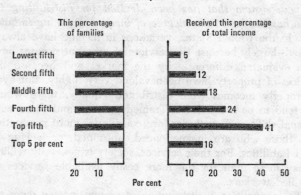

Source: U. S. Bureau of the Census. *Current Population Reports*
P-60, 116. The figures are for 1977 and are rounded.

[11] Arthur F. Burns, *"Looking Forward,"* National Bureau of
Economic Research, 31st Annual Report (1951), p. 4. Note that
this tabulation refers to income only. It does not indicate distribution of wealth.

Who are the rich? The very largest incomes arise primarily from large holdings of property—real estate, mining properties, oil wells, buildings, or factories. Professional and business earnings also account for a large part of the income received by those in the upper brackets. Doctors, lawyers, business executives, and salesmen work their way up the income scale year by year as they become older and gain efficiency and judgment. However, some individuals by-pass this gradual route and shoot into a higher income level in a short period of time. Successful speculators, actors, writers, and salesmen, for example, may "get rich quick." A change of luck, a shift in consumers' tastes, a brilliant idea, or a change in the weather can move people into and out of the high income class in a short time.

Who are the poor? Aged people, families headed by women or those supported by a wage earner who is sick or handicapped are often among the poor. So are part-time workers and those who do not move out of low-value production (for instance, farming on low-grade land) and into occupations where their efforts would be worth more. Many are kept from seeking better opportunities by racial and other types of discrimination. Geographical location may also play a part; education, job opportunities, and the over-all standard of living are lower in some sections than in others.

The accompanying table shows that black families' incomes are substantially lower than white families' incomes and that families headed by women are far worse off than families headed by men. Data from the same study show that incomes are lower among young and old families. One out of four families headed by persons twenty-four years old or younger and sixty-five years and over received incomes of less than five thousand dollars in 1975.

One of the continuing challenges to the American economy is to find ways to improve the economic status of the low-income groups. For example, in his *Economic Report to Congress* in 1966, the President of the United States said: ". . . 32 million Americans remain in poverty and millions more are unable to realize their full economic potential." The President was supporting a "War on Poverty," designed to develop the earning capacity of these people. Political and

INCOME OF AMERICAN FAMILIES, 1977

Type of family	Number of families[12] (in thousands)	Median income
All families	57,215	$16,009
White families	50,530	16,740
Black families	5,806	9,563
Families of Spanish origin	2,764	11,421
Families headed by a male	48,979	17,517
Families headed by a female	8,236	7,765

administrative difficulties in carrying out the program, compounded by the strains of the Vietnam War, seriously undercut this effort. A decade later, the incoming President faced a similar challenge to reduce poverty.

Generally, the living standards of the lowest-income groups can be improved in two ways: first, by increasing the output of the American economy so that more goods are available for everyone; and second, by changing the distribution of what is available so that the poor get a bigger share. The first method will be discussed in Chapter 8, on economic growth, and the second method might be explored as follows:

The Problems and the Issues

We have seen that the unequal distribution of incomes is the result of two influences: decisions in the market and decisions by the government.

When the market decides how income shall be distributed, it does so on the basis of economic criteria—supply, demand, and bargaining. Generally, it gives more income to those considered more productive. But individuals are not helpless in the market. In addition to increasing their actual output of goods and services, they can also use various devices to in-

12 Source: *Consumer Income*, Current Population Reports, Series P-60, No. 116, U. S. Bureau of the Census, July 1978, p. 6. These figures are for aggregate income and are not directly comparable to those used earlier. If 20 million individuals not living with families are included in the tabulation, the median income is $13,572.

crease the dollar value of what they produce. They can join with others to hold up the price of what they sell, and they can attempt to persuade consumers that they should want (and pay more for) their product. Individuals can also enlist the aid of the government to control the supply or the prices of the things they are selling.

When the government (society) decides how income will be distributed, it may use economic and noneconomic standards for distributing income. Policy makers may decide that society owes a moral obligation to some groups. Government may provide more income for some groups as a part of a political bargain, or because it feels that our social customs result in an unfair treatment of some people. In other words, when the government intervenes directly, it views the distribution of income not only as an economic problem but as a social, moral, or political problem as well.

If we are concerned about inequality, then the basic issue may be to decide how much the distribution of income should be based on the economic rules of the market system and how much it should be based on the other rules that government can impose. More specifically, the issue may be how much the powers of the government should be used to reduce the degree of inequality of income distribution.

The Objectives

Let us assume that we want to improve living conditions for low-income groups. In addition, we may want to create more economic equality to correspond with our concept of political equality. To attain these objectives, we may want to curtail what seems to be wasteful consumption by those in the upper-income brackets and eliminate the advantages or disadvantages that arise from an inherited economic status. Or we may want to make the economic system seem more "fair" to some people in order to avert political unrest.

At the same time, we may want our economic system to produce a growing volume of goods and services. We may want to preserve incentives so that people will want to improve themselves economically and culturally. We may also require that our system be free from rapid fluctuations of output and prices. Suppose, on balance, we decide that our central objective should be to raise the income of the nation's poorest families while pursuing as many of our other objectives as we can.

Some of these objectives and requirements may be in conflict, as shown in Chapter 1. For instance, we may think that large fortunes are needed to finance the continued growth of our productive capacity. If we do, we shall either have to change our objective or find a substitute way to obtain capital. In thinking through such problems, it is vitally important to define these objectives and requirements so that such conflicts can be identified. We must try to identify the costs of achieving the goals we seek and compare them with prospective benefits.

The Alternatives and Consequences

We might consider three principal courses of action: (1) allowing the forces of the market to drive individuals to whatever economic status their initiative and surrounding conditions will permit, in the belief that in the long run greater equality will be achieved; (2) redistributing some of the income received by the rich, by giving it to the poor; and (3) dealing with the physical and social causes of low productivity. Each of these approaches may involve a variety of specific proposals that should be explored. Moreover, they are not mutually exclusive. More training and more equal opportunities (possibilities under alternative 3) would be consistent with possibilities under either alternative 1 or alternative 2.

Those who would rely exclusively on the market system say that economic pressure will induce people to improve their productivity. Critics claim that this approach has only limited possibilities. Greater effort will hardly help the income earner who is handicapped. It will do little good for those persons who, because of sex, race, or national origin, are excluded from various occupations. It won't help mothers with dependent children unless free day care is provided. In general, unless people in the low-income groups have access to adequate educational, training, job, and promotion opportunities, they may be thwarted in their desire to improve their economic status, regardless of how much harder they work or are willing to work.

A second approach to the problem is to transfer some income from the rich to the poor. A progressive income tax, together with welfare payments and other subsidies for low-income groups, is one way in which inequalities of income have been reduced. One limitation of this approach is that it may reduce the incentive of some recipients to improve their status, and it may have a harmful effect on the initiative of those who are paying the costs. But studies have shown the difficulty of making generalizations about how people react to income support programs and to higher taxes. The task of the policy maker is to devise specific proposals to advance us toward our economic goals without causing bad side effects.

A third approach to the problem involves a variety of specific programs designed to attack the various causes of poverty. Crop insurance and training in farming techniques may help small farmers; vocational rehabilitation may help the handicapped. Better enforcement of fair-employment laws may reduce arbitrary restraints caused by racial and other types of discrimination; social security and unemployment insurance may help sustain the flow of income after retirement or during layoffs; vocational high schools and on-the-job training may improve the skills of youths. Altogether, it is argued, such programs offer economic protection to some groups and open up greater opportunities that it is hoped will pay off both for individuals and for society.

Some programs of this sort, such as social security, were introduced in the 1930s. During the 1960s, the so-called Great Society established programs to remove barriers to the economic advancement of women, blacks, and Hispanic Americans. We have had four decades of experiments with social programs, but how much of the gain in real income during that time has resulted from these programs and how much from market forces is hard to sort out. Some of the gains have resulted primarily from the better use of our resources, from technological developments, and from other factors that will be discussed in Chapter 8. But social programs have also enabled large numbers of Americans to climb out of poverty. Nevertheless, the inequality of income distribution (and the inequality in the distribution of wealth as well) remains an important problem for the nation's agenda.

This chapter has stressed these basic ideas:

1. We indicate through the market and through the government what we want produced, how we want it produced, and who is to get it. Because each of us is a producer, an income receiver, and a spender, these decisions are linked to one another.

2. The economic process may be viewed as a circular flow of income and production. Income arises from production. In the last analysis, our income *is* what we produce. Broadly speaking, we are concerned with two aspects of this circular flow: (1) the total amount of income and production available for society, and (2) the way that the total flow is distributed and used. The national income and gross national product accounts are comprehensive measures of the sources and uses of this flow of income.

3. Proposals for changing the distribution of income must be judged with an understanding of their effects on the operation of the entire economic system. There may be moral or political grounds for proposing changes, but, before accepting or rejecting such proposals, they should be explored for their economic consequences. Proposals that are economically desirable may be found to be politically or morally inadequate, or vice versa.

Suggested Reading

Paul A. Samuelson, *Economics*, Chaps. 3 and 4, pp. 41–78, Chap. 6, pp. 100–20, Chap. 10, pp. 179–204. George L. Bach, *Economics: An Introduction to Analysis and Policy*, Chap. 8. These readings give further information on how our economy operates, how the national income is created, and how the national income is distributed. See also "Free Private Enterprise," by Sumner Slichter, in *Readings in Economics* (Samuelson et al., eds.), pp. 14–20. This is one of the best short statements of the theory and practice of a free enterprise system. Some of the issues it discusses will be especially helpful in preparation for Chapter 3. See also "The Economic Organization of a P.O.W. Camp," by R. A. Radford, in the same volume, pp. 21–28.

Chapter 3

COMPETITION IN THE ECONOMY

One of the satisfactions of shopping is to encounter rival retailers who are vigorously competing for our business. A chain store advertises lower prices; an independent retailer offers better service. Sometimes it is a heady experience to find many sellers vying for our favor, and we conclude that the consumer is a rather important individual after all.

Of course, we can't choose between rival electric power companies or among several different water suppliers. We cannot haggle over our telephone bill as we might haggle over the price of a used car. But at the same time we know that usually where we have no choice in the matter, the sellers are not free to charge what they please. If a single utility firm serves the community, a regulatory commission is likely to be on the job to see that the community is properly served and that the firm makes no more than a reasonable profit.

Most of us know from experience that competition and monopoly exist side by side. We have been told that competition is desirable and monopoly undesirable. Somehow competition is supposed to provide, at favorable terms, the goods and services most wanted by the public, while monopoly must be regulated to ensure the same result. Thus competition is supposed to foster the efficient use of the nation's resources and to discourage the inefficient use of these resources. In brief, we support competition because we believe it to be a means to greater economic welfare. But how does competition work? How does it promote economic welfare? Why is it self-regulating? And why is monopoly considered

less dependable for serving the welfare of the general public?
What is the justification for regulating monopoly?

THE FUNCTION OF COMPETITION IN AN ECONOMIC SYSTEM

A first step in understanding competition is to recognize that there are differences in markets. At one extreme is the broad "American Market." It includes all the things bought and sold in this country. In this "market," all sellers compete vigorously for their shares of the consumer's dollar. At the other extreme, the market for Tiffany diamonds is extremely narrow; as the product is defined, there is only one seller. In the first case, everything can be considered in some measure a substitute for everything else in the consumer's living standard; and in the second case, there is no substitute at all. In defining such markets, the concept used by the economist is the "degree of product substitutability." Sellers tend to be more competitive when their products can be readily substituted for one another.

Some firms compete almost exclusively with rivals that produce the same or nearly identical products. Tool makers, for instance, compete primarily with one another—on the basis of their ability to design and produce tools to meet various specifications. There may be alternative tool makers—and thus competition within the industry—but there is no alternative industry to which a buyer can turn to meet his needs. The degree of substitutability is low between the tool industry and any other.

On the other hand, movie theaters compete not only with other movie theaters but also with plays, sports events, and television. Similarly, steel competes directly with steel, less directly with aluminum, and more remotely with wood. In other words, the breadth of the market depends on the degree to which goods can be substituted for one another, and this in turn influences the range of competition.

In general, competition exists when there are a number of sellers of a product or a service and no single seller can exercise control over the market price. In a sense, this means the individual seller is "controlled" by the market. Competition means that in the search for income new firms are free to enter into any kind of production, and workers are free to shift from job to job. Ultimately, it means that the distribution of workers, capital, and other resources is determined by the "votes" in the market.

Competition also implies freedom of choice for consumers; and it helps to guide production in accordance with consumer desires. All consumers are free to allocate their income in a way they believe will yield them the greatest satisfaction. This spending pattern tends to direct production into a pattern that reflects the wishes of consumers.

The price system is the prime mover. A simple illustration will show in theory how a competitive price system works.

A company producing nails must pay its workers as much as they could get by working elsewhere. (Competition means there are alternative places for them to work.) Similarly, the company must pay the going price for all the other materials and services it uses in producing nails. In other words, competition determines what the firm pays for productive resources. That is, competition determines the price of labor (the wage rate) and the price of all the other things the firm buys.

Competition also determines how much the seller can charge for nails. If the price consumers are willing to pay for nails is not high enough to cover all these costs, the company will lose money, and ultimately it will have to stop producing nails. The workers and the other productive resources that have been used by the firm will then tend to move to other firms where consumer demand for the product is great enough to cover all the costs. The resources move to firms where the prospects of earnings are greater.

On the other hand, if the demand for nails increases, the price of them will tend to rise, permitting nail producers to earn larger profits. These larger profits will attract new producers and induce the original producers to expand production and to bid for more labor and other productive resources. These resources will be diverted from other production where demand is weaker. As a result, the supply of nails will increase, and this will tend to bring the price down to the point where the nail producers are "in equilibrium"—they are covering their costs and earning a normal profit.

Price competition also helps to weed out the less efficient producers. The successful firms will be those nail producers who, through efficient operation, can sell nails at the lowest price. Those who cannot pay the "going wage" (the competitive wage) or earn the normal profit at the prevailing price for nails will eventually have to give up production.

Clearly, the role of prices is important in a competitive system. A rise in prices, for example, will accomplish two things. First, as noted above, it will offer producers an opportunity to bid workers and other resources away from other activities and into the production of nails. Second, a price increase will eliminate some buyers from the market; only those who can afford the higher price will continue to buy nails. In brief, there will be high prices to match the limited supply, but there will be no "shortage" (just as there is usually no "shortage" of Cadillac automobiles today, even though a lot of people cannot buy them). Falling prices would, of course, tend to bring the opposite results—less incentive to produce and more buyers. Thus flexible prices can help bring about the necessary adjustments in purchases and production.

However, if competition is restrained so that prices cannot move up, an increase in consumers' demand for a certain quality of nails may only result in "shortages"; people may be willing to buy them at the fixed price, but the supply will not be adequate. In such circumstances, the nails will go to those buyers who get to the store early and buy while the supply lasts. On the other hand, if the price cannot move down, a decrease in consumer demand may merely mean unsold goods on sellers' shelves.

The price system, even in highly competitive markets, seldom works perfectly. Its operation is sometimes impaired by the presence of too few buyers or sellers, lack of knowledge of alternative opportunities, and too many restrictions on competitive practices. Because real markets seldom operate with perfect smoothness, the economist has developed the concept of "perfect competition" to describe an "ideal" market in which adjustments in production and distribution would work out as smoothly as our nail illustration. This type of perfect market never exists, but the concept is a useful theoretical tool with which to compare the actual performance in a market.

Monopolistic firms may perform like competitive firms, but there is no assurance that they will. Monopoly is at the other end of the scale from competition; it means literally "one seller," but the term is commonly used to mean any producer who has substantial control over prices in the market.

A monopoly, as sole or dominant supplier of a product, occupies a sheltered position. If its product is a necessity, and if no good substitutes are immediately available, the monopolistic firm may restrict its output and increase its profits by charging high prices. It will not be obliged to heed the desires of consumers or the pressures of competition. In its sheltered position, it can operate in a settled way, without modernizing equipment and without keeping abreast of new technology.

Monopoly distorts the workings of the free market. It does not yield the checks and incentives that are provided by competition. Nor does it always provide an automatic stimulus to innovation and economic growth. In order to perpetuate itself, it must regularly prevent rivals from developing. In other words, monopoly may not only permit resources to be used in an inefficient manner but it may also obstruct or prevent the entry of firms that would correct the situation.

The monopolistic firm, however, may not take advantage of its sheltered position; it may never try to exploit the public. But the fact that it has the power to act contrary to the best interests of society is often considered justification for curbing that power. For these reasons, whenever it is more practical to serve the public by means of a monopoly, such enterprises usually are regulated to prevent the abuse of monopoly power.

These general comments about the theory of competition and monopoly give us some indication why economists have a tendency to prefer competition. However, the preference for competition is not absolute. As we shall see, there are a number of instances in which governmental restraints or private restraints on competition have been judged to be preferable to free competition.

AMERICAN EXPERIENCE WITH
COMPETITION AND MONOPOLY

Laissez faire, the philosophy of minimum governmental interference in economic affairs, guided our economy during its first century. A growing population and an open frontier fostered the competitive notion of "every man for himself." With abundant resources to develop, there were widespread economic opportunities—and those who accepted these opportunities were not likely to be controlled by government. Competition for expanding markets was heightened by the richness of the rewards for success. Competition in the market helped direct production, and in doing so probably speeded the economic development of the nation.

However, a laissez faire policy did not create a wholly competitive economy. Monopolies existed in nearly every town and city. As a small community could support only one "general store" or blacksmith, many a tradesman was spared any competitive challenge in his locality. We have no way of knowing how much of the work of the economy was done under such conditions, but we do know that improved transportation and the growth of markets spelled the end of many of these local monopolies. In other words, as the economy grew, competition often became more vigorous.

Economic expansion also fostered the development of the so-called "natural" monopoly. This is a firm that can provide service at lower cost than two or more competing firms. The railroads were early "natural" monopolies. Because wagon trains were comparatively slow and inconvenient, and because it was too costly or risky to build a competing railroad alongside an existing one, the first railroad in operation was generally able to maintain its market advantage.

Some of the railroads used their monopoly power to exploit the public. As a result, some state governments attempted to control railroad activities, but the laws were often ineffective. As public resentment against the monopolistic practices of railroads grew, and as more railroads crossed state lines, there was a growing demand for federal regulation.

The establishment of the Interstate Commerce Commission in 1887 was one of the earliest efforts of the federal government to regulate monopolistic activities. It had been the practice of many railroads to cut their rates for preferred customers and to raise rates for others; as usually there was no competing railroad for "short hauls" along the area between large cities, they charged what the traffic would bear; and on "long hauls" they occasionally embarked on "rate wars," which were designed to destroy rivals so that rates could subsequently be increased. The ICC was formed to prevent these and related practices and to require the railroads to perform more in the public interest.

The rise of cities led to the growth of additional "natural" monopolies. Water, sewage disposal, urban transportation, and later, electricity and gas became necessary for the community. Because competitive utility services were generally inferior or wasteful, the community usually gave one firm an exclusive franchise. In return, the firm accepted some municipal or state regulation. More recently, the federal government has also regulated public utilities that cross state lines. Telephone service, electric power, and gas pipelines are but a few of the industries in which federal regulation has supplemented state and local regulation.

The intent of regulation was seldom to impose competitive conditions, for in most instances competition would have been costly and wasteful. Rather, regulation attempted to cause the monopolist to operate in the public interest as well as his own interest. Government regulation of "legal monopolies" was a substitute for control by the competitive market.

As business expanded, a new challenge to competition arose. Many producers began to combine with competing firms or to destroy other competing firms by a variety of cutthroat practices. The formation of the Standard Oil Trust in 1881 is a familiar illustration.

John D. Rockefeller engaged in price wars to smash rivals and experimented with various kinds of pooling agreements and rebates from railways to tighten control of supply in the richest markets. His most effective innovation was the voting trust, by which stockholders of competing companies gave their voting rights to a central group of trustees who thereby were able to manage production and prices of all the participating companies as though they were one large firm. The success of the trust movement in the oil industry led quickly to similar devices in the sugar, whiskey, match, steel, tobacco, and other industries.

The development of these trusts provoked widespread public resentment and eventually led to restrictive federal legislation. In 1890, a decade after the organization of Standard Oil, the Sherman Antitrust Act was passed. It sought to prohibit all kinds of agreements, contracts, and voting trusts that restrained trade. But the law was written in general terms, and enforcement was difficult. Hence, despite the publicized "trust-busting" activities of President Theodore Roosevelt's administration, business sought and found new ways to diminish competition—by establishing holding companies, buying up assets of other firms, and engaging in many discriminatory trade practices.

In 1914, new legislation—the Federal Trade Commission Act and the Clayton Act—was passed in an effort to control practices that were not clearly subject to regulation under the Sherman Act. Price discrimination among different buyers, tie-in sales that required the buyer of a given product also to buy other products from the same seller, and purchasing the stock of competing firms were some of the practices attacked under the Clayton Act. The Robinson-Patman Act was passed in 1936 to further regulate the pricing policies of firms. The Antimerger Act of 1950 made it unlawful for one firm to acquire the assets of another where the effect may be to substantially lessen competition or tend to create a monopoly.

Apart from the regulation of natural monopolies, governmental policy has thus attempted to prevent practices that tend to restrain competition. By enacting the antitrust laws (more accurately, the "antimonopoly" laws) and establishing the machinery to enforce them, Congress has worked toward some "rules of the game" designed to maintain an effective market system. These laws, primarily the Sherman Act and the Clayton Act, do not catalogue all the things that business can and cannot do—that would be impossible. They cite some general practices that can lead to monopoly, and give the courts wide discretion in deciding what constitutes illegal "restraint of trade" or what practices "substantially lessen" competition.

Over the years, the interpretation of these laws has changed as circumstances have changed. The enforcement agencies, the United States Department of Justice and the Federal Trade Commission, and the courts have changed their views a number of times about what business firms can and cannot do. The process of judicial review, whereby cases or rulings are decided in the federal courts, has enabled the changing ideas of the members of the judiciary to play a crucial role in the changing interpretation of the laws.

In general, the antitrust laws do not punish the mere size of firms. On the issue of large firms that seemingly had the power to control the level of prices and determine the degree of competition, the courts said in two cases:

1. A firm that produced 95 per cent of the shoe machinery output—

> The company, indeed, has magnitude, but it is at once the result and cause of efficiency, and the charge that it has been oppressively used is not sustained.[1]

2. A firm that controlled about 50 per cent of the output of steel products—

> The Corporation is undoubtedly of impressive size and it takes an effort of resolution not to be affected by it or to exaggerate its influence. But we must adhere to the law and the law does not make mere size an offense or the existence of unexerted power an offense.[2]

Later, however, the Aluminum Company of America, which produced about 90 per cent of the aluminum ingots, was held to have acquired a monopoly in violation of the law. "Nothing compelled it to keep doubling and redoubling

[1] *U. S. v. United Shoe Machinery Company*, 247 U. S. 56 (1918).
[2] *U. S. v. United States Steel Corporation*, 251 U. S. 451 (1920).

its capacity before others entered the field,"[3] said the court. Other decisions involving the tobacco and taxicab industries also implied that the magnitude of market domination should be considered in antitrust cases. But even this view has been modified by subsequent decisions, so that the prevailing stress seems to be less on the share of the market held by a firm and more on the particular practices a firm may use to restrain trade and control prices.

In deciding what constitutes illegal restraint of trade, the court has maintained a flexible attitude. In 1911, the court said it was guided by the "rule of reason"—that it did not condemn all restraints of trade, but only those that appeared to exert an *unreasonable* restraint on competition and trade. Some such statement was necessary, as the Sherman Act prohibited "every contract, conspiracy or combination in restraint of trade." This broad terminology seemed to conflict with established rights of contract. The "rule of reason" was simply a statement that the legality of the behavior of any firm must be judged in terms of the particular facts of the case; absolute standards simply could not be applied in a complex economic system.

As the American economy has encountered new problems, it has frequently modified its policy on free competition. In the period before the Civil War, for instance, competition in the banking field led to a number of abuses that harmed the operation of the monetary and banking system. The National Banking Act of 1863 was passed partly in order to control some of these abusive practices. Pure food laws, child labor laws, "truth in advertising" laws, are all results of the attempt of society to make competition conform to certain standards—they are attempts to restrict competitive practices in order that the market mechanism will yield results that conform with the desires of the community.

Various amendments to the antitrust laws have also been made, permitting certain groups of producers to work together in combination. The Webb-Pomerene Act (1918) permits firms engaged in selling goods abroad to combine in

[3] *U. S.* v. *Aluminum Corporation of America, et al.*, 148 Fed. (2d) 431 (1945).

their export operations. The act was designed primarily to enable American firms to compete with similar combinations in other countries. The Miller-Tydings Act (1937), and the McGuire Act (1952) permit manufacturers to restrict competition among retailers by setting "fair trade" prices. The Clayton Act, one of the basic antimonopoly laws, specifically excludes agriculture and labor associations from the provisions of the law, and subsequent legislation has also been passed to strengthen this position. Both of these groups were apparently felt to be at a competitive disadvantage in the developing industrial economy and, therefore, were given special opportunities to combine.

The biggest departure from the policy of free competition was the National Industrial Recovery Act (1933). This act, which encouraged business, labor, agriculture, and professional groups to work together to determine price and output policies, was designed to combat the depression. In words that are similar to those that were used later by supporters of "fair trade" laws, President Franklin D. Roosevelt said about the act:

> Its goal is the assurance of a reasonable profit to industry and living wages for labor with the elimination of the piratical methods and practices which have not only harassed honest business but also contributed to the ills of labor.[4]

The NRA "codes," which were the government-approved restrictions on competition drawn up by each industry, lasted only two years, but in that time they became the nation's guides for competitive behavior. They were a product of the depression and a reflection of the hope that by stabilizing prices and competitive practices, the nation could find the way to recovery.

How do we account for the enactment of these laws that seem to contradict the general principles of our antitrust legislation? Some people think they merely reflect the power of small, self-seeking pressure groups. Others think they reflect

[4] *The Public Papers and Addresses of Franklin D. Roosevelt,* Vol. II (1933), p. 246.

the defects in the competitive system. There is some truth in both of these views, but there is more to the problem than that.

Competition needs rules, and society uses these rules to achieve a variety of objectives. For example, the American people have generally been sympathetic to the under-privileged. Therefore, some laws are designed to strengthen the position of those who appear to be in a relatively weak bargaining position. This was clearly an important reason for the legislation permitting workers to combine into labor un-ions and farmers into co-operatives. It is interesting to note that, unless such combinations are thought to be "abusing" their power, they are seldom even called "monopolistic."

Public opinion also seems sensitive to the adverse effects of vigorous price competition. It is also sensitive to the needs of small businesses. Thus even though the independent retail firm may charge more for a product than a chain store or a "discount house," it is protected by "fair trade" laws. The public has not always been sensitive to these issues—nor should it always be expected to be sensitive to them in the future.

Clearly, the American public is not concerned with the preservation of competition merely for the sake of competition. It desires competition because in most circumstances the competitive market provides an efficient means of allocating the productive resources of the nation. But there is no measure to show how much a given deviation from competition harms this allocation mechanism.

When the practices of a particular firm clearly violate our loosely defined ideals of competition, the government makes an effort to stop them. But governmental action may also have an undesirable effect on other objectives such as the in-creased productivity of large-scale enterprises, the incomes of farmers, workers, or other groups, the continued existence of small business, or the growth of research and technology.

MARKET FAILURES

Rising concern about pollution in the 1960s focused atten-tion on a problem that had been relatively neglected: the management of common property resources, such as the atmosphere, rivers, and oceans. Like the public goods discussed in Chapter 2, these resources are used by all of us collectively and are not traded in the market. Unlike public goods such as weapons and roads, they cannot be replaced through production and they have generally been free—a gift of nature. And there's the rub.

Goods and services that are free tend to be overused, and our common property resources have proved especially vulnerable to exploitation. For a long time, it seemed that the simplest and most economical way to get rid of household or industrial waste was to dump it into the river or spew it into the air—and then rely on nature to purify it, recycle it, or hide it. Any other disposal effort seemed unnecessarily costly. This system seemed to work for hundreds of years, until the population explosion and the enormous increase in industrial output began to overtax nature's capacity. By the beginning of the 1960s, it began to be widely recognized that clean air and clean water are scarce resources, not unlimited ones, and that since we can't manufacture more of either, we need to ration their use more effectively.

Since puffs of air and drops of water are not traded in the market, the services provided by the atmosphere and waterways in carrying off wastes are not included in the cost of production. Suppose a manufacturer of widgets dumps the wastes from his plant into a river, making water downstream unfit to drink. Waste disposal will show up as a cost to the downstream community, which had no part in widget production and perhaps no interest at all in widget consumption, rather than to the producer. This is what economists call an "external cost" or "externality." In the foregoing example, widget making prospers, and the value of a common resource declines. As for the community downstream, its residents can either look for another source of water, invest in a water purification system, or persuade the upstream polluters either to stop polluting or to foot the bill for a cleanup.

Two consequences of not including all costs in the price of a product should be stressed. First, drawing on the example used above, if all costs are not included, the price of widgets may be lower relative to other products, and more may be sold. Second, if waste disposal is not included in the cost of production, the producer has no incentive to economize in the use of air and water.

There are various ways to cope with this so-called market failure. One is to impose regulations to ban or reduce the discharge of pollutants. Another is to encourage the treatment of wastes, through the federal subsidies that have been provided for the construction of municipal sewage treatment plants, for example. Still another is to impose a charge on the disposal of wastes into the air and rivers in an effort to discourage the practice and to give producers an incentive to seek alternative means of waste disposal, including recycling. The use of such effluent charges is a device for incorporating the cost of waste disposal into the cost of the product. If a charge system can be made to work, the need for regulation will be reduced. Competitive pressures will induce the producer to change his method of production, to recycle wastes, or to take other steps to find a cheaper alternative to the dumping of wastes into the river or air.

The use of regulation to compensate for the lack of competition or absence of a market has had mixed results. It has provided consumers with an element of protection against excessive prices by natural monopolies. But, at the same time, according to its critics, it has been time-consuming and inefficient, imposing costs on producers and ultimately on consumers, that are greater than would occur in a competitive market. Regulation has also sometimes proved to be ineffective, partly because of the co-operation that develops between the regulatory agency and the regulated industry.

Defenders of regulation who acknowledge shortcomings in regulatory performance say that the remedy is to be found in improving the regulatory process. Critics, particularly economists, are likely to stress the desirability of eliminating regulation wherever markets can function, to determine efficiently what should be produced at what price. In the field of transportation especially, a series of studies has claimed that if regulations of the Interstate Commerce Commission were largely eliminated, costs would be lower and service better.

Greater efforts to encourage experimentation in the use of

economic incentives have been made in recent years in a number of areas, such as job training and pollution control, but regulation, despite its shortcomings, remains the major alternative to the competitive market.

KINDS OF MONOPOLY IN EXISTENCE TODAY

Many practices that seem competitive are also in some degree monopolistic. For instance, brand names and product differentiation are attempts by sellers to distinguish their products and to acquire a special advantage for them. They are competitive efforts to attract consumers. At the same time, they provide some protection from the actions of rival producers. The difference, in other words, between what is called competition and what is called monopoly is to some extent a matter of degree—the degree of control the seller has over the market price.

Collusive activities among sellers are clearly monopolistic. Competitors who get together to decide on a uniform pricing policy or a division of the market, or to impose restrictions on the area of competition, violate the law. Such agreements between competitors are illegal in themselves. The government does not need to prove that the effect of these agreements will be to lessen competition. It only has to prove that the agreement was made.

But it is often difficult to find out whether agreements have been made. A casual conversation during a game of golf or a trade association meeting may accomplish the same uniformity of practice that the "Gary Dinners" did when they brought steel producers together to agree on competitive practices in the steel industry. The conviction of several executives in 1961 for price-fixing in the electrical industry was a reminder that agreements to limit competition still posed a problem nearly fifty years after they had been made illegal, but we have no way of knowing how prevalent such collusion continues to be.

Mergers, consolidations, and holding companies can also restrain competition. These legal combinations are subject to review and prosecution by government, but in each case the government must show that competition has been restrained or will be substantially lessened by the combination. However, the very elusiveness of the concept of competition frequently makes it difficult for the government to prove its case.

A central issue for all concerned with antitrust has been the problem of defining the market. To conclude that a merger will give a firm too large a share of the market requires first that the market be defined. The general criterion, as indicated in this chapter, is that firms are considered to be in the same market if the products they produce are substitutes for one another.

But are glass containers and metal cans in the same market? The court held that they were in blocking the merger of the Continental Can Company, second largest producer of metal cans, and Hazel-Atlas Glass Company, the third largest producer of glass containers. The company argued in vain that the markets were separate, and a minority of the court accused the majority of inventing a single market by joining glass and metal containers—but not including plastic or other kinds of containers in that market.

The definition of the market was the crux of the famous cellophane case. Here a broad definition worked to the advantage of the company. The court cleared Du Pont of monopolizing cellophane because it interpreted the market broadly to include all flexible wrapping materials—aluminum, waxed papers, glassine, and others—rather than cellophane alone.

But in a later case, a merger was struck down because the FTC defined the market narrowly to include only steel wool pads instead of all kinds of scouring pads.

Many people regard the growth of big business as an indication that our economy is highly monopolistic. Much of the production of the nation comes from giant firms that dominate an industry. For example, the nation's fifty largest manufacturing companies account for one fourth of our manufacturing production, and the two hundred largest for more than 40 per cent.

Concentration varies from industry to industry, as the accompanying table indicates, and it varies over time. These figures tell only part of the story about market power, however, and it is dangerous to generalize about the effectiveness of competition from statistics about concentration.

SHARE OF THE MARKET BY BIG FIRMS

Industry	Percentage of value of shipments by 4 largest companies	
	1947	1972
Blast furnaces and steel	50	45
Cereal breakfast foods	79	90
Cigarettes	90	84
Meat-packing	41	22
Milk	22	18
Petroleum refining	37	31
Women's coats and dresses	3	13

Source: *Concentration Ratios in Manufacturing*, U. S. Bureau of Census, 1972 Census of Manufacturing, October 1975.

It should be pointed out that these figures are for *manufacturing* industries, and manufacturing accounts for slightly less than a third of our national income. In other industries, such as retail and wholesale trade, construction, and the service industries, production is far less concentrated. It is important to remember, therefore, that the 8 million non-farm businesses of the nation operate under a variety of market conditions, and that despite the concentration of assets among large firms in the economy, competition has not declined. The number of firms has, in fact, grown along with our population.

Some economists contend that monopolistic behavior is fostered when one or a few sellers are much more powerful than all the rest in the market. Others argue that competition can be more vigorous. Most economists would probably agree that competition can exist in industries in which oligopoly (a few sellers) exists, but that it will be very different from the competition among a large number of sellers of similar size. For example, in a market where there are many small firms, each firm tends to operate on the assumption that if it cuts prices, other sellers will not promptly retaliate. It supplies too small a part of the total market to seriously injure its rivals. But if there are only a few producers, each firm must consider the possible reactions of the other firms. Thus if a large producer is contemplating a price cut that might increase its share of the market from, say, 25 to 30 per cent of the total sales, it must expect the other large producers to retaliate. Seemingly, this fact limits price competition—without any collusion on the part of the sellers.

The view has been expressed that large enterprises are held in check by "countervailing power." Bigness in one sector of the economy may beget bigness in another, and a new set of checks and balances may result. It is argued that these centers of power offset each other, and perform a function similar to the role played by competition among many small producers. In addition to giant manufacturing corporations, there are large labor unions and large farm organizations that also wield tremendous economic power. The government itself is one of the strongest bargaining forces. When these groups bargain with each other, the power of one limits the power of the other.

This display of power against power is apparent when government enters into contracts with industry, when labor bargains with management, and so on. But it is also more specific. The giant buyer confronts the giant seller within an industry. The giant steel companies are confronted by giant automobile manufacturers as buyers of sheet steel, and by giant can manufacturers as buyers of tin plate. And the giant steel companies must compete against giant aluminum or other metal producers in order to hold their markets. Large electrical manufacturers buy from large copper producers, and large food processors must bargain with large chain store distributors. Thus it is suggested that however remote this system of power versus power seems from the ideal of perfect competition, its results may be somewhat similar. Countervailing power, in other words, may help keep prices within bounds and check the abuse of economic power.

But these powerful units do not always compete with each other. They may find it advantageous to pool their interests or combine their power. For example, building contractors and trade unions have occasionally formed collusive agreements designed to close local markets to new workers and new builders and thereby to control prices. The fact that big firms frequently merge with competitors or integrate their operations to avoid bargaining with suppliers or distributors suggests that countervailing power cannot be considered an adequate regulator of economic power. Moreover, big firms and government may also work hand in hand.

It has also been argued that large firms will operate in the public interest because big business has bred a new type of leader who has a greater sense of social responsibility. The "robber baron" seems to be passé. "Industrial statesmen" may be more typical of the American scene today than at the turn of the century. Certainly there is good evidence that business leaders today are *likely to be* far more aware of their public responsibilities. Either because they are sensitive to the needs of the public or because they fear the consequences of public criticism, more business leaders appear to be responsive to public opinion.

A faith in "good leadership" as a substitute for public enforcement of a competitive society assumes that private interests and public interests are the same, or that executives can always wisely compromise conflicting private and public claims. But these are questionable assumptions. Although the rise of better qualified executives with a broader vision of their private and public responsibilities is to be applauded, this development does not in itself seem to provide a satisfactory regulating mechanism for economic life. A system of checks and balances provided by competition or governmental policy has generally proved to be safer for the American economy.

The monopolistic features of our economy are not always easy to identify, nor are the best measures for coping with them easily determined. As we have seen, agreements among sellers, mergers, and consolidations may be used to eliminate rivalry between competing firms. Some forms of rivalry may also be diminished if a few firms become considerably stronger than all the rest. If this happens as a result of greater efficiency or more vigorous competition, the economist must generally evaluate the specific performance of the industry. But as the following section shows, there are different types of competition, and we cannot always be sure which types are best for the American economy.

HOW DO FIRMS COMPETE TODAY?

Product variation, advertising and promotional activities, and price cutting are the major competitive weapons. However, the use of these weapons varies from industry to industry. Automobile manufacturers ordinarily put relatively little emphasis on price competition, but maintain a vigorous rivalry in terms of the style and quality of cars. Automobile dealers, on the other hand, heavily emphasize price in their ads. Many retail firms compete primarily by the services they supply with the product, or the credit terms on which the product is sold. In some industries, such as the cigarette industry, competition appears to be largely a matter of advertising, with relatively little rivalry in either the product or the prices charged by competing firms.

Product improvement is a widespread form of competition in the American economy. Creating new products and improving old products has frequently taken the place of price competition as the principal basis for economic rivalry. Accordingly, over the years the range of products and the opportunities for the exercise of consumer choice has steadily broadened. For example, wool suits now compete not only with other wool suits but also with dacron suits and suits made of a blend of wool and synthetic fibers. Continued multiplication of grades and of varieties of products has increased the range of substitution and inter-product rivalry.

Product variation implies that each producer will sell a product that is partially different from that sold by any other producer. Thus the market consists of a number of partial monopolies in which each producer has more control over his price policy than he would if a number of producers were selling an identical product. In the fabled mouse-trap market, the man who "built a better mouse trap" was somewhat free of the check of competition—and, accordingly, he could behave in some degree like a monopolist (until someone built one that was even better).

An increasing degree of product variation is clearly one

way to meet the variety of wants of the public. It is also a way to improve the quality of the things we consume. But the problem of choosing the right product has become a more complicated task for consumers; for sellers the cost of stocking all grades and varieties has become greater and greater. These and the costs of product research and experiments are the price we pay for variety and improvement; they are the price we pay for this form of competition.

Promotional activity is the most familiar form of competition. Advertising, branding of products, and the services of salesmen and dealers supplied with products, are well known to consumers today. It is sometimes claimed that these activities impose unnecessary costs on the public, but in general, promotional activities perform an important function. They bring information about products to the attention of consumers, and as a consequence the degree of competition may be heightened. If they expand markets, they may result in lower costs through mass production.

In some respects, promotional activities come close to being variations in product. Many selling campaigns are designed to make the consumer feel that one product is different from all others when in fact it may be quite similar. For example, a brand name is designed to make the consumer think specifically of a given product: "Don't ask for a widget; ask for an Acme Widget with a super-horizontal-platidone—just ask your dealer for S-H-P." The services of the dealer combine with the advertising and brand name to make the product appear, in the mind of the consumer, as a complex package of services for which he may have a slight preference. The creation of this preference is the objective of the promotional activities.

When the product cannot be distinguished from its near-substitutes either by its own characteristics or by the services and promotion of its seller, price variation is the main basis of competition. This was the basis of competition in our earlier illustration of the nail producer. But price competition can also operate alongside the other forms of competition. The television industry is a familiar example. Since the first (black-and-white) television sets were produced for large commercial sales after World War II, they have undergone major changes. Quality has improved, and costs of production have declined. These cost savings have led to greater price competition. The introduction of color led to another competitive cycle. At the same time, television manufacturers expanded promotional activities in an effort to increase consumer preference for a particular make or model. More recently, product innovation has led to television games and videocassettes.

However, price competition has diminished in a number of industries where a "live and let live" policy prevails. Druggists, jewelers, and a number of other retailing groups have supported laws to prevent unrestricted price competition. Automobile dealers have tried to stop what they call "bootlegging" cars—selling them at reduced prices. Manufacturers' groups have established a variety of pricing schemes to control price competition. Labor unions have exerted a high degree of control over wage competition among individual workers. Agricultural groups have limited competition by participating in production quotas and marketing agreements.

Understanding of the long-run effect of these limitations on price competition requires individual market studies. Broad generalization cannot be applied to so diverse and complex an economy as that of modern America. Most economists, on principle, would urge that price competition should be expanded, but many recommend exceptions to meet special circumstances in today's economy. It is on the specific exceptions that economists mostly disagree; for example, labor, agriculture, steel, banks, to mention a few. Some indication of the complexity of the problem can be seen if now we take a further look at our policy toward mergers. We shall use the framework outline in Chapter 1.

The Problem and the Issues

Mergers are a natural part of the economic process. They may enhance competition as well as weaken it. Mergers enable firms to acquire new technology quickly and economically, to achieve diversification that will lead to stronger and more stable operations, and to achieve more reliable sources of supply. Sometimes there may be tax advantages and other financial incentives. However, under some circumstances mergers may reduce competition or threaten to do so.

Over the years, public concern about mergers has risen and fallen, depending in part on the prominence of the merging firms and the over-all level of merger activity. Political and social factors also play a role. We have had at least three big merger waves since the Sherman Antitrust Act was passed, in 1890. At the turn of the century, huge combines were built up in such industries as sugar, tobacco, steel, and petroleum. In the 1920s the automotive, farm-machinery, chemical, and electrical industries were focal points of activity. After World War II there was a rather steady increase in mergers throughout the 1950s and 1960s. This trend exploded into the great merger wave of 1967–70, which was marked by the growth of the big conglomerates, such as Ling-Temco-Vought, Litton Industries, Gulf & Western, and others. These giant firms were built by combining a number of unrelated companies.

Merger activity has been relatively modest in the 1970s, but the quadrupling of oil prices in 1973–74 by the Organization of Petroleum Exporting Countries (OPEC) provided a dramatic reminder of how producers can act together to exert monopoly power. Although the OPEC cartel is unlike a U.S. antitrust case, it revived fears in the United States of concentrated economic power. Public frustration was reflected in calls to break up big oil companies or to pass laws that would keep them from acquiring coal companies and other firms in the energy business.

The rise in merger activity in the 1950s and 1960s was accompanied by an unprecedented government drive to enforce antimerger laws. More mergers were blocked during 1950–65 than during the previous thirty-five years. Among the more noteworthy cases was the Justice Department's success in blocking the proposed merger of Bethlehem Steel, the nation's second largest producer of steel, and Youngstown Sheet and Tube, the sixth largest. The court rejected the companies' argument that the merger would increase the ability of Bethlehem to compete with U. S. Steel, the number-one firm. It was more concerned with the fact that Bethlehem's share of the market would be increased from 15 to 20 per cent and that this might give impetus to further mergers in the industry as other firms sought to strengthen their capacity to compete against the Big Two.

In 1962, in the first case under the 1950 Antimerger Act to reach the Supreme Court, the Brown Shoe Company was ordered to divest itself of the Kinney Shoe Company. The court said that this merger between the eighth and third largest shoe distributors would accelerate a trend toward concentration in the shoe industry.

Cases such as these made it clear that the government would probably attack mergers by competitors in the same line of commerce (horizontal mergers) when one or both of the firms involved held a substantial share of the market.

Acquisition of suppliers or outlets (vertical mergers) has presented issues of greater complexity, since economic evidence on the competitive effects of a vertical merger is more debatable. But vertical mergers have also been challenged. The Brown Shoe case had vertical as well as horizontal aspects. Brown was a manufacturer as well as a distributor, and the court feared that Brown might require Kinney stores to carry Brown shoes, thereby closing part of the market to Brown's rivals. An especially dramatic and controversial vertical-merger decision (based on the original Clayton Act) was the 1957 order that required Du Pont to dispose of its holdings of General Motors stock acquired forty years earlier.

Consequences of acquiring quite unrelated firms (conglomerate mergers) are especially difficult to assess. The firms are neither rivals in the same market nor customers of one another. Until the mid-1960s, there was no indication that conglomerate mergers would be challenged. But the size of some conglomerate mergers and the increase in their number led the government to re-examine the possible consequences of such mergers and to file a number of suits. Today there is much greater uncertainty over the competitive consequences of conglomerate mergers than over horizontal or vertical mergers, but it is clear that conglomerates are not immune from prosecution.

The Objectives

The broad purpose of antitrust policy is to help keep the economy vigorously competitive so that production will be efficient, prices low, and innovation encouraged. Merger policy is aimed more specifically at blocking or breaking up combinations that impair competition or are likely to impair it. Mergers may reduce the number of effective rivals, for example, or make it more difficult for new firms to enter the market.

At the same time, there appears to be no interest in prohibiting all mergers. Thus, a requirement of policy may be to keep the merger route open as a useful way of achieving business expansion and reorganization.

The Alternatives

One alternative is to accept the existing legislation as adequate. The 1950 Act, it is said, closed an important loophole, and the government is now able to attack mergers that would have been immune under the original Clayton Act. The government should, therefore, concentrate on the maintenance of vigorous enforcement efforts and on the development of better tools for determining which mergers should be halted.

Another alternative is based on the assumption that antimerger legislation is not really effective, since the 1950 law didn't prevent the 1967 burst of mergers. Therefore, a remedy should be sought through modification of governmental policies other than antitrust policies. An antitrust program, it is argued, cannot by itself maintain a competitive economy if governmental policies on taxation, the award of military and other contracts, international trade, and so on undermine competition by continually favoring one or another group of firms.

Another alternative is to enact tougher antimerger laws. If the rise of conglomerate mergers is interpreted as evidence that business firms have turned away from horizontal and vertical mergers because of antitrust policy and enforcement, perhaps the time has come for legislation aimed specifically at conglomerates.

Still another alternative would be to eliminate all antimerger legislation and confine antitrust prosecution to instances of monopolizing or collusive behavior. The great merger wave of the late 1960s, which saw the total number of acquisitions jump from 1,746 in 1966 to 4,542 in 1969, subsided of its own accord by 1972, and, in the words of one observer, "hardly transformed the industrial landscape." Perhaps the emphasis on mergers as a threat to competition is misplaced.

Appraising the Alternatives

Choices among such alternatives as these may be related to three different approaches to antitrust problems.

One is the *market structure* approach. Some observers argue that there is a very close relationship between the number of firms in a market and their relative size, on the one hand, and the behavior of firms on the other. They give great weight to data about the level of concentration in any industry—the proportion of assets, sales, or employment that are accounted for by the four largest or twenty largest firms in the industry. The antitrust program should strike at possession of undue market power, irrespective of a firm's conduct. This line of reasoning could be used to buttress the case for tougher legislation, particularly against conglomerates.

A second approach is to put major stress on *conduct*. While structural evidence is relevant, some experts argue that in the type of economy we have today, with its many monopolistic elements, it is futile, if not harmful, to insist on any particular structure. The essential issue is the firm's conduct—such as its pricing practices. Is it engaged in collusive activities or monopolistic practices in which mergers form one aspect of a broad effort aimed at obtaining and maintaining undue market power? This approach might lead to less emphasis on antimerger activity and greater concern with monopolistic practices and the effects of other government policies.

A third approach is to stress *performance*. After all, say proponents of this view, if our objective is maximum growth consistent with price stability and full employment, we should judge firms by their contribution to these goals. If the firm produces high-quality products and is an innovator, if it is efficient, and so on, questions of structure, and perhaps even of conduct, are secondary.

The relative quiet in merger activity that has followed the 1960s explosion of activity (and the intense concern it caused) provides a good setting for a dispassionate analysis of these alternatives.

This chapter has stressed the following ideas:

1. Competition, especially price competition, is a basic characteristic of a free market system. It can perform the function of a regulator of production and consumption and provide a framework of incentives for the achievement of greater economic efficiency.

2. However, competition does not regulate the use of common property resources, such as air and water, so these must be managed by public policies.

3. Unrestrained competition does not always yield results that agree with our social objectives. First, competition may actually destroy itself as some firms destroy others. Second, competition may harm certain groups that are weak in bargaining power. Third, in some instances competition may be more wasteful than monopoly. Therefore, in order to obtain socially desirable results the government has imposed certain "rules of the game."

4. Rivalry by product improvement and advertising is not the same as price competition. Economists differ in their views of which provides better service to consumers, but most economists would urge the maximum degree of price competition consistent with developing technology and an expansion of production.

5. In evaluating the desirability of restrictions on price competition, we must consider not only the interests of the persons directly affected, but also the long-run interests of the American people as a whole. We are able to do this only if we make an effort to trace the consequences of the restrictions and then see how well they serve our objectives.

Suggested Reading

Paul A. Samuelson, *Economics*, Chap. 26, pp. 508–34. George L. Bach, *Economics: An Introduction to Analysis and*

Policy, Chaps. 24–27. See also "A Policy for Antitrust Law," by Carl Kaysen and Donald F. Turner, in *Readings in Economics,* pp. 189–95, and "In My New Industrial State Trust Busting Not Needed," by J. Kenneth Galbraith, in the same volume, pp. 195–99.

Chapter 4

LABOR AND UNIONS

One of the continuing questions in any economy is: Who gets how much? In an economy of competitive markets, this question is answered by a stream of decisions in the market place. But in the American economy impersonal relations among buyers and sellers do not rule alone. The government helps decide who gets how much when it taxes one group more heavily than it taxes another, or makes payments to one group and not another. When farmers organize co-operatives, they too are trying to do the same thing—alter the distribution of income. Doctors, businessmen, and other groups have used various devices from time to time in attempts to enlarge their share of the output of the nation. So have labor unions.

Labor union activity is of particular interest because about one fourth of our employed population belongs to labor unions or employee associations. In such key industries as steel, autos, and trucking, nearly all employees are union members. Unions are also important because they can exert substantial pressure on wages and working conditions, not only for themselves but for all workers. They sometimes create pressures on prices and employment. They exert political power, they occasionally fight among themselves, and they sometimes challenge or defend basic aspects of a free market economy.

In this chapter we shall explore some of the effects of labor union action. We shall also examine one of the pressing problems of governmental policy—what to do about work stoppages in vital industries. Some people believe that such stoppages should be strictly controlled, others believe that these stoppages must be tolerated as a necessary cost of our kind of economic system. In a broad sense, the discussion that follows illustrates the way we might examine other economic groups—farmers, electric power producers, or any other group. We want to find out what they are, what they want, how they try to get it, and the consequences of their behavior.

OBJECTIVES AND GROWTH OF UNIONISM

The avowed objective of American labor unions has been to obtain higher wages and better working conditions for their members. In contrast to the more politically minded labor movements in foreign countries, American unions have been predominantly business-minded. They have sought to get "more" without overturning the economic system. Since the early 1930s, labor unions have been far more active politically than they had been for the preceding half-century. They have sought to gain more of their goals through legislation. Yet the biggest job of the union is still its direct dealings with management.

Labor organizations of some sort—fraternal orders and unions of craftsmen—date back to colonial times. They existed in isolated local communities, frequently as secret societies in order to avoid retaliation by employers. The era of industrial strife following the Civil War brought an increase in union activity and in attempts to form national organizations.

In 1869, the formation of the Knights of Labor brought many unions together in a loose federation. The Knights of Labor was predominantly utopian and politically motivated, although it pursued some immediate economic objectives and engaged in strikes for better working conditions. Its influence declined, however, after the organization of the American Federation of Labor in 1886. The AFL, which was composed mostly of skilled workers, espoused the cause of business unionism and opposed intervention in political affairs, except those directly affecting unions, and it was this philosophy of unionism that triumphed.

The immediate goal of the early union was to sign up members and win recognition as the bargaining agent for the workers it represented. This was the essential preliminary to bargaining for higher wages and better working conditions. The battle for union recognition progressed slowly against the opposition of employers, the apathy of workers, and the distrust of the public.

Union membership grew slowly and irregularly from 1890 until the First World War. Then came an increased demand for labor, and wartime government officials recognized union leaders as spokesmen for the workers. As a result, the prestige—and the membership—of unions increased. By 1920, 5 million workers were organized. A large proportion of them were skilled craftsmen, and only a few industries, such as the coal mines, were unionized on an industry basis. The mass production industries were virtually unorganized.

Union strength waned during the twelve-year period following the depression of 1920–21. The decline was a result of several factors: competition from nonunion workers and labor-saving devices, public and governmental antagonism to unions, complacency of many union leaders, and aggressive antiunion policies pursued by business firms. The law and its interpretation by the courts also generally favored employers. Many employers maintained peaceful relations with their employees, but others fought the rise of unionism by suing union workers for damages or obtaining injunctions prohibiting unions from organizing or striking to enforce their demands. Some employers used spies to check on employees who were spreading the doctrine of unionism. At times they imported strikebreakers to take the jobs of striking workers and to fight them if necessary. Workers who joined unions were not only fired, but they were also "blacklisted"—that is, their names were circulated among other employers, who would refuse to give them jobs. Sometimes, in order to get employment, workers were required to sign "yellow dog" contracts, which bound them not to join a union if hired. These practices contributed to the shrinkage in union membership during the twenties.

The long history of conflict between unions and management, together with the violent and often bloody strikes, gradually awakened the public to the need for a constructive policy to govern industrial relations. One of the first positive steps by government was the Railway Labor Act of 1926, which guaranteed railroad employees the right to organize and bargain collectively. The act also set up machinery for the mediation and arbitration of disputes between the workers and the employers. Another step was the Norris-La Guardia Act of 1932, which limited the use of injunctions in labor disputes and outlawed the yellow dog contract. With these laws, the government was again making some "rules of the game"—only this time they applied to the rivalry between labor and employers.

The passage of the National Industrial Recovery Act in 1933 marked the beginning of a new spurt in union growth. The act provided for a number of changes in the economic structure of the nation; one of these was that "employees shall have the right to organize and bargain collectively through representatives of their own chosing." This right of labor was declared a parallel to the power given to employers to control competition, and it had an immediate impact. The new stature given to unions brought a sharp increase in membership. The act was later declared unconstitutional, but the provision that applied to the newly-won rights of labor was re-enacted in another law—the National Labor Relations Act of 1935 (the Wagner Act).

The Wagner Act declared that peaceful collective bargaining is an objective of federal public policy. It defined unfair labor practices on the part of employers. It created the National Labor Relations Board to supervise union elections, to certify newly organized unions, and to ensure good faith in collective bargaining. Given this legal stimulus, trade union membership jumped from about 3.5 million in 1935 to almost 9 million in 1940. This was a period of bitter organizing drives and vigorous employer opposition to unions, but gradually more and more unions won recognition.

This period also saw the formation of the Congress of Industrial Organizations (CIO) after the American Federation of Labor (AFL) could not decide how to organize workers in mass production industries. The AFL was basically a federation of unions organized along craft lines—carpenters, plumbers, and so on. In organizing an entire industry, such as steel or automobile manufacturing, these AFL unions wanted workers to join the established craft unions. But the supporters of industrial unions wanted to organize workers by industries—one union for steel workers, another for auto workers, and so on. As a result of this conflict, some of the unions broke away from the AFL and formed the CIO.

For 20 years these two organizations competed and grew and then, in 1955, they merged into a single federation which embraced five out of six organized workers. The unity of the labor movement proved short-lived, however. The biggest union within the AFL-CIO, the Teamsters, was expelled for corrupt practices in 1957, the automobile workers withdrew in 1968, and other defections followed.

The trend of union membership, which leveled off for a decade after the early 1950s, began rising again in the 1960s. The new recruits were predominantly white-collar workers from the private sector and government workers. This was the period of transition to a so-called service economy, one in which production workers lost their dominance in the work force. As employment growth faltered in industry, which had been the traditional source of union strength, organizers began shifting their attention to service workers, such as retail clerks, and to the government. At the same time, associations of professional employees, such as teachers, nurses, and police, began to act as collective bargaining agents for their members, thus blurring the distinction between trade unions and associations. The government directory of trade unions was renamed to include "Employee Associations." The membership of major unions—AFL-CIO affiliates and independents—and employee associations is given in the following table.

After the Second World War, unions began to lose public support. The labor shortage and sympathetic aid of the government had contributed to the growth of unions during the war. But strikes in vital industries, jurisdictional disputes between rival unions, and defiance of the government by some union leaders caused a reaction that resulted in the passage of the Taft-Hartley Act in 1947. This law, which amended the Wagner Act, reaffirmed the principle of collective bargaining, but placed a variety of restraints on the powers of the unions. The closed shop was outlawed, the union shop

National Unions and Employee Associations
Reporting 100,000 or More Members

Unions[1]	Members
Teamsters (Ind.)	1,973,000
Automobile Workers (Ind.)	1,545,000
Steelworkers	1,300,000
Electrical (IBEW)	991,000
Machinists	943,000
Carpenters	820,000
Retail Clerks	651,000
Laborers	650,000
State, County	648,000
Service Employees	550,000
Meat Cutters	525,000
Communications Workers	499,000
Hotel	452,000
Teachers	444,000
Operating Engineers	415,000
Ladies' Garment	405,000
Clothing Workers	350,000
Musicians	330,000
Paperworkers	301,000
Government (AFGE)	300,000
Electrical (IUE)	298,000
Postal Workers	249,000
Transportation Union	238,000
Railway Clerks	235,000
Letter Carriers	232,000
Plumbers	228,000
Mine Workers (Ind.)	220,000
Painters	211,000
Rubber	191,000
Iron Workers	182,000
Retail, Wholesale	180,000

[1] All unions not identified as independent (Ind.) are affiliated with the AFL-CIO. Other abbreviations: IBEW for International Brotherhood of Electrical Workers; AFGE for American Federation of Government Employees; IUE for International Union of Electrical, Radio, and Machine Workers; UE for United Electrical, Radio, and Machine Workers; NAGE for National Association of Government Employees; and NFFE for National Federation of Federal Employees.

Unions	Members
Oil, Chemical	177,000
Fire Fighters	172,000
Textile Workers	167,000
Electrical (UE) (Ind.)	163,000
Sheet Metal	161,000
Transport Workers	150,000
Bricklayers	148,000
Transit Union	140,000
Boilermakers	138,000
Bakery	134,000
Printing and Graphic	129,000
Maintenance of Way	119,000
Typographical	111,000
Woodworkers	108,000
Government (NAGE) (Ind.)	([2])
Graphic Arts	100,000
Federal Employees (NFFE) (Ind.)	100,000

Associations	
Education Association	1,470,000
Civil Service (NYS)	207,000
Nurses Association	196,000
Police	147,000
California	106,000

Source: U. S. Bureau of Labor Statistics, *Directory of National Unions and Employee Associations, 1975,* Bulletin 1937 (1977), p. 65. Based on union and association reports for 1974 to the Bureau of Labor Statistics.

came under regulation, as did the check-off, welfare funds, and certain other union programs.[3] Some "unfair labor practices" were listed, employers were given more freedom to move against unions, and restrictions were imposed on certain strikes. All in all, the law changed the "rules of the game" by restricting union practices.

Dissatisfaction with portions of the Taft-Hartley Act and evidence of corruption in some unions led to the passage of

[2] Estimated by the Bureau as exceeding 100,000.

[3] In a closed shop, only union members are hired; in a union shop, new workers must join the union; and the check-off means the employer collects the dues for the union.

the Labor-Management Reporting and Disclosure Act of 1959 (Landrum-Griffin Act), which permitted federal intervention into internal union affairs. The act put restrictions on the use of union funds by union officers and sought to protect certain rights of individual union members. It required unions to file annual financial statements and required employers to report nonwage payments to union officials, as well as payments to consultants. Amendments to the Taft-Hartley Act included outlawing secondary boycotts, limiting organization picketing, giving strikers on economic issues the right to vote in representation elections under certain conditions, and exempting the building trades from the prohibition on the closed shop.[4]

While seeking to improve working conditions and wages by collective bargaining, unions have also used political action to achieve their objectives. Unions have supported such legislation as minimum wages and maximum hours of work, occupational safety and health regulations, and workmen's compensation. Through their political action groups, they tend to support friendly candidates and oppose those they consider to be unfriendly. Their interest in legislation and public policy ranges beyond the trade union field. The major objective of unions is still to get more for their members, but on some issues this can be done only by getting more for others by governmental action. Thus unions have generally supported social welfare programs of local, state, national, and even international magnitude. However, union members do not present a solid political front. On such issues as tariff reduction or the role of government in labor affairs, union workers have a variety of political views and, like any other group in the economy, their voting decisions reflect a number of considerations.

Today, the typical collective bargaining contract covers two major types of issues: those that pertain to the worker, and those that pertain to the union. The contract sets forth the wage rates to be paid, the hours to be worked in a normal work week, payment for overtime work, vacation rights,

[4] A secondary boycott is an action by a union against an employer to prevent that employer from dealing with another firm which is really the objective of the union's opposition.

and various other conditions of employment. These provisions cover the issues that first led workers to join unions.

The contract also includes provisions affecting the survival of the union. The union has objectives of its own in addition to those affecting the welfare of its members. It seeks to protect its status as the bargaining agent and to maintain its membership and financial solvency. The union leader may recognize that in the long run these provisions are as important as those governing conditions of employment. They are also important to business, because of the stability they may bring to the union-management relationship.

Frequently, conditions of employment—wages, hours, and so on—are not the key issues in a dispute. If the strength of the union is at stake, the so-called group objectives of the workers may take precedence over their immediate economic objectives. Thus the union should be viewed not only as an economic group but also as a social and political institution that holds the loyalty of its members. In the eyes of many workers, the union gives the laborer a chance to "speak up"; it serves his desire for self-respect; it promises security and protection from some of the economic and social forces of the modern world; and it gives him the feeling of belonging to a group—a basic desire of all of us. For these reasons, it is generally irrelevant arithmetic to calculate the length of time it will take a worker to make up the income lost as a result of a strike.

To achieve their goals by direct action or at the bargaining table, unions have developed many tactical approaches. Some unions have imposed restrictions on the number of apprentices entering a trade or used high union dues in order to limit the number of available workers. These measures (found mainly in craft unions) were based on awareness of how changes in the supply of labor can affect wages. Some other aims and practices of unions are:

To achieve uniformity in wage rates—the slogan is "equal pay for equal work"—some unions have used an agreement with one employer as the basis of negotiation with another (pattern bargaining). Such bargaining is not only less complicated, but it eliminates competition among employers at the expense of workers.

To organize nonunion workers, they have employed full-time organizers and launched extensive organizational drives.

To maintain the interest and support of their members, they have established newspapers and published educational material.

To simplify the collection of dues, some unions have negotiated the check-off, whereby dues are deducted from the worker's pay and turned over directly to the union.

To maintain membership, some have sought "union shop" contracts, seniority rules, and other rules governing the discharge or demotion of their members.

The strongest and costliest weapon of a union is the strike. When collective bargaining fails and the existing agreement has expired, the union may attempt to halt production by withholding the supply of labor. In general, it does so because it expects that the loss of income and markets will prove more costly to the employer than the loss of wages will be to the worker. The employer, on the other hand, may attempt to stay in operation with a skeleton work-force or nonunion labor. Any strike thus raises two major questions: (1) whether the union can effectively withhold the supply of labor and (2) whether the workers or the owners can best stand the losses if a work stoppage occurs. A strike can be made effective or "broken" on the first issue; on the second issue, it may evolve into a contest of endurance.

Because the strike causes economic loss, it is frequently criticized. But the right to strike is firmly established in public policy and law in the private sector and in some public jurisdictions. It is recognized as a legitimate and necessary part of a free economic system. It represents the final test of bargaining power between the union and management. Indeed, it is often the threat of a strike that forces the opposing sides to reach a meeting of minds at the bargaining table. No other alternative short of government regulation of industrial relations appears available.

To offset the efforts of the employer to "break" the strike, a union may take additional steps to make the strike effective. For example, it may resort to *picketing*, stationing workers at the entrances to the plant with placards charging the employer with unfair practices. On occasion, the entire union membership has barricaded the plant to prevent workers or customers from entering. Another supporting weapon has been the *boycott*. Unions have discouraged their members and the public from buying the products of the firm engaged in the dispute. An extension of this device is the outlawed *secondary boycott*, which is the refusal of union members of one firm to work on materials purchased from a firm that has a dispute with a union. These are actions that help make the strike effective; they are actions to prevent the employer from conducting "business as usual."

WHAT HAVE THE UNIONS ACHIEVED FOR WORKERS?

Organized workers look primarily to their unions to obtain higher wages, better working conditions, and protection from the power of management. In the long run, the stability and further growth of union membership is likely to depend on how well the unions can fulfill these expectations. Therefore, let us examine two questions in more detail: Do unions raise wages? Do they protect the workers from the possible abuse of power by management?

On the face of things, it seems a foolish question to ask whether unions increase wages. Daily newspaper reports of wage increases negotiated by unions suggest that the answer is obvious. But is it? We know that wages tend to be higher in unionized industries—but they were generally higher in these industries before the unions came into being. Studies show that union wages tended to increase slightly faster than nonunion wages after the Second World War—but some of the largest increases occurred in some of the low-wage, nonunion occupations (domestic workers, for instance). But, actually, comparisons between union and nonunion wage rates are not too helpful; the existence of unions has influenced *all* wages. For example, in some of the nonunion industries, employers have granted wage increases to prevent unionization of their firms, and some nonunion firms have been forced to increase their wages in order to keep their employees from taking more attractive union jobs elsewhere.

Union workers and employers will seldom question the

view that unions increase wages. However, some observers argue that wages are necessarily determined by the supply of and demand for labor; that regardless of union pressure, wages rise and fall as the national income and employment rise and fall. Thus they argue that the wage increases of the postwar years merely reflect the fact that the demand for labor was high. Others argue that wages would not have risen as sharply if unions had not maintained pressure on employers. Unions, they say, shorten the lag between the time the employer is willing to pay more and the time the market makes him pay more. But there is general agreement about the fact that some union workers have from time to time been able to gain relative to other wage earners.

As the compensation of all employees comprises roughly two thirds of the national income, it follows that the general level of "real" wages and salaries (the goods and services the income will buy) cannot advance for long without increased productivity. Wages can, for a time, grow at the expense of profits or other shares, but in the long run the rate of increased productivity sets a ceiling on the increase of real wages.

This truism was once translated into a statement of public policy by the President's Council of Economic Advisers. In 1962, the Council introduced wage-price guideposts to provide standards for noninflationary wage and price behavior. The general guide for wages was that the rate of increases in each industry, including fringe benefits, should be equal to the rate of productivity increases for the economy. The need for specific modifications was recognized; for example, more rapid rates of increase would be justified in low wage industries or in industries that needed to attract additional labor. Opinions differ on the role of the guideposts, but for the period 1962–66 the pattern of wage and price changes did approximate the Council's description. Unions and management, however, have generally preferred free collective bargaining without governmental constraints or pressures.

In the long run, competition for labor might cause real wages to keep pace with rising productivity, but there is no assurance that it will. Certainly, the bulk of organized workers are not likely to resign themselves either to the be-

nevolent dispositions of their employers or the gradual workings of a free, nonunion labor market. The role of unions,
then, is to maintain pressure on employers to keep wages rising. From industry to industry and from plant to plant,
differences in productivity and the relative economic strength
of labor and management will yield wage differences. But
the overall effect of the unions will be to strengthen the long-
run tendency for wages to rise with productivity.

*Wages alone do not tell the full story of employee com-
pensation because "fringe benefits" have accounted for an increasing share of the wage bill in recent years.* These supplements to regular wages are now an important part of the
payroll of American business. Indeed, they have become so
large that the term "fringe benefits" is hardly appropriate.
These benefits include pay for time not worked (such as vacation pay, sick leave, and holiday pay); monetary awards
and prizes; bonuses; profit-sharing plans; educational subsidies; pensions; payments for death; hospitalization, medical, and surgical insurance; and minor services such as credit
union facilities and employee discounts.

Some of these wage supplements have resulted from legislation (old-age and survivors' insurance, unemployment insurance, and workmen's compensation), and some from the
greater concern of management with employee morale. There
is little doubt, however, that the growth and prevalence of
these supplements largely reflects union bargaining power.
Much of the growth in wage supplements took place during
the wage stabilization programs of the Second World War
and the Korean conflict. When unions were unable to obtain
increases in wage rates, they sought instead to obtain nonwage payments. By 1960, negotiated health and insurance
plans covered 14.5 million workers and pension plans 11 million (or 80 per cent and 60 per cent, respectively, of all
workers covered by union contracts). By the mid-1970s,
nearly 85 per cent of union workers were covered by health
and insurance plans and 95 per cent by pension plans. Meanwhile federal legislation was passed that strengthened the
pension rights of all workers, organized and unorganized
alike.

Unions have also shown a strong interest in more stable income and protection against the impact of technological change. For example, demands for a "guaranteed annual wage" in the 1950s led to the introduction of supplementary unemployment benefits in labor contracts. These SUB plans generally provide for employer contributions to a trust fund that makes weekly cash payments to employees who are out of work and eligible for state unemployment compensation.

To workers, one of the most significant contributions of unions has been the improvement of working rules, protection from employer dictation, and an increase in security. Some observers contend that the orderly and judicial procedure for settling grievances is the most important union contribution to the welfare of the workers and to industrial relations in general. The grievance procedure is the machinery for handling the disputes and complaints that arise out of the interpretation and enforcement of union contracts. Collective bargaining contracts usually provide for procedures whereby individuals—representing the company or the union—can appeal for redress. Procedures provide that the worker and his shop representative can appeal to foremen and then to successive levels of authority up to representatives of top management and the national union. Finally, there is wide acceptance of the right of either side to appeal to an umpire or arbitrator whose decision may be accepted as final and binding on both parties.

For the individual worker, the singular importance of the grievance procedure negotiated by a union is that it helps assure the full and just consideration of complaints. Most companies, too, have been equally interested in perfecting workable grievance procedures, as they help to maintain employee morale, eliminate many causes of industrial unrest, and avert work stoppages resulting from unsolved issues. Seniority rules may provide additional protection to the workers by assuring a measure of job security and a chance for promotion. These rules play much the same role as civil service regulations and tenure for teachers. They serve the desire of the workers for security.

But not all unions are equally concerned with the welfare of the workers. Like any group they may occasionally fall under the domination of unscrupulous leaders. Fortunately, however, most American labor unions have responsible leadership. The AFL-CIO has taken strong measures in recent years to deal with crooked union leaders and has expelled several unions from membership in the national organization.

HOW DO UNIONS AFFECT MANAGEMENT?

To the employer, the growth of unionism has often resulted in some loss of managerial control. He has lost the power to set wages unilaterally, subject only to the factors of supply and demand of the market place; his power to promote or fire workers has been limited; his power to discipline employees has been curbed. Moreover, he has frequently been forced to fall in line with the wage pattern set by a dominant firm in the industry. He has been persuaded to change his organizational structure to include a division or department of industrial relations, and at times to accept the decisions of outside arbitrators regarding working conditions in his plant.

Observing the spread of collective bargaining contracts into areas that once appeared to be the sole prerogatives of management, we may ask: How far can labor be allowed to assert its voice in the formulation of policies that were once the exclusive concern of management? At what point will the ability of management to manage be dangerously hampered?

There are few laws or accepted rules limiting the range of collective bargaining. Therefore, these questions are not readily answered. It is not easy to determine the point at which union demands for self-determination seriously obstruct the operations of management. Fifty years ago, the attempts of unions to bargain over wages were opposed as an invasion of the rights of management. Today, bargaining over wages has become established, while union bargaining on the rate and timing of production is generally being resisted.

For the most part, unions have sought a role in deciding affairs they believed affected the welfare of their members. Over the years, they have expanded their notion of what affects the welfare of their members. Consequently, the scope of collective bargaining has increased. It seems likely that unions will continue to press for a greater voice in many business practices and policies. However, there is little evidence that they desire real joint management-labor direction of enterprise. Generally, American union leaders feel that they can better serve the workers by bargaining with management than by assuming the managerial role.

Although labor usually appears to be the aggressor, it is not always. During a period of rising income and employment, demands for wage increases and other benefits tend to be initiated by the union. If the economy is prosperous, unions have a better chance for success in their bargaining. However, in a period of declining income, many of the pressures generated at the bargaining table will arise from management. When incomes and sales are falling, employers may seek to reduce expenses by cutting wages and other labor costs. A sustained period of such negotiations initiated by management would make management appear, in the eyes of labor, as the party that is "encroaching" on the other.

The failure of firms has occasionally been blamed on unions. From time to time, firms have announced that they were going out of business because "unreasonable demands" by labor had made operations unprofitable. It has seldom been clear, however, whether the union demands were *the* cause, or the final straw, or merely an alibi. There is no doubt that a strong union has the power to impose demands that would make profitable operations impossible. On occasion, especially when the union has greatly miscalculated the ability of management to meet higher labor costs, unions have probably caused significant business losses. But when the union is merely trying to raise wages to a level being paid by competing firms, the failure of a firm may not be attributed to abuse of union power. When wages are the same in competitive firms, business failure is generally a result of the inability of management to meet business competition.

On the positive side, management has often found the union a helpful ally. The union may provide management with useful information about the status of employee morale. Co-operation in the grievance procedure can prevent minor complaints from growing into major issues. Some unions maintain expert staffs that seek ways to improve production.

It is not unusual to find labor and management combining to lobby for the passage or defeat of legislation that affects the interests of their industry.

In some instances, unions have accepted lower wages in an attempt to keep some firms in operation. For example, some New England textile workers accepted wage cuts in order to prevent manufacturers from closing down their plants in New England and moving to the South. At the same time, unions have attempted to raise wages in the South. Generally, unions attempt to maintain the same scale throughout a given industry—preventing one firm from gaining an advantage over another in wage rates.

It is not possible to catalogue all the ways in which unions affect management. The rapid growth of the field of "industrial relations" reflects the importance of their influence. Even firms that are not unionized are affected by the existence of unions. They usually have to meet the prevailing wages and conditions of employment established by bargaining elsewhere, and some firms modify their employment practices in an effort to keep employees out of the unions. The labor union, like the corporation, has become an institution affecting the operation of most American businesses, and it is the task of each firm to deal with this institution in a way that will best serve the objectives of the firm.

THE IMPACT OF UNIONISM ON THE ECONOMY

The union may affect the productivity of the economy, its prices and employment, the distribution of its national income, industrial peace, and the operations of federal, state, and local governmental agencies, which have become increasingly unionized. With union influence becoming more and more a part of our national economic life, there is no doubt that the public interest is increasingly concerned with the day-to-day operations of labor unions, with the conduct of their collective bargaining negotiations, and with the provisions of their collective bargaining contracts.

Some union practices may reduce labor productivity. Union controls over hirings, layoffs, and promotion by seniority may have an indirect adverse effect on productive efficiency. More direct limitations on productivity come from make-work or "featherbedding"—such as restrictions on the number of bricks a bricklayer can put in place per day, stand-by musicians, and extra workers on railroads. On occasion, union opposition to technological advances has retarded the expansion of labor productivity. Unions support these restrictions on the ground that they are necessary for the health, safety, or security of their members.

Some union restraints on productivity are a heritage of the early struggle for recognition. Some result from a fear that new jobs may be hard to find. Because conditions that lead to restraints are more pressing in some industries than they are in others, union policies toward them differ from industry to industry. However, most union leaders recognize that economic growth requires technological change and increased productivity. The major concern of most unions is to see that the adjustment to new technology is made without serious harm to the welfare of the workers.

Union wage policy—the pressure for more labor income—may be a stimulant to economic growth. It induces management to find new and better ways of reducing costs. Mechanization of the coal mines and dieselization of the railroads, for example, are generally considered to be partially the result of union pressure for higher wages. Similarly, unionization of the clothing workers eliminated the "sweatshop" and forced employers to adopt more productive means of operation. Demands made by unions for shorter hours, sanitary and safety standards, and other better working conditions have likewise at times contributed to increased productivity and larger total output. But not all economists accept this "shock" theory of increasing productivity. Some believe that strong unions can force employers to share the gains of new technology with workers; if they do, they argue, it will reduce the incentive for innovation.

The impact of union policies on prices and employment is difficult to assess. If unions succeed through collective bargaining in raising wages only by the amount of increased productivity, the effect on prices or employment will tend to be slight, although, as shown later, there may be an effect on the distribution of income. If, however, the increased wages (the cost of labor) are not matched by increased productivity, the effects on prices and employment may be far-reaching. Confronted by higher labor costs, management must either absorb them, pass them on through price increases to consumers, or cut costs elsewhere.

If the wage increase occurs in an industry where the product involved has a highly elastic demand—that is, where a price increase would deter a large number of buyers—the firm will generally have to absorb the increase. A firm with large enough profits can do this, and the effect will be a shift in the distribution of income. However, if the profits of a firm are small, a wage increase may have to be passed on. One of the continuing debates between labor and management has dealt with this point—whether wage increases can be absorbed or have to be passed on. The arguments over "the ability to pay" have never been resolved, largely because people, even those on the same side, cannot agree on what is a "necessary" profit or how much of the additional cost can be passed on.

When the cost of wage increases is passed on to consumers, the output of the firm may be affected. Except where the demand for the product is inelastic—that is, where sales do not appreciably change when the price changes—price increases by an individual producer will tend to reduce his sales; consumers will tend to reduce their purchases and spend their money for other items. A decline in sales will lead to a decline in production; a decline in production will result in the layoff of some workers. These workers may be absorbed by the firms whose output has expanded. But if the demand for labor in other firms does not increase, the workers will remain jobless. As the saying goes, they will have been "priced out of the market."

But a firm's output and employment do not always change when wages change. Reductions in profit margins, in other production costs, or increased productivity of workers may offset the rise in the wage bill. Declining production and employment may also be averted if the wage increase becomes widespread—that is, if a wage increase in a pace-setting industry is followed by wage increases in other industries. The cost of these increases may be passed along to consumers, leading to a general rise in prices that leaves the firm's relative position unaffected. Indeed, higher wages may help sustain the higher prices; if this income effect is sufficiently widespread, total demand and total output may remain unchanged.

When labor is fully employed, widespread wage increases that outstrip the growth in labor productivity will tend to feed inflation. Monetary gains will be illusory to the degree that they are offset by rises in the price level. For example, after the Second World War successive "rounds" of wage increases did not lead to unemployment, but rather contributed to an increase in incomes and prices. Each union generally felt that it had to get more to "catch up." When it did "catch up" under a new contract, other unions had to do the same.

Because it is hard to forecast the effects of wage increases, it is understandable that union leaders give relatively little attention to the effect of a wage demand on employment. A wage increase occurs in the present, and the price and employment effects generally occur in the uncertain future.

Unionism has encouraged "the downward rigidity and the upward flexibility" of wages and prices. When national income is falling, wage and price cuts are less likely to occur in organized industries. The union may foresee future difficulties in restoring a wage cut, but it is less able to foresee how much a wage cut may help or harm employment. Thus it will generally resist wage cuts—even in the face of a general decline in economic activity. The fact that workers can fall back on unemployment compensation encourages unions to allow the pressure of a recession (lower national income) to fall on employment rather than lower wages. In the industrial sphere, this behavior reinforces the tendency of firms to hold their prices relatively stable and adjust to the recession by curtailing production and employment.

Unions maintain upward pressure on wages to increase the share of their members in the growth of the national product. Theoretically, labor could share in the increased output of our economy without getting increased wages. For instance, if our economy becomes more productive, that is, if more goods and services are produced per worker, the prices of goods and services could fall. If prices are lower, workers will obtain more with the same money income. In other words, workers with stable wages will share the gains of greater productivity if the economy is so competitive that producers must reduce prices in order to sell their larger output.

Broadly speaking, however, unions are not likely to rely on this process; first, because they doubt whether lower prices would result; second, because even if they believe that price cuts will increase the real value of money wages, each union wants to improve the incomes of its own workers a little bit more; third, because a union leader who tried to sell his members on the prospects of future price cuts in the things they buy, instead of higher wages, would soon be out of a job.

Unions may also directly affect governmental operations. Since the early 1960s, public-employee unions have been the fastest growing segment of organized labor, and they have posed new challenges for federal, state, and local government managers. Over a 15-year period, membership in the American Federation of Government Employees has doubled; the American Federation of State, County and Municipal Employees grew threefold, and teachers' unions grew sevenfold.

This growth can be largely explained by two developments. One is the enormous growth of employment in state and local governments. The other is an increasing acceptance of the right of government employees to organize and bargain collectively. An executive order signed by the president in 1962 granted federal workers these rights, and since that time, as unionism has spread, additional executive orders have spelled out some responsibilities of unions, protected the authority of management, and provided a mechanism for the settlement of disputes between unions and government. Recognition of unions by states and municipalities has been spotty; practices vary throughout the country. Thus today the right to organize is still an issue in some areas, whereas the special problems posed by unions of policemen and firemen are the focus of concern in others. The most troubling issue is whether government employees should have the right to strike. Two states, Hawaii and Pennsylvania, legalized the right to strike in 1970, provided that other approaches to a settlement have been exhausted and provided that a strike will not endanger public health and safety. But generally strikes against government are illegal—a fact that hasn't prevented occasional walkouts in defiance of the law. For the federal government, a new problem was posed in the mid-1970s by efforts to organize the armed forces.

Work stoppages are another way in which unions affect the economy. Work stoppages usually result from a breakdown of collective bargaining. Therefore as both unions and management are involved in the bargaining, we can seldom say a stoppage has been "caused by the union" or "caused by management." Actually, most work stoppages result from miscalculations in the collective bargaining process. There are exceptions, however; for instance, the "wildcat strike" (workers defy their leaders and by-pass collective bargaining in order to stop work over some grievance) and "union busting" (employers refuse to bargain, in the hope that a prolonged strike will break the power of the union). The work stoppages that result from these conditions occur because collective bargaining is not used in good faith.

But most collective bargaining sessions are concluded without a strike. Estimates of the United States Bureau of Labor Statistics show that even during the great "strike year," 1946, over one thousand new labor contracts were peacefully settled each week and strikes resulted in a loss of only about 1.4 per cent of total days worked. In 1947, about 100,000 labor contracts were negotiated, twenty-four out of twenty-five of them peacefully. Since that time, the number of contracts has increased to about 150,000 and all but 3 or 4 per cent are renegotiated without a strike. When strikes occur, they are usually settled promptly—within two weeks. The strike that makes headlines is an exceptional case.

A major contribution to industrial peace has been the increase in agreements lasting two years or more. The one-year contract, once typical of collective bargaining, had become the exception to the rule by the early 1960s. Long-term contracts frequently provided for automatic wage adjustments during the life of the contract, geared to changes in productivity or the price level or both.

THE QUALITY OF WORKING LIFE

Although unions continue to emphasize traditional goals such as wages, job security, and union security, a number of them have taken a greater interest in a host of issues that can be bundled together under the heading of "quality of working life." This is a broad term that is often used without precise definition, and it is employed more by sociologists, industrial relations specialists and government policy makers than by labor leaders. It is used to suggest increasing concern about the hazards of the workplace and the meaning of work as an activity that occupies nearly half the waking hours of those who are employed full time.

Of special interest to unions such as the Machinists and the Oil, Chemical and Atomic Workers has been the issue of industrial accidents and illnesses. The enactment of the Occupational Safety and Health Act (OSHA) in 1970 greatly increased the visibility of workplace hazards, but the enforcement of the act has disappointed those who had supported it as well as those who hadn't. Unions have argued that the Department of Labor has moved too slowly both in identifying hazards to health and in doing anything about the hazards that have been identified—particularly the toxic substances that lead to asbestosis, cancer, and other serious diseases. Employers, including those who favored legislation to improve safety and health conditions in the workplace, have criticized the Department for capricious and counterproductive enforcement practices.

The full seriousness of work hazards is still partly a matter of guesswork. Before 1970, estimates of the National Safety Council had indicated that about fourteen thousand workers were killed every year in industrial accidents. A survey by the Department of Health, Education and Welfare indicated that about 390,000 cases of industrial illness occur each year. But such statistics were not considered very reliable, and OSHA officials have sought more reliable data.

One of the objectives of OSHA was to put greater emphasis on prevention and to shift the cost of accidents and illnesses to the employers or the public. A major obstacle to achieving this goal has been the difficulty of identifying illnesses that are related to working conditions. Most troublesome have been illnesses with long latency periods—that is, illnesses that do not show up until five, ten, or twenty years after workers have been exposed to them on the job.

Problems of worker satisfaction are also receiving greater attention. Business managers, interested in raising productivity, have experimented with the redesign of jobs to make them more interesting and to give workers a greater say in how work tasks should be organized. They believe that if jobs could be made more satisfying, workers would be more productive. In some instances, unions and management have co-operated in such efforts.

Another experiment to improve job satisfaction has focused on hours of work. Instead of the established routine of five eight-hour days a week, some firms introduced the four-day work week of ten hours a day or four days with a shorter work week. A variant is so-called flexitime, which gives workers the option of establishing their own work schedules so long as they are all present for a period known as "core time."

Experiments in job redesign, flexitime, and other efforts to improve worker satisfaction have thus far touched only a small percentage of workers. Their significance is not in the numbers affected but, rather, in the fact that job satisfaction is being given specific attention in the world of work and that some firms are willing to experiment in an effort to cope with the problem.

How satisfied or dissatisfied are workers with their jobs? During the late 1960s, it became fashionable to talk of the "blue collar blues" and worker alienation, but the prevalence of such discontent remains a matter of debate. Some observers pointed to wildcat strikes and slowdowns to buttress their views that discontent was growing. Others cited statistical surveys, such as the surveys on working conditions conducted in 1972–73 by the Survey Research Center, at the University of Michigan, to back their view that there had been no measurable change in workers' attitudes (except perhaps a slight increase in dissatisfaction among women and blacks). More than 90 per cent of those interviewed in the 1972–73 Survey Research studies described themselves as reasonably satisfied with their work. When the survey was repeated, five years later, expressions of dissatisfaction were slightly higher, largely because of discontent among college-educated workers. But no one knows whether a 10 per cent—or 5 or 15 per cent—expression of dissatisfaction is tolerable for a society. And few would deny that an improvement in job satisfaction is a good goal to aim for.

There is no doubt that the economy has come a long way from the time when indifference to the worker's welfare and the desire to "bust the union" were a part of the everyday creed of business, and when union leaders were claiming that the businessman was a "soulless exploiter of human suffering." Today, the old phrases are sometimes brought out again in the heat of battle, but they generally do not have the ring of an earlier period.

This brings us to the question of government policy toward strikes that directly affect public safety, health, or welfare. We shall use this question to illustrate again the steps in economic analysis.

The Problem and the Issues

An important task of public policy toward labor has been to help establish an environment in which labor and management will reach a bargain that will be mutually acceptable and fair to the public. The legal framework that has developed encourages the formation of unions and the use of collective bargaining by labor and management. The Wagner Act established the basic "rules of the game" by saying that employers must allow workers to organize into unions, must not make attempts to break the power of the union, and must bargain with the union in good faith (that is, must honestly attempt to reach a settlement). The law said, in effect, that labor unions are legitimate economic bargaining units that must be treated by the same rules that apply to any bargaining unit in a competitive economy, and efforts to destroy them are illegal.

The Taft-Hartley Act and the Landrum-Griffin Act placed

restraints on the powers of the unions—saying, in effect, that they, too, must abide by certain rules. They must reflect the actual desires of their workers, they must not impose certain restraints on the ability of workers to obtain employment, they cannot employ certain "unfair labor practices," and they must disclose certain information about the officers and the finances of the union. Also, strikes in vital industries were made subject to certain controls.

Most of the time, the strike is not needed, but occasionally it is used. When a strike occurs in a major industry, the whole economy feels some of the effects. When most of the coal industry is shut down, or the railroads or airlines are tied up, or schools and hospitals are shut down, the impact on the public is great.

Occasionally, a strike means that the public may be deprived of goods and services that, even if not essential for health and safety, are important to comfort. In addition, employees are deprived of employment and income, and this loss may depress business activity in the affected area. The consequences of a strike may also spill over into other industries: a strike in the steel industry, for example, can cause loss of work in the automobile industry. Under many conditions, therefore, a strike is a public calamity rather than a purely private contest over wages, hours, or working conditions.

Public pressure for settlement of industrial disputes usually exists. Generally, the public is less interested in the terms of settlement than in the settlement itself. Both labor and management recognize this. They recognize that there are three parties to the dispute, not two, and that the third party—the public—grants labor and management the right to pursue free collective bargaining in the expectation that both sides will actively seek agreement.

In general, the public is willing to bear some occasional inconvenience in order to allow labor and management to settle their differences by negotiation, but there are limits to public forbearance. During the 1970s, a different kind of strike has posed a particular problem for the public—a strike in which a governmental unit is a party to the dispute. Strikes by garbage collectors, teachers, firefighters, and police have made headlines across the country. The total number of such strikes is low, but they are highly visible and they are especially disturbing to the communities affected.

When public health or safety is endangered or when an important part of the production of the nation or vital government service will be halted by a strike, public intervention may be necessary. The major issue, then, is to determine what steps may be taken. The principal questions to be answered are: What will different measures do to our system of collective bargaining? How effective will different measures be in ending the work stoppage? What measures will be most fair to all parties?

Objectives

When a strike has curtailed the flow of indispensable goods or services, the basic objective of the public is to restore the flow of production. At the same time, the public also has the goal of preserving our pattern of free collective bargaining. The requirements for a solution to a dispute in the private sector might be that neither labor nor management will receive any special advantage, that the government will not continue to intervene indefinitely, that any government action will not hinder a private agreement, or that force will or will not be used. Here again, there may be conflicts; conflicts that will have to be settled in order to reach a decision.

The Alternatives

The importance of preserving free and voluntary solutions of industrial conflicts suggests the use of *mediation and fact-finding* as a first step. Mediation in a labor dispute is the intervention of a third party—usually appointed by the government. The go-between may enter the dispute at the request of either side or when the government offers mediation in the public interest. The mediator tries to find a compromise solution but is not empowered to compel either party to accept the compromise. The mediator tries to keep tempers down so that both sides can continue to work toward a solution, depending instead on an understanding of the issues, the individuals, and the bargaining process to bring the parties together so the deadlock can be broken.

Fact-finding involves the appointment of an impartial board to investigate and report on the facts of the dispute. Fact-finding boards at times recommend solutions, although they do not have the power to enforce them. The purpose of these fact-finding reports is to clarify the issues and to help build up public opinion that will put pressure on the parties to accept a solution.

Both methods have been used to deal with serious strikes, and sometimes they have been useful in expediting a solution. They have the advantage of preserving the freedom of union-management relations. But they do not guarantee the continued flow of indispensable goods and services. If they fail to bring about a solution, the public may demand more drastic action.

To compel the performance of indispensable services or the production and delivery of essential goods, *compulsory arbitration* is sometimes proposed. Several states have passed laws calling for compulsory arbitration of disputes involving public utilities. These laws generally provide for the appointment of an impartial board that investigates the dispute and decides on a settlement that the state can enforce. However, in some states where these laws have been tested in the courts, compulsory arbitration has been held unconstitutional when it affects interstate commerce.

Generally, proposals for compulsory arbitration have not had wide support. One reason is the feeling that it would concentrate too much power in the hands of a few people. A more basic objection is the view that if labor and management can get along well enough to make the system work, they probably do not need it. In brief, this approach has received little use and little support in this country.

The *injunction,* a court order that prohibits both employers and employees from shutting down operations, has been used for some emergencies. It usually requires operations to continue under existing conditions. The Taft-Hartley Act, for example, empowers the federal government to obtain an eighty-day injunction against a work stoppage in an essential industry. This injunction is intended to provide a "cooling-off" period during which labor and management will have additional time to resolve their disputes. In practice, however, the injunction has not always proved to be effective, because the union is free to strike when the injunction expires. The injunction may merely change the deadline for a strike. Another criticism of the injunction is that it works to the benefit of the party resisting change. Typically, this has been the employer, but in a period of declining business activity, it could act to the disadvantage of an employer who seeks a reduction in pay or an increase in hours worked. An injunction of indefinite length obviously would be grossly unfair in a society in which economic conditions change as they do in the United States.

The seizure of a strikebound firm is a last-ditch way in which the government can safeguard the flow of production. It has been used primarily in wartime, but not exclusively; its use was discussed during the 1978 coal strike. When the government seizes a plant, it continues operations either under existing conditions (with a deduction of a percentage of net income as compensation for its services), or under temporary new wage scales established by a special board. The advocates of seizure as a weapon of last resort point out that it averts public hardship, while leaving to the union and the company the task of arriving at a final settlement by the bargaining process. When agreement is reached, the firm is returned to the management of the company.

However, the terms of seizure do not make agreement equally urgent to both parties. If the seizure provides for maintaining the status quo, it is open to the same objections that are raised against the injunction: it works to the benefit of the party resisting change; this party has little incentive to push for a solution that would involve important concessions. If the terms of seizure allow for changes in wage rates and working conditions, the party that benefits has no incentive to seek a permanent solution. Moreover, a change in the working conditions may have the effect of compulsory arbitration; that is, the new terms would represent the minimum acceptable to the favored party. In this instance, the claim that seizure preserves the free bargaining process would be illusory.

In public policy toward serious strikes, the government must consider not only the alternatives available but also the way in which they are used. If the government lets the parties to the dispute know which weapon it will use to compel fulfillment of the demands of the public, it will tend to weaken the chances for settlement. For example, if the employer feels assured that the government will resort to an injunction that will favor him, he will have less incentive to bargain in good faith. The same is true in the case of the union. If it is assured that the weapon of compulsion will work in its favor, it will have less incentive to bargain in good faith.

In strikes affecting the public sector, the same tools of mediation, injunction, or takeover of an operation (such as the use of military units to operate the Postal Service) may also be used, but political considerations may bear more heavily on the decisions of how to proceed and how much to yield.

It has sometimes been argued that political pressures lead to unduly generous settlements, especially on pension issues, where costs are deferred into the future. On the other hand, it has been argued that the ban on union organization in some jurisdictions and the almost universal ban on strikes is unwarranted, since the work of most government employees is not vital to public health. The extension of governmental activities over the past half century has meant that a number of jobs in the public sector are about the same as jobs in the private sector. Bus drivers and truck drivers are free to strike a private employer but not the government. Employees of private insurance companies may strike, but not employees of the Social Security Administration. Employees of private hospitals may strike, but not employees of government hospitals. And so on. Should all government employees be treated differently from employees in the private sector, or just some?

Strikes by police and firefighters pose the greatest challenge, because of the threat to public safety resulting from the walkouts. On the one hand, government cannot tolerate defiance of its authority. On the other, it is not feasible to jail hundreds or thousands of employees. Compulsory arbitration has been urged for such disputes, and it may prove useful in some circumstances, but there is no assurance that a union that is willing to defy a law outlawing strikes will accept an unsatisfactory arbitration award. There is no wholly satisfactory substitute for steps that will encourage both parties to arrive at a mutually acceptable agreement.

So far, such challenges to governmental authority have been short-lived—or at least have been resolved short of an ultimate test of strength—as a result of prolonged and patient negotiation and testing of wills. Whether we will have to live with occasional illegal strikes in the public sector or whether an effective procedure can be developed to head them off is an unanswerable question today.

Appraising the Alternatives

The threat of governmental action in a dispute in the private sector stresses an important aspect of collective bargaining—that it is a contest in which economic strength, the persuasive abilities of the parties, the ability to bluff, the backing of workers or other employers, and many other economic and noneconomic factors all play a part. To resolve such a contest, both parties must strongly desire a settlement. The function of public policy is to increase the desirability to both parties for settlement and thereby to reduce the probability of a strike.

The *threat* of an arsenal of government weapons can help the situation, but it cannot provide a complete solution. In some cases, each disputing party may foresee, correctly or incorrectly, governmental intervention as an aid to its position. Each party may feel it is futile even to consider such an uncertainty as governmental control, or may not strongly care whether there is a strike or not. Eventually, therefore, such stoppages may have to be settled by the only alternative—compulsion.

In the public sector, the settlement of impasses may be even more difficult because of political considerations. Each of us must decide personally whether compulsion is or is not necessary. If compulsion is deemed necessary, which of the alternative forms of compulsion best meets our needs? Also, what about the specific conditions to be imposed? Shall the existing wage level continue while the government has control? How can we bring equal pressure on unions and management to settle their differences? Our ultimate decision on such questions will be based on our objectives and our understanding of the consequences of different courses of action.

This chapter has stressed the following basic ideas:

1. Labor unions are among the most important groups in this country; they play an established role in our economic system. Like many other economic groups, their primary objective is to enhance the welfare of their members. However, they are not motivated solely by economic considerations; they have their own internal political objectives, and they have social objectives. Occasionally, these other goals actually conflict with their economic interests.

2. One of the most important achievements of unions is the maintenance of pressure on employers for wage increases and other economic benefits. Unions have also provided the individual worker with a greater degree of control over his working conditions. Many decisions formerly made exclusively by management are now influenced by unions. The economy has thus shifted from an arrangement in which management provided most of the directive influence over economic activity to an arrangement in which both management and labor direct economic affairs.

3. Wages, employment, and prices are affected by collective bargaining. However, wage increases gained by collective bargaining may or may not be inflationary. Similarly, wage increases may result in an expansion of employment or unemployment. Their effects at any given time will depend on a number of other factors: how much employment already exists, how much output per worker has changed, whether consumers are willing to pay higher prices for a given amount of a product, and so forth. In order to evaluate the economic effects of the demands of the union for wage increases or the demands of management for wage cuts, it is necessary to understand many relevant circumstances.

4. In recent years, the concern for the welfare of workers as been broadened to include job satisfaction and other issues related to the "quality of life."

5. Work stoppages that halt production can be considered

an economic loss. However, this loss may be measured against the gains that result from free collective bargaining. Broadly speaking, the American people have decided that the gains outweigh the losses. However, there are occasions when the effects of a work stoppage extend far beyond the immediate area of union-management conflict, and the cost exceeds the gains. These cases, particularly in the public sector, raise some of the most difficult issues of public policy toward labor.

Suggested Reading

Paul A. Samuelson, *Economics*, Chap. 7, pp. 131–46, Chap. 29, pp. 572–97. George L. Bach, *Economics: An Introduction to Analysis and Policy*, Chaps. 30–32, pp. 398–430. These selections explore the practices and goals of labor unions and some of the economic consequences of union policies. (In a few sections the discussion may be somewhat advanced for those who have not read earlier chapters in the books.) See also *Brief History of the American Labor Movement*, U. S. Bureau of Labor Statistics Bulletin 1000 (Washington: Government Printing Office, 1976), and "The Role of Labor Unions," by George W. Taylor, in *Readings*, pp. 66–72.

Chapter 5

DEBTS AND MONEY

The preceding chapters have described some characteristics of our "mixed economy." They have indicated the way the market regulates production and distributes economic rewards. They showed the roles that competition, governmental controls and regulations, labor unions, and a variety of other influences play in economic life. Now we turn to a new topic—the role of money and debt in our economy.

American economic growth has been accompanied by an increase in public and private debt. By 1978, the gross debts of consumers, business firms, state, local, and national governments (excluding currency), and private financial institutions were an estimated $6.5 trillion. They had almost doubled during the 1970s and are still rising.

As the chart on page 114 shows, financial institutions—banks, insurance companies, and other financial organizations—have the largest debts, and governments and businesses owe considerably more debts than they hold. As a debt is merely the promise of a person, group, or institution to pay another at some future date, the graph also shows the obvious fact that for every borrower there is a lender. For the whole economy, the volume of debt is equal to the volume of credit.

Surprisingly enough, this total volume of debt has been built up faster during prosperity than during recessions. As individuals, we might expect to go into debt in bad times and to pay off in good times. But actually this offhand, commonsense expectation does not hold for the economy. Total debt (public and private) has tended to grow as gross national product has grown.

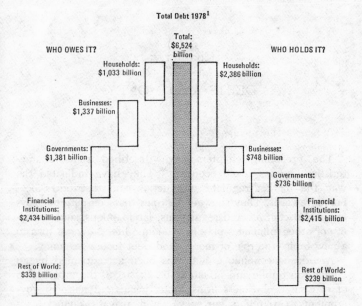

Total Debt 1978[1]

WHO OWES IT?

Total: $6,524 billion

WHO HOLDS IT?

Households: $1,033 billion

Businesses: $1,337 billion

Governments: $1,381 billion

Financial Institutions: $2,434 billion

Rest of World: $339 billion

Households: $2,386 billion

Businesses: $748 billion

Governments: $736 billion

Financial Institutions: $2,415 billion

Rest of World: $239 billion

Basically, the growth of income and the growth of debt go together, because the amount that many people want to spend is influenced by their incomes. Businessmen, for example, are optimistic about the future when their income is growing; thus, they are more willing to borrow during prosperity. At the same time, many people tend to save more as their incomes increase. As their incomes rise, their spending rises, but not as rapidly; hence, their savings also rise. The growth of debt is the way that the deficits of one group and the surpluses of another are brought together. As these surpluses and deficits tend to grow with income, the growth of income contributes to the growth of debt.

[1] These figures are estimates based in part on flow-of-funds data developed by the Board of Governors of the Federal Reserve System and in part by the Federal Reserve Bank of Chicago (*Two Faces of Debt*, 1979). All figures are rounded to the nearest $1 billion. Nonprofit associations and trust funds are included in the group labeled "consumers."

One of the most important things to learn about our economic system is that it requires the use of debts. The objective of public policy is not to eliminate debt, but to manage it so as to maintain the flow of income and production. We shall see later what specific functions debts play for various groups, but let us list here the major functions they play for the economy as a whole.

Debt enables us to adjust the timing of our spending. By freeing us from the day-to-day restraint imposed by our income, debt enables us to meet emergencies and to enjoy consumption, build factories, or make major governmental outlays when we most want them and then pay for them out of future income.

Debt enables us to build new productive equipment. Savers are not necessarily directly interested in creating capital (building factories, tools, or other productive equipment), hence debts bridge the gap between them and the people who create capital. Moreover, debts enable a large number of persons to pool their savings to buy equipment that would be too expensive to be financed by a few. It also helps existing enterprises over temporary periods of inadequate income. In each of these respects, debt facilitates economic growth.

Debt provides us with our money supply. Not only our currency but our main medium of exchange, commercial bank deposits, is a form of debt. In the specialized industrial economy based on exchange, this money provides a convenient and readily acceptable means of payment.

We can see how these functions are performed by looking at the debts of the four major groups—consumers, business, governments, and financial institutions. Of course, each of these groups contains some borrowers and some lenders, and each does some borrowing from the other groups. Each borrows for different reasons, and when it borrows, it has different effects on the economy.

THE ROLE OF CONSUMER DEBT

The opportunity to "buy now and pay later" has radically changed the living conditions of American consumers. Without the use of credit, consumers might have to put off buying a house, a car, or a kitchen range until they had saved enough money for the purchase. With credit, they enjoy the use of the house, car, or range while paying for it.

Debt, in short, enables consumers to enjoy a richer way of life. Are they "living beyond their incomes"? For the most part, they are not. If a man has an income of $20,000 per year, he obviously cannot buy a $50,000 house with that year's income. But over a twenty-year period his income will total $400,000—quite enough to permit a $50,000 purchase—and a twenty-year mortgage recognizes this fact. Consumers may appear to live beyond their incomes because they go into debt for a major purpose, but they generally do not live beyond their present-plus-future incomes; only those who consume their inherited wealth and those who die in debt live beyond their income over the long run.

Some people argue that if individuals would save as much before they buy as they do after they go into debt, they could still have what they want—without paying interest. But it is not quite that simple.

In the first place, unless people can borrow, frequently they will have to wait before they can buy. Debt enables them to buy more nearly at the time they choose. In addition, many people apparently will not or cannot save except under the pressure of an overhanging debt. If they could not borrow to buy a car, they might never have a car at all, for they might never put aside enough money beforehand to buy it.

Debt is especially useful for the purchase of houses. The people who most want housing are young couples with growing families. Most of them have not saved enough money to buy outright the kind of house they need. By the time they could save enough, they would no longer want big houses: their children would have grown up, married, and moved away, and would probably be buying homes of their own—on credit. So they go into debt. Consumer credit enables families to grow up in bigger and better homes by permitting the bit-by-bit purchases of houses.

Despite their borrowing, consumers on the average spend less than their total income. Although they owed $1,033 billion in 1978, they held debt or claims on others amounting to

$2,386 billion. They are, as the accompanying chart shows, a group with surplus income—although some of the group borrows, as a whole the group has tended to spend less than its

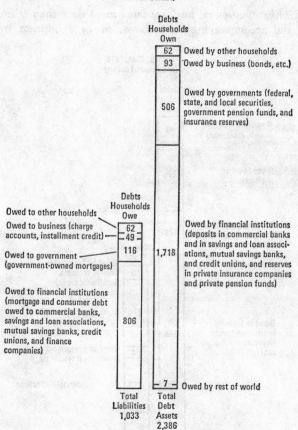

Household Debt, 1978
(in billions of dollars)

Debts Households Own

62 Owed by other households

93 Owed by business (bonds, etc.)

506 Owed by governments (federal, state, and local securities, government pension funds, and insurance reserves)

Debts Households Owe

Owed to other households

Owed to business (charge accounts, installment credit)

62

49

Owed to government (government-owned mortgages)

116

1,718 Owed by financial institutions (deposits in commercial banks and in savings and loan associations, mutual savings banks, and credit unions, and reserves in private insurance companies and private pension funds)

Owed to financial institutions (mortgage and consumer debt owed to commercial banks, savings and loan associations, mutual savings banks, credit unions, and finance companies)

806

7 Owed by rest of world

Total Liabilities 1,033

Total Debt Assets 2,386

income. Consumers hold some of the debts of other consumers. They hold a large part of the business debt and a large part of the debt of the federal government. They also hold a large share of the insurance policies and bank deposits, which are the debts of financial institutions. In other words, consumers as a group have transferred (loaned) their surplus to the other groups.

THE ROLE OF BUSINESS DEBT

Unlike consumers, business owes more debt than it holds. As the accompanying chart shows, in 1978 business owed

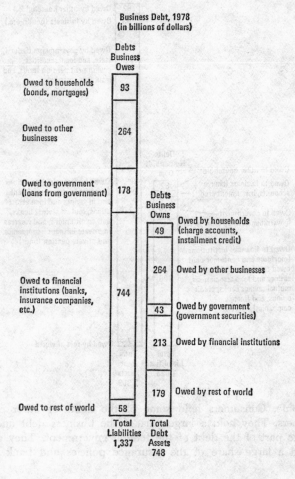

Business Debt, 1978
(in billions of dollars)

Debts Business Owes

Owed to households (bonds, mortgages)	93
Owed to other businesses	264
Owed to government (loans from government)	178
Owed to financial institutions (banks, insurance companies, etc.)	744
Owed to rest of world	58
Total Liabilities	**1,337**

Debts Business Owns

49	Owed by households (charge accounts, installment credit)
264	Owed by other businesses
43	Owed by government (government securities)
213	Owed by financial institutions
179	Owed by rest of world
Total Debt Assets	**748**

$1,337 billion, mainly to individuals (consumers) and financial institutions. It held only $748 billion of the debts of others, and some of that includes the debts of individual businesses. These figures do not mean, however, that business is "insolvent." Each business has other assets, such as plants, machines, and its position as a going concern, which generally more than offset its debts.

Business debts are commonly considered the most desirable debts in the American economy. Most of us understand and approve debts to increase the production and distribution of goods; for example, when a department store borrows a hundred thousand dollars to finance the purchase of new stocks of merchandise or when a steel company sells $10 million in bonds in order to modernize its blast furnaces.

Businessmen, however, do not go into debt merely for the sake of increasing production. They have another, more basic motivation. They want to make profits. Whether a loan is for a steel plant or a dance studio, the ultimate test will be whether it can make an adequate return. That is the test that will be posed by both borrower and lender.

Business borrows for two broad purposes: to maintain day-to-day operations and to finance major capital improvements. Day-to-day borrowing is necessary because workers must be paid promptly, materials have to be purchased, inventories have to be held for certain periods, and slow-paying customers must be financed—in short, a steady stream of bills must be paid when due. Few businesses can schedule their operations so that incoming revenue can always be counted on to meet the demands for outgoing cash. Therefore, most enterprises find it necessary to borrow additional funds to make up the difference.

The most changeable of these short-term loans are those for inventory, that is, goods on shelves, in the production line, or in warehouses. Inventory loans are characterized by seasonal fluctuations. Manufacturers increase their stocks of raw materials in preparation for their busy season, and retailers start laying in goods in advance of seasonal peaks in consumer spending—for example, Christmas holiday buying. Generally, they finance this stocking-up by inventory loans. Such loans run from three to six months and are presumably paid off as soon as the goods are sold. Different firms have different seasonal peaks, but almost all of them follow a similar practice—they build up inventory at one time and gradually "sell it off" at a later date.

Inventory borrowing is clearly based on an expectation of future sales. Thus a firm borrows and agrees to a plan of repayment that will fit in with these future sales. But if sales fall below expectations, the firm may find itself in trouble. In order to meet its obligations on time, the business may be forced to liquidate a part of the previously acquired inventory at reduced prices. Unfortunately for economic stability, business executives tend to follow this erratic pattern because they must (1) anticipate their sales on the basis of forecasts and (2) meet their fixed credit obligations. Of course, without inventory debts, the occasional pressure to get rid of inventory would be milder, but apparently we prefer to pay the price of this instability for the convenience of having our businesses well-stocked.

The economic decline that occurred in 1974 and early 1975 was due partly to a cutback in business buying for inventory. In the fourth quarter of 1974, business was still adding to its inventories at an annual rate of over $10 billion a year. During the worst of the recession, however, business not only stopped buying new goods but also began selling off the stocks it already had on hand—at an annual rate, in the second quarter of 1975, of around $26 billion a year. In other words, business not only stopped buying goods to add to stocks in its warehouses, it didn't buy even enough to keep the stocks at the old level.

Business debt incurred for the purchase of plant and equipment also changes from time to time. It tends to increase more rapidly during prosperity than during periods of declining income. Businessmen wax optimistic and pessimistic like the rest of us, so they tend to expand their equipment when sales are growing and to put off new capital purchases when they are having trouble disposing of all the goods produced with equipment on hand. Their rate of borrowing and spending is therefore highly dependent on their expectations of changes in the level of our national income and employment.

But this is a circular process. Business spending is also an important part of our total spending. Thus a change in the level of investment spending can lead to a change in the level of income and employment. This circular process is discussed in Chapters 6 and 7.

Some of our most prosperous businesses have always been "in debt." They can remain "in debt" because their earning power continues, and people are willing to lend them their money. A business corporation does not have to plan on getting "paid up" when it becomes old. Because it does not have to die, it can remain in debt indefinitely. People, of course, must redeem their debts during their lifetime or leave an estate to pay them. They may borrow during their lifetime, and they may even "refund" their debts (borrow to pay debts that are coming due) for a while, but a corporation can continue to grow and accumulate new equipment and new debts indefinitely—as long as the way it uses the funds is economically useful.

THE ROLE OF GOVERNMENT DEBT

Most of the outstanding government debt is owed by the federal government. About 30 per cent of the total government debt is owed by state and local governments. The federal debt—swollen by the cost of fighting wars and meeting various emergencies—accounts for the rest. But this has not always been the case. Throughout most of our history, state and local government debt tended to exceed the federal debt. During the past half century, however, the federal debt has generally become larger and more important to our economy, although in recent years state and local debt has been growing at a faster rate.

Like business, government borrows more than it lends. In other words, over the years, it has spent more than its income. As the chart on page 122 shows, in 1978 government owed $1,381 billion and held only $736 billion of outstanding claims against consumers, businesses, and financial institutions. But, also like business, it cannot be said that government is insolvent. Government has vast investments in

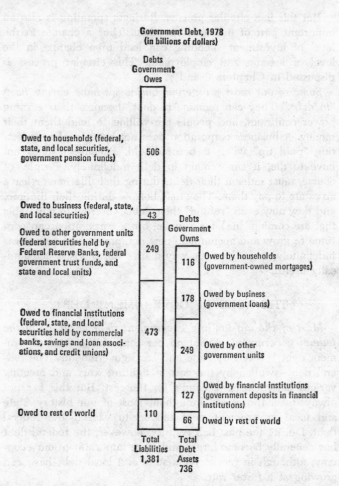

Government Debt, 1978
(in billions of dollars)

Debts
Government
Owes

Owed to households (federal, state, and local securities, government pension funds) — 506

Owed to business (federal, state, and local securities) — 43

Owed to other government units (federal securities held by Federal Reserve Banks, federal government trust funds, and state and local units) — 249

Owed to financial institutions (federal, state, and local securities held by commercial banks, savings and loan associations, and credit unions) — 473

Owed to rest of world — 110

Total Liabilities 1,381

Debts
Government
Owns

116 — Owed by households (government-owned mortgages)

178 — Owed by business (government loans)

249 — Owed by other government units

127 — Owed by financial institutions (government deposits in financial institutions)

66 — Owed by rest of world

Total Debt Assets 736

roads, land, military equipment, schools, and many other tangible and intangible assets, including the power to tax.

State and local government debts arise for the most part, from spending for tangible things: schools, fire houses, parks, playgrounds, and streets. Most state and local governments cannot pile up large funds out of tax revenues with the idea of spending the funds later in a lump sum for some major project. If they do accumulate funds, pressure for tax reduction tends to curtail their savings. So they pay for such projects by issuing bonds and then pay off a certain amount of the bonds year by year.

Unfortunately, state and local governments generally tend to borrow and spend when most of the rest of the economy is doing the same thing. When incomes are high and people have jobs, tax receipts are high, and cities and states have more income available for servicing bonds. Therefore, they

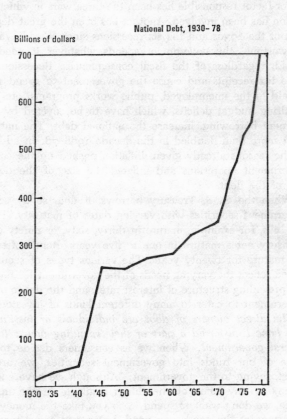

National Debt, 1930–78

Billions of dollars

700

600

500

400

300

200

100

1930 '35 '40 '45 '50 '55 '60 '65 '70 '75 '78

Source: *Historical Statistics of the United States* and *Federal Reserve Bulletin*.

borrow during periods of prosperity and cease borrowing in periods of depression when tax receipts fall off. In following this pattern, they tend to aggravate our cycles of prosperity and depression. In addition, this pattern is uneconomical. A local government unit often ends up buying some of its projects when they cost the most—and paying for them when incomes are lower.

As shown by the chart on page 123, the national debt has increased enormously during the past half century. One major factor responsible has been the three wars in which the nation has been involved. Another has been the great depression of the 1930s and the six recessions since World War II. In wartime, the government spends whatever it needs to spend, regardless of the fiscal consequences. Recessions reduce tax receipts and cause the government to spend more on aid to the unemployed, public works programs, etc. The resulting budget deficits, which have to be covered by government borrowing, increase the national debt. The national debt more than doubled in the decade 1968–78. In addition to the reasons already given, inflation pushed up the cost of government operations and inflated the size of the deficits and of the debt.

When the U. S. Treasury borrows, it does so by selling government securities with varying dates of maturity. Treasury bills, for example, mature in thirty, sixty, or ninety days. Treasury notes mature in one to five years. Bonds often do not mature for twenty years. The various types of securities issued reflect the varying needs of the government for money, the prevailing structure of interest rates, and the desire of the government to cater to many different kinds of investors.

The direct owners of debt are individuals or institutions that have transferred a part of their spending power to the federal government. When we as consumers decide to put some of our funds into government securities, we are, in effect, saying to the government: "Although we have enough money to buy some of the things available in the market place, we don't want to spend it, so you take the money and buy some of the goods you need. Later, you can return the money to us—with interest." The effect of such a transaction is to switch the pattern of spending from the consumer goods we would have purchased to government goods. From washing machines, perhaps, to spacecraft. The same type of transfer takes place when corporations or other investors buy government securities.

OWNERSHIP OF THE FEDERAL DEBT, JULY 1978

Owner	Amount (billions)
Direct owners	469
Individuals	108
Corporations	20
State and local governments	62
U. S. Government trust funds	159
Foreigners	120
Financial institutions	281
Commercial banks	98
Federal Reserve banks	109
Savings banks	6
Insurance companies	15
Other	53
Total federal debt	750

Source: *Federal Reserve Bulletin,* October 1978, p. A32. Figures rounded.

They decide to hold government securities rather than the other things they might have purchased.

The federal government therefore can borrow from the public when it wants to control private spending. In wartime, for example, the government wants to divert much of the resources of the nation from production of consumer goods to war goods. So it asks the public to buy bonds "to help in the war effort." The request is not made because the government cannot get along without our money. It is made so that the public will stop trying to buy consumer goods— stop trying to bid materials away from the government. In wartime, the government will get the things it wants anyway, but it prefers to get them at stable prices in order to avert a general inflation.

Superficially, it might seem that all that should be necessary in such circumstances would be to tax the spending power away from people. But the problem is not that easy to solve. One of the ways war industries persuaded people to move from garages in Iowa to airplane plants in Los Angeles and induced housewives to become welders was to offer them more money. If the government had then turned around and taxed all of the extra money (it did tax some of it), people would have had little reason for making the changes. Therefore, the government did the next best thing— it tried to persuade people to save their new earnings until after the emergency was over. It asked them to buy government securities.

The key to public debt policy is to borrow from the right people at the right time. In depression, the government should attempt to borrow from people who are not planning to spend much of their income. Actually, as we shall see later, it should try to borrow from banks. It would do the economy little good, and might even do harm, to borrow from people who planned to spend their money anyhow.

During a war or inflation, the government should attempt to do the opposite; it should try to borrow funds that otherwise would have been spent. Of course, if people are already saving and holding their cash idle, the government would not need to borrow to put a damper on consumer spending, but if people tend to spend their incomes as fast as they earn them, the Treasury could help prevent price inflation by getting them to buy bonds instead.

The other group of government debt holders—financial institutions—permit the "indirect purchase" of government securities by the public. The public holds bank deposits, life insurance policies, and other assets, which are the debts of banks, insurance companies, and other financial institutions. These financial institutions lend money to the government by buying government securities. They are financial intermediaries, which owe debt to the public and own some of the debt of the federal government. Thus the public can hold the kinds of assets it wants and yet at the same time indirectly lend to the government.

THE ROLE OF THE DEBT OF FINANCIAL INSTITUTIONS

Financial institutions channel funds from savers to borrowers. As intermediaries in the flow of savings, their role is vital to the steady growth of national income. They also provide the economy with most of its money supply as well as other liquid assets. Savings and loan associations, savings banks, insurance companies, and commercial banks owe a variety of debts to the people who have funds deposited with them. These debts occur in many forms.

Savings accounts, sometimes called time deposits, are claims against a savings bank. They do not have to be paid by the savings bank at once. The savings bank may require several months' notice. For this privilege, the savings bank generally pays *interest* to the owner of the account. Savings and loan shares work the same way, but the time before the savings and loan association makes payment may be longer. Most life insurance policies grow in value as premiums are paid, and on very short notice, the owner can obtain the accumulated value by surrendering his policy.

Checking accounts (sometimes called demand deposits) are claims against a commercial bank. They must be paid immediately on the request of the owner. A check is an order from the owner of a deposit to the bank; it orders the bank to pay so and so much to the holder of the check.

As the chart on page 128 suggests, financial institutions perform an intermediary function; they create one form of debt in exchange for another. They exchange their debts for those of others. If the people of a community want to save $100,000 and put it in a savings bank, they will receive $100,000 credit in their pass books. The savings bank can then loan the $100,000 to borrowers who will spend it. So the savings bank gives two things to the public—a pass-book credit and $100,000. It has also received two things from the public—an IOU from the borrowers and $100,000. The whole transaction has transferred spending power from the deposi-

The Debt of Financial Institutions, 1978
(in billions of dollars)

Debts Financial Institutions Owe	Debts Financial Institutions Own	
	806	Owed by households (consumer credit and mortgages owed to banks, insurance companies, finance companies, etc.)
Owed to households (deposits in commercial banks, mutual savings banks, savings and loan associations, and credit unions; reserves in private insurance companies and private pension funds) — 1,718		
	744	Owed by business (business loans, bonds, and mortgages held by banks, savings and loan associations, insurance companies, and pension funds)
Owed to business (deposits) — 213	473	Owed by government (federal, state, and local securities held by financial institutions)
Owed to government (deposits) — 127		
Owed to other financial institutions — 305	305	Owed by other financial institutions
Owed to rest of world — 71	87	Owed by rest of world
Total Liabilities 2,434	Total Debt Assets 2,415	

tors (those with a surplus of funds) to the borrowers (those with a deficit of funds).

Financial institutions are necessary because people do not want to invest all of their savings themselves or to lend their funds directly to the people who want to borrow. Some people do not like to hold the IOU's of other people or the bonds and notes of business or government. They prefer to hold their savings in bank deposits or insurance policies—they prefer the IOU's of financial institutions. The main function of financial institutions is to supply these savers with the kinds of assets they want to own and at the same time to provide funds for the people who want to borrow. Thus when people hold more bank deposits, this indicates that banks have done more lending. If people hold something else, some other institution has done more lending.

But are the financial institutions purely passive in these transactions? Not at all! A commercial bank, for instance, can go out and find customers to whom it can lend money and so can the savings institutions. The commercial bank can offer to take the customer's IOU, and, in return, give him a checking account (a debt of the bank). The other financial institutions also make loans, but not quite in the same way. Savings banks and insurance companies must first find someone who will deposit money and hold a savings account or an insurance policy.

This tells us that there is something special about the commercial bank. What is special is that it supplies society with a special kind of debt which we call money. Let us look at money in more detail.

Throughout history, many different things have been used as money, including wampum, furs, stones, precious metals, and, in Germany after World War II, cigarettes. Actually, money can be almost anything, as long as most people will accept it and agree to use it in setting the prices of what they buy and sell. At the present time, we use coins issued by the Treasury, paper money issued by the Federal Reserve Banks, and checking accounts as money. In fact, all that is required for something to be used as money is social acceptance. In our economy and in most modern societies we use *debts* for our money—not all debts but certain types. In short, money can be anything that is generally acceptable as a medium of exchange. This includes checking accounts, which people spend by writing checks. The fact that some people will not accept checks for payments does not alter the fact that they are *generally* acceptable. After all, in earlier times, some people would not accept gold coins unless they could weigh them on the spot; yet the coins were still considered money.

But money is more than a medium of exchange; it is also an abstract unit of measure. As an inch is a measure of length, and a pound is a unit of weight, the dollar is the unit we use to measure value. And the money we handle is merely the thing that shows we have a claim for so and so many dollars' worth of goods and services. The fact that money is a generally acceptable *claim* also means that it is a "store of value." Instead of collecting a lot of goods and services for the future, we can hold money with the expectation that we can buy the needed goods and services when we want them.

Certainly, the balance we hold in a checking account at the commercial bank performs the functions of money. But what about the balance we hold in a pass-book savings account or in an insurance policy? Is this also money? Almost, but not quite. It is a "store of value"—a claim for a certain amount of dollars—but it cannot be used for the purchase of goods and services without some intermediate steps. We cannot exchange our savings book for groceries, nor can we use our insurance policy to buy a car—but we can convert them to the cash needed for such purchases. For this reason, these other debts of financial institutions are sometimes called *near-money.* They are similar to currency and demand deposits in some ways, but they are not a means of payment.

In fact, there are today three official definitions of money, labeled M-1, M-2, and M-3. M-1 is currency and privately owned checking accounts (demand deposits)—what most people think of as "spending money." M-2 is M-1 plus time and savings deposits in commercial banks (except for very large negotiable certificates of deposit). M-3 is M-2 plus deposits in savings banks, savings and loan associations, and credit unions—the so-called nonbank thrift institutions. When we discuss monetary policy, in Chapter 7, we will see that all three concepts are important, since "near-money" (included in M-2 and M-3) can easily be converted into "spending money."

There are two ways in which commercial banks can increase the money supply. They can create new money by making loans to their customers—to consumers, business, farmers, home buyers, etc. They can also create new money by buying government securities. In both cases, the banks will usually create checking accounts or demand deposits, which are money and can be spent when their owners write checks.

The rate at which commercial banks can create money by expanding lending to the public is limited partly by the willingness of the public to borrow. At any time the number of people who are willing to borrow is limited. Borrowing costs something—interest—and some people are not willing to pay this cost. Also, some people are too uncertain about the future to know whether they will be able to repay the loan on schedule—and some people do not even bother to ask for a loan because they know the banker would not regard them as sound risks. Whatever the reason, when the public becomes less willing to borrow, it will put a damper on the creation of money.

Banks can, of course, attempt to influence the attitude of the public toward borrowing. They can raise or lower the interest rates they charge, or they can ease or tighten their standards for acceptable loans. But the response to these changes is not always prompt or substantial.

If banks cannot increase the demand for loans, they can still create deposits by buying outstanding debts. When banks buy government securities or other debts that are held by the public, they pay for them with increased bank deposits.

The ability to expand total deposits this way depends upon the attitudes of the public and the banks toward holding deposits and other debts. Bankers may be unwilling to buy securities, as they were in the 1930s, because their yields are too low to offer a satisfactory return. And there are times when the public prefers to hold other debts instead of bank deposits. When a person sends a check to be deposited in a savings and loan association he is saying, in effect, "I prefer to hold savings and loan shares instead of a checking account"; when he buys a government bond he is saying he prefers a bond to a demand deposit; when he draws a check on his account to pay off his note at the bank, he is saying that he prefers less debt rather than more deposits.

Let us use an illustration to show why, if demand deposits are to grow, the public must be willing to hold them. Suppose Mr. A decides to pay off a $1,000 loan he owes the bank; he will write a $1,000 check, payable to the bank, and get back his IOU—the bank will cancel the $1,000 deposit and the $1,000 debt.

Because Mr. A wanted to cancel his IOU rather than hold a bank deposit, he made total deposits fall. And the bank, in order to restore its deposits to their former level, must now try to obtain another security to take the place of the one retired by Mr. A. But this may not be easy. If many people act like Mr. A, the supply of debts will become more scarce, their prices will rise, and the banks may decide that their yield is not worth the price. Thus when the public becomes less willing to hold deposits the willingness of banks to buy securities and create deposits may also be restrained.

The impact on the banks will be similar if Mr. A wants to buy government bonds, savings and loan shares, or any other type of IOU. His funds may compete, directly or indirectly, for the same things that the bank needs to create deposits. Banks can, of course, attempt to persuade depositors to keep their funds in the bank. They may advertise and offer their customers a variety of services to induce them to hold bank deposits. But there are limits to the amount of competition banks can afford and still make a profit. Therefore, if their customers do not readily respond to these efforts, the growth of bank deposits will tend to be retarded.

Legal controls impose an important limit on the ability of the banks to create deposits. For most banks, this limitation is imposed by the Federal Reserve System.[2] The banks that are members of the Federal Reserve System can only create deposits if they have adequate reserve accounts at a Federal Reserve Bank (that is, if they own some of the debts of the Federal Reserve Banks). Generally speaking, the larger the reserves (the more debts of the Federal Reserve Banks the commercial banks own), the more deposits they can create.

What is the Federal Reserve System? It is a group of

---

[2] About 75 per cent of our commercial bank deposits are owed by members of the Federal Reserve System—the rest are under state regulation.

twelve banks (Federal Reserve Banks) located in different sections of the country and operated under the central direction of the Board of Governors of the Federal Reserve System in Washington, D.C. The Federal Reserve System is not a part of the Treasury or any other agency of the federal government; it is a separate agency, whose primary purpose is to supervise the activities of commercial banks and regulate the money supply. The Board of Governors has seven members appointed for fourteen-year terms by the President with the consent of the United States Senate. These terms are staggered so the Board will be relatively free from control by any single presidential administration.

Each of the twelve Federal Reserve Banks is actually "a banker's bank." Commercial banks use a Federal Reserve Bank in much the same way that we use a commercial bank. The commercial banks own deposits—debts of the Federal Reserve Bank—and they can obtain currency by writing checks on their deposits. They can also write checks to pay what they owe to other banks. They can also borrow from the Federal Reserve Bank in order to build up their deposits.

The important control exercised by the Federal Reserve System is its requirement that each of its member banks must have a deposit of a certain size in a Federal Reserve Bank. This deposit is called its *legal reserve.* The amount of reserves that a bank must own is a prescribed percentage of its deposits. In other words, if a bank has $1 million of demand deposits and a 20 per cent reserve requirement, it will need a $200,000 deposit at the Federal Reserve Bank. If the bank wants to increase its customers' deposits, by receiving cash from the public or by making new loans (accepting the IOU of a borrower), it will have to increase its reserve account at the Federal Reserve Bank. If it cannot do this, it cannot increase its deposits—that is the law.

By controlling the amount of reserves, the Federal Reserve authorities can impose a limit on the amount of deposits commercial banks can create. We shall not stop here to go into the various ways that the authorities can change the amount of reserves—this is discussed in Chapter 7—but we should note that the control over these reserves is one of our principal means for influencing the level of national income and employment.

In summary, there are certain requirements for issuing the debts (money or near-money) that financial institutions can create. They can create them only if: (1) they are willing and able to lend to consumers, business, and government, (2) the public wants to hold the money or near-money, and (3) the regulating authorities will permit the institutions to create them.

There is one more financial debt that should be mentioned —Federal Reserve notes. These are another part of our money supply—currency issued by the Federal Reserve Banks. Our total supply of coins and currency was about $100 billion in mid-1979. The currency is a debt of the Federal Reserve Banks. The Federal Reserve Banks create these notes when the banks ask for them. All the banker has to do is to write a check on his deposit at the Federal Reserve Bank and he can get the cash. The note is merely a paper evidence of the IOU of the Federal Reserve—another debt that we use as money.

We can now see that our money today is a mixture of debts of banks (deposits), debts of the Federal Reserve System (currency), and, if we include "near-money" (M-2 and M-3), the debts of many nonbank thrift institutions. But demand deposits on which the public can write checks are the most important form of money in the United States.

As shown in the accompanying tabulation for mid-1979, demand deposits (M-1) account for slightly under three quarters of the money supply. All of this money is a form of debt obligation of the banks; but by law and by custom they are accepted as our medium of exchange.[3]

---

[3] A note is appropriate here on credit card spending. Consumers spend approximately $80 billion a year through the use of credit cards. In mid-1978, they owed $15 billion to banks and another $21 billion to department stores, oil companies, and organizations like American Express and Diners Club for credit card charges. When people use their Visa or Master Charge cards, they are, of course, borrowing from the banks that issue the cards. When using a gasoline credit card, a department store charge card, or an American Express card, they are being extended credit by the organization in question. Credit card charges are thus really no dif-

THE MONEY STOCK OF THE UNITED STATES, APRIL 1979
(BILLIONS OF DOLLARS)

Currency	100.2
Commercial bank demand deposits	264.1
Total: M-1 (money)	364.3
Commercial bank time and savings deposits[4]	525.5
Total: M-2	889.8
Deposits in nonbank thrift institutions[5]	641.6
Total: M-3 (money and "near-money")	1,531.4

Source: *Federal Reserve Bulletin,* June 1979.

We will now examine briefly a problem dealing with money and debt. What is the impact of the national debt on the American economy? What problems face us as a result of the continued growth of this debt? As in earlier chapters, we will follow the outline used in Chapter 1.

The Problem and the Issues

With the exception of one year (1836), when it was paid off, the United States has had a national debt since 1789. As noted earlier, the greatest increases in the debt have occurred in the past fifty years as a result of depression, war, inflation, and the expansion of the government's role in the economy. In 1978, when the debt was more than $750 billion, the total interest cost of this debt was $43.8 billion a year, or 7½ per cent of total federal spending—a sizable item in the federal budget.

People have many concerns over the national debt, some of them justified and some of them not justified. Some people believe that the nation will "go bankrupt" if the debt contin-

---

ferent from other forms of credit, such as a bank loan to buy a car. They permit consumers to "buy now and pay later."

[4] Excluding negotiable certificates of deposit over $100,000.

[5] Mutual savings banks, savings and loan associations, and credit unions.

ues to increase, just as an individual or a business might go bankrupt if its debts continued to increase. Others fear that we are imposing a heavy burden on future generations who will have to pay off the debts we are contracting today. Still others believe that increases in the debt will cause inflation.

Some of these popular fears stem from a lack of understanding of the nature and role of debt in our economy. There are indeed things to worry about, but most of them relate to such technical matters as the impact of the debt on money markets, on interest rates, and on the availability of funds for private investment. We cannot afford to be cavalier about the national debt, because it can create problems. But on the other hand we should worry about the right things and not the wrong ones.

We will focus here on just one aspect of the national debt. This is its relationship to the nation's goals of growth, stable prices, and full employment. What might be the consequences of a policy of substantially reducing the national debt? What might be the consequences of allowing it to increase?

The Objectives

It is generally agreed today that preventing an increase in the national debt (that is, balancing the federal budget) is not an objective to be pursued for its own sake regardless of the consequences. The prime objective of public policy is to maintain full employment and price stability in the short run and to promote economic growth in the long run. These objectives may require that the national debt be increased at certain times and reduced at other times. Putting a balanced budget ahead of these basic objectives could lead the government into raising taxes and cutting spending during a recession, which would make the recession worse. On the other hand, allowing the national debt to increase—that is, running budget deficits, which have to be covered by the creation of new money—when the nation is experiencing inflationary pressures may make the inflation worse. Thus the objective is wise debt management—managing the debt in such a way as to contribute to the nation's over-all economic goals.

The Alternatives

Is the national debt a threat to our national solvency? Could the nation "go bankrupt"? The fact is we do not really know how big the national debt can become before we run into serious trouble. We do know, however, that it could be much higher than it is today—even though we do not know the precise amount. We should remember, too, that as recently as 1940 many persons "viewed with alarm" the fact that the national debt had reached the "enormous" total of $40 billion. Most Americans at that time would have been unable to conceive a debt of over $750 billion, the figure reached in 1978.

Bankruptcy is the legal condition that may result when debtors do not have the ability to pay their debts. It is the device society uses to decide how much an insolvent borrower can pay to each of his creditors. In the legal sense, these terms cannot be applied to the debts of the federal government to the public. The capacity of the federal government to pay its debts is virtually limitless—it can use taxes or it can create the funds necessary to pay whatever it owes to its citizens. For these and a host of other reasons the state of bankruptcy is not applicable to a national government.

Second, will the national debt ever be paid off? The answer to this question is both yes and no! Yes, because individual securities are being paid off every day as they come due. The U. S. Government has always paid off the holders of maturing securities, and it is inconceivable that it will not continue to do so. But the debt in the aggregate will not be paid off, because new securities are constantly being issued to new lenders as the old ones are being paid off.

Finally, does the national debt cause inflation? The answer here is that it all depends. If most of the increase in debt results from the government's borrowing from commercial banks, new money is being created and total spending is likely to rise. This was not inflationary in the 1930s, when the nation had many idle resources. The increase in spending simply put some of these idle resources to work and increased production. But it was inflationary in the late 1960s, when increased government spending, financed by increases in the national debt, pushed up total spending at a time when our resources were more fully employed and we could not increase production very much.

This analysis suggests that it is unwise to try to reduce the national debt during periods of recession or depression. Debt reduction means running a budget surplus and using that surplus to pay off the government's creditors. To the extent that these creditors are banks, which originally created new money to buy the government securities when they were issued, paying them off means "abolishing" money, that is, canceling the demand deposits originally created. Reducing the money supply at a time when the demand for goods and services is already so low that some of the nation's productive resources are idle will only make the recession worse.

On the other hand, when the nation is experiencing inflationary pressures, reducing the size of the federal budget deficit (and, if possible, balancing the budget) may be very desirable. The less the government has to borrow, the less money the banking system has to create. The less the money supply increases at such a time, the less the inflationary pressure. Conversely, increases in the national debt during periods of inflation may make it worse.

Appraising the Alternatives

The national debt *is* large, but it must be viewed in the perspective of a growing economy in which the use of credit (increase in debt) is an important element. In the thirty years following the end of World War II, the net debt of the federal government—that is, the debt of the federal government itself and federally sponsored credit agencies—held by the public increased from $229.5 billion in 1946 to over $750 billion in 1978. But the debts of state and local governments, business, consumers, and homeowners increased much more, as can be seen from the following table.

These figures should be encouraging for those who fear the national debt. Note first that in 1946 the national debt was 59 per cent of total debt. In 1976, it was 18 per cent. While the national debt has grown over the thirty-year period, other forms of debt have grown much faster, particularly corporate, mortgage, and consumer debt. These figures

NET PUBLIC AND PRIVATE DEBT, 1946 AND 1976
(BILLIONS OF DOLLARS)

	1946	1976	Increase	Per Cent Increase
National debt	229.5	597.2	367.7	160
State and local debt	13.7	236.3	222.6	1,625
Corporations	93.5	1,414.7	1,321.2	1,413
Farmers	7.6	108.5	100.9	1,328
Mortgage debt	31.8	684.1	652.3	2,051
Consumers	8.4	217.8	209.4	2,493
Commercial and financial	12.1	96.4	84.3	697
	396.6	3,354.9	2,958.3	

Source: *Economic Report of the President, 1978,* p. 337.

show that the enormous growth of the American economy since World War II, with real GNP almost tripling, has been financed largely by an expansion of private debt—by business borrowing to build factories, by citizens borrowing to buy houses and cars, and so on. Even in the public sector, state and local borrowing to finance schools, hospitals, roads, etc., has grown faster than federal borrowing.

Our analysis of how to manage the national debt—whether to try to reduce it or let it increase—suggests that policy at any particular time must be formulated with a full comprehension of the current state of the economy, of the nation's broad economic goals, and of both the long-run performance of the economy and its short-run problems.

The technical problems relating to debt management referred to earlier are important, but in general the growth of the national debt has not prevented our economy from growing and prospering. Our analysis has illustrated some of the reasoning we must do. We have concentrated here on some of the financial effects in order to throw additional light on our debt structure. The national debt, we have seen, must be viewed along with all of our other debts; and, like all debts, it has an impact that may extend far beyond the borrower and lender. In deciding what should be done with it, we must have some understanding of these effects, particularly the relationship of the debt to the nation's goals of growth, price stability, and full employment.

This chapter has stressed these basic ideas:

1. Debts are a necessary part of our economic system. They represent an economic relationship between those who wish to spend more than their income and those who wish to spend less than their income. Our arrangements for borrowing and lending contribute to the growth of our income and production. The fact that some people abuse this arrangement by incurring debts that they are unable to meet causes some individual problems, but it does not indicate that the over-all arrangement is economically unsound.

2. There are different types of debts for different borrowers. They perform different functions, and they have different effects. Consumers buy automobiles, businesses buy raw materials, governments buy roads, and financial institutions buy the debts of everyone else. They all foster the growth of spending, the growth of markets, production, and employment.

3. When financial institutions buy the debts of consumers, business, and government, they contribute to the growth of liquid assets. Some of these liquid assets are called *money*. For this reason, the role of the financial institutions is particularly important. They do more than merely transfer funds from one person to another—they create a particular type of debt that has special effects of its own. The growth of the money supply influences our spending and, in turn, the level of production for the entire economy.

Suggested Reading

Paul A. Samuelson, *Economics,* Chaps. 15 and 16, pp. 269–313. George L. Bach, *Economics: An Introduction to Analysis and Policy,* Chap. 16, pp. 201–7, and Chap. 17. Federal Reserve Bank of Chicago, *Two Faces of Debt,* 1979. This pamphlet presents clearly and simply the role of debt in our economy.

Federal Reserve Bank of New York, *Money: Master or Servant,* 7th ed., 1974. This pamphlet gives an excellent picture of the role of money in our society, how our banking system creates it, and how the Federal Reserve authorities try to manage it.

Chapter 6

INFLATION AND RECESSION

Over the years, the American economy has been plagued by short-run instability. Incomes, employment, and production have moved ahead rapidly for a few years, only to slip back temporarily before moving on to new peaks. Periodically too, the nation has experienced bursts of inflation when the general price level has risen sharply. Many names have been given to these economic fluctuations, including "the business cycle," "prosperity and depression," "inflation and deflation," or simply "boom and bust." They all signify disturbances that interrupt the long-run improvement in the level of living.

The preceding chapter gave us some indication of how money and debt are related to these disturbances. The main purpose of this chapter is to identify some of the other causes of changes in the level of economic activity. To do so, it will be necessary to explore more fully the nature of economic fluctuations—to look inside them and see how they come about.

WHAT ARE ECONOMIC FLUCTUATIONS?

All of us know something about economic instability from our own experiences. Some elderly people still remember the inflation that followed World War I. In 1919, the cost of living almost doubled, and the average citizen had to try to make ends meet on an income that failed to keep pace with prices. Then, in the middle of 1920, farm prices fell precipitously, and many businesses failed. During 1921, unemployment averaged 10 per cent of the labor force. Gradually, the nation recovered, and the late twenties saw most people, but not most farmers, enjoying higher levels of living than before. This upswing reached a peak in the hectic get-rich atmosphere of the stock market boom of 1928 and 1929 when many people thought America had at last attained permanent prosperity.

The 1929 crash and the great depression of the 1930s are still vivid memories to many older people. The bank failures, the bread lines, the farm surpluses, the vast army of unemployed made many people think our economic system had disintegrated, that capitalism was through. By 1940, however, the United States was rearming. War entirely changed the economic picture. Ten years after the unemployment crisis of 1933, the United States found itself trying to hold down prices, rationing food and gasoline, and recruiting housewives and others to meet a labor shortage.

The fear of depression was well entrenched, however. Long before the end of World War II, there were many predictions of a postwar collapse that would throw millions out of work. But it didn't occur. After the Second World War, employment remained high, shortages continued, and prices soared. In the summer of 1948, Congress was called into special session to deal with price inflation. But a year later we were in a "recession" and unemployment rose above the 4 million mark (over 6.5 per cent of the civilian labor force).

Since World War II, the economy has escaped a major depression but it has suffered six recessions—the recessions of 1948–49, 1953–54, 1957–58, 1960–61, 1969–70, and 1974–75. In 1949 the rate of industrial production fell to a level 10 per cent below that of the previous year. Business improved again in early 1950, and then came the Korean War and a new surge of price inflation as well as new records in employment and production. By the fall of 1953, however, the nation began to curtail defense spending, and business activity began to decline. By March 1954, unemployment had risen to 3.7 million (5.8 per cent of the labor force), and industrial production had declined about 10 per cent. In 1955, however, production and employment once again broke all records. Between September 1957 and April 1958, industrial production fell by 12.5 per cent and unemployment more than doubled, reaching 7.5 per cent of the labor force. By March 1959, however, industrial output was exceeding the pre-recession level and GNP was at an all-time high. In the presidential election campaign of 1960 a new slowdown in economic activity became a major issue, but, by July of 1961, industrial production had regained its previous peak, and it continued to expand for the following eight years.

The eight years from 1961 to 1969, culminating in the mild recession of 1969–70, constituted the longest period of uninterrupted growth in recent American history. Starting in 1966, however, inflation gathered force, and during 1970 the general price level rose by 5.5 per cent. The years 1971–73 were years of renewed economic growth, but in 1974–75 the nation experienced a severe recession, with total production dropping by 1.4 per cent in 1974 and by another 1.2 per cent in 1975. At the same time, the annual rate of inflation accelerated to more than 10 per cent and the phrasemakers coined a new one: "double-digit inflation." In 1975, economic recovery began and continued through 1978, although inflation remained stubbornly high by historical standards.

This quick survey of the American economy's performance over a period of almost sixty years shows that the goal of sustained high levels of income and employment has been an elusive one. Over the long run, the nation's economy has grown spectacularly, doubling in size roughly every twenty years. In the short run, however, it has been characterized by much instability. Trying to achieve a more stable growth remains one of our major economic goals.

The 1970s have been a particularly disturbing period for two reasons. First, until recently recession was regarded as the primary problem, with inflation a threat only when the nation was involved in a war. All of the great periods of inflation of the twentieth century before the 1970s were associated with the nation's four wars—World Wars I and II, Korea, and Vietnam—or with their aftermaths. But the 1970s have shown us that inflation can also be a major problem in peacetime.

Second, we used to think that we could have either a recession or inflation but not both at the same time. But the

1970s have shown that we can have both at the same time. In 1970, the real GNP dropped by 0.4 per cent, but the price level rose by 5.5 per cent. In 1974 and 1975, when the real GNP was dropping by 1.4 per cent and 1.2 per cent, the price level rose by 9.7 per cent and 8.7 per cent. Traditional theory does not explain such a state of affairs. Economists and public policy makers are now grappling with a new and baffling phenomenon for which there is no precedent and also as yet no satisfactory answer.

The business cycle is a highly complex process, and no two cycles are alike. The great "peaks" of prosperity such as 1929, the inflationary crises such as 1920, 1948, 1951, and 1974, and the deep "valleys" of depression such as 1933 are spectacular events that nearly everyone remembers. It is more important, however, to understand the continuous and varied nature of the business cycle and to recognize that the term "business cycle" is not a description of evenly spaced changes in business activity. Business activity does not fluctuate rhythmically between the extremes of price inflation and depression, nor does it fluctuate around a norm of full employment. In order to understand what does happen, let us now distinguish the phases of the business cycle as follows:

> The Upswing (prosperity phase, expansion)
> The Upper Turning Point (downturn, crisis)
> The Downswing (depression phase, contraction)
> The Lower Turning Point (upturn, revival)

Keeping this division in mind, we should note that the upswing does not *necessarily* culminate in inflation. It did in 1920, in 1948, and in 1966, but it did not in 1926 and 1937. In 1937, for example, an upswing terminated, and a downswing began when unemployment was still over 7 million. Nor does the downswing *necessarily* culminate in deep depression. It did in 1921 and in 1933, but it did not in 1949, 1954, 1958, 1961, and 1970.

On the basis of historical knowledge, we can say that economic fluctuations vary in length, amplitude, and scope. Some downswings and upswings, like the cycle from 1929 to 1937, can be measured in years. Others, such as the "reces-

sions" of 1949, 1961, and 1969–70, can be measured in
months. Some cycles have reached extremes such as the crisis
of 1933 and the inflation of 1946–48 and 1974–75; others,
such as the recession of 1954, have been mild and have even
gone unnoticed by large sections of the population. Finally,
some recessions have involved all kinds of economic activity
—manufacturing, construction, agriculture, and so on—as in
1933, while others have touched only particular areas, such
as the so-called "inventory recession" of 1949.

*Sections of the economy are affected in different ways by
these fluctuations.* For example, agricultural production and
employment do not change rapidly, but the prices of farm
products tend to fluctuate widely. On the other hand, in the
steel and automobile industries prices do not go up and
down as much, but production and employment fluctuate
widely. In fact, in recent years there has been an increasing
tendency for all prices to become "sticky"—to resist downward adjustment. Many farm prices are supported by the
government; minimum wage laws and long-term union contracts put something of a floor under wages; many prices, including utility and transportation rates, are regulated by governmental agencies. Thus one big difference between recent
business recessions and those of years ago is that prices in
general seem to go down much less than formerly; a recession is now likely to affect industrial output and employment
more than the price level.

Why worry about these short-term fluctuations if in the
long run each generation is better off than its predecessor?
The answer, of course, is that depression means idle production facilities, men and women out of work, businesses fail-
ing, and farmers unable to get satisfactory prices for their
crops. Inflation means housewives are unable to stretch their
dollars far enough at the grocery store. It means that retired
people and others who receive fixed incomes suffer a decline
in real purchasing power. It means that the value of people's
savings is eroded.

EXPLAINING ECONOMIC FLUCTUATIONS

Unfortunately, a simple statement of the cause of economic fluctuations is not possible. In the first place, there seems to be no single "cause." The American economy is extremely complex, and a variety of factors influence its operation. Many theories "explaining" business cycles have been put forward over the years, but not one of them has been accepted alone as an adequate answer. For example, some economists have viewed the banking system as a major source of instability. Others have attributed economic fluctuations to under-consumption—the inability of consumers to buy continually all the goods produced; to psychology—alternating "waves" of optimism and pessimism; to distortions in "the structure of production"—changes in the balanced relationship between capital goods and consumer goods industries; to the irregular rate of industrial innovations; to improper government policies; and even to cycles of sunspots!

While economists are generally agreed that no single theory provides *the* explanation, today they do put major emphasis on changes in the level of total spending, or aggregate demand, as an important cause of economic instability. In this chapter we will examine this theory and also some other factors that seem to play an important role in the performance of our economy today. We do not know all the answers by any means, but as a result of the research that has been done, there is a better appreciation today than ever before of the key elements and relationships involved in economic fluctuations.

The concept of the gross national product can help us explain economic fluctuations. As described in Chapter 2, the figures for gross national product show us that there are three major groups who buy the things our economy produces for the market—consumers, producers, and government.[1] We refer to the total demand of these buyers as "aggregate demand or total spending." The following figures for 1977 and 1979 (first-quarter annual rate) illustrate this:

[1] For simplification, net exports are included with producers.

	Billions of dollars	
	1977	*1979*
Gross national product	1,887	2,265
Consumers (personal consumption expenditures)	1,206	1,440
Producers (gross private domestic investment and net foreign investment)	287	366
Government, federal, state, and local (government purchases of goods and services)	394	459

Aggregate supply, on the other hand, is the total amount of goods and services our economy can produce when all its productive resources are fully and efficiently employed. The relationship between aggregate demand and aggregate supply is crucial in determining the level of income and employment and the behavior of the price level at any particular time.

If aggregate demand is rising—if the three buyers are trying to buy more goods and services—at a time when the nation has idle productive resources (unemployed workers and idle factory capacity), production and employment will be stimulated and the economy will grow. Since idle productive resources can be put to work, the supply of goods and services will increase in response to the growing demand and there is no reason for prices to rise very much. This was the situation between 1961 and 1965, when real GNP rose by 22 per cent but the price level only inched up at about 1.5 per cent per year. But if aggregate demand continues to rise once full employment of resources has been achieved, then inflation results. This is what happened between 1966 and 1969, when real GNP rose by 10 per cent but inflation accelerated to a 5 per cent annual rate. Inflation of this type, which has been described as "too many dollars chasing too few goods," means that the buyers are spending more than is needed to buy a limited supply of goods and services at prevailing prices. Therefore they bid up the price level.

If aggregate demand is falling—that is, if the three buyers are buying less—then production and employment will tend to fall. Declining aggregate demand generally results in less employment, idle factories, and farm surpluses. Ultimately, it results in depression.

The objective of public policy, then, is to see that aggregate demand is maintained at the right level—not too high, and not too low. The "right level," of course, is not a fixed level. Because our capacity to produce increases about 4 per cent a year as a result of growth in the labor force and gains in productivity, the "right level" must gradually increase.

THE SOURCES OF AGGREGATE DEMAND

To the economist, "demand" means more than just "want" or "need." It is wanting something and being able to back up that want with purchasing power. At any moment, millions of persons "want" things but are unable to enter the market as buyers because of lack of money. Where then does aggregate demand come from and why does it vary?

The principal source of aggregate demand is current income. As shown in Chapter 2, the production of goods generates income in the form of wages and salaries paid to workers, profits earned by independent businessmen, farmers, and corporations, rent paid to those who permit the use of their property in the productive process, and interest paid to those who lend money. Thus the process of production generates the purchasing power needed to buy the goods and services that are produced.

There is no guarantee, however, that total spending will exactly equal income received. To begin with, a sizable part of income—almost one third, in fact—is taken from income earners by the government in the form of *taxes*. Of course, the government usually uses tax revenues to buy goods and services. But its total expenditures will not necessarily equal its total tax collections. It may spend more than it collects, supplementing its tax receipts with borrowed money, or it may spend less. So the government, through budgetary or fiscal policy, can help expand or contract total spending. As we shall see later, fiscal policy is one of the important tools for influencing aggregate demand.

Another part of income is likely to be *saved* rather than spent on consumer goods and services or paid in taxes. Some of these savings may be directly invested by the savers: a consumer may use his savings to buy a house, or a business may use its savings to buy new machinery. As we saw in the preceding chapter, some of these funds also accumulate in the form of bank deposits, savings accounts, insurance reserves, and so on. When the financial institutions lend funds to producers who invest in new capital, these funds are also being spent. They are not being spent by savers themselves; they are being spent by businessmen and are part of gross private domestic investment.

But there is no assurance that at any given income level producers will want to invest the same amount of money that the savers of the community decide to save at that same income level. Producers may want to invest more, or they may want to invest less. The decision to save and the decision to invest are made to a certain extent by different groups and for different reasons. Therefore, it would be a coincidence if the plans of the groups were exactly the same. Producers may want to spend more currently than the public wants to lend; in this case, they may draw on previously accumulated bank balances or on new deposits created by borrowing from the banking system. Or they may want to invest less; in this case, some goods will remain unsold, and the level of income will fall.

In other words, if investors try to spend more than the public currently wants to save, they will tend to increase aggregate demand and thus exert an upward pressure on income, employment, and prices. But if the savers try to save more than the investors want to invest, total spending will tend to decline, and the decline will exert downward pressure on prices, production, employment, and income. What we are saying in both situations is that upward or downward movements in the national income are likely to result when there are divergences between the plans of investors and savers. It is through these changes in the level of economic activity that savings and investment are made equal.

It should be emphasized that the buyers of the national product can supplement the purchasing power derived from their current incomes by borrowing from financial institutions or by drawing on their own accumulated assets. As we have seen, consumers, businessmen, and the government can and do spend beyond their incomes by borrowing from the banks and other financial institutions. Thus whether aggregate demands go up or down depends in part on government controls over these financial institutions. These controls will be discussed in the next chapter.

WHY DOES AGGREGATE DEMAND FLUCTUATE?

We must now identify the chief influences on spending for investment, consumption, and government services. First, we shall consider changes in the level of investment because these, historically, have been the most dynamic, the most unpredictable, and the most difficult to influence by economic policy.

Investment spending is based largely on the businessman's expectations of profits. Producers invest in the construction of new factories, the purchase of new equipment, and so on, because they believe there will be a demand for the new or better goods and services that will be produced as a result of their investment. Investments, in short, are made because producers expect they will yield a profit. Investment spending, therefore, is affected by technological change—by inventions that improve the output of the firm. It is also affected by the costs and the risks of replacing or expanding plants and equipment. However, experience shows that investments for entering new markets or to use new technology can and will be postponed if expectations of profits are uncertain.

Here we begin to see some reasons for the extreme variability of private investment. For example, in constant dollars (to eliminate the effect of price changes), it fell by 85 per cent between 1929 and 1933 and by 32 per cent between 1973 and 1975. On the other hand, it rose by 45 per cent between 1961 and 1965 and by 59 per cent between the second quarter of 1975 and the second quarter of 1978. Investment decisions are made by thousands of producers whose expectations of future profit are affected by many factors. Some of these, such as the evaluation of the international situation or the "friendliness" or "unfriendliness" of an administration in Washington toward business, are quite intangible. That is the reason so much emphasis is often placed on creating a favorable political, social, and economic "climate" to encourage investment. Tax laws designed to encourage the movement of venture capital into industry, harmonious labor-management relations, a rapid population growth, and the development of new industries and products as a result of research are all examples of factors likely to encourage investment. There are also unfavorable factors, which can have the reverse effect. For example, business expectation of more inflation or changes in the tax laws unfavorable to business can be an important deterrent to investment.

The expansion of investment in itself will, of course, generate more purchasing power. The consequent higher demand for goods will in turn stimulate more investment. This is the reason that an upturn in one area can lead to a much broader upswing. Isolated cycles in different industries may synchronize into major cycles when each is helped along by the others. A contraction of spending may also lead to a further contraction of spending—especially in spending for capital equipment.

Investment is also influenced by changes in technology. Many economists have pointed out that our economy is extremely dynamic; it is characterized by technological change or "innovation." These innovations take the form of new industries, new products, improved versions of old products, new marketing techniques, and so on. The industrial history of America is full of such stimulating innovations as automobiles, chemicals, plastics, supermarkets, air-conditioning, frozen foods, motels, automation, and jet aircraft, to mention a few.

These innovations do not occur in a steady stream but come at irregular intervals. When one does come, the economic chain reaction works something like this: "Innovators" pioneer with a new product. If it is well received by the public, they reap their reward in the form of profits. But their success will attract competitors. The upswing or prosperity phase of the cycle of the industry then develops as competing producers vie with one another to borrow money, hire skilled workers, buy raw materials, build new plants, and develop advertising campaigns. There will be what might be called a "bunching" effect in investment.

Later, however, the market may be temporarily satiated, and increased competition will reduce profit margins. The less efficient producers and the speculators will be squeezed out, the demand for machinery and raw materials will fall, and business activity will decline until some new innovation comes along to give fresh impetus to expansion.

In this concept of the business cycle, borrowing also plays an important role. Prosperity—when the imitators are imitating the innovator—will be fed by an expansion of debt if banks and other lenders are able and willing to make loans. If banks have excess reserves and are optimistic about the future of the economy, they can supply new credit at low interest rates and help the expansion of income. But when the wave of expansion loses its force, or when the banks run short of reserves, interest rates will tend to rise and new loans will decline in volume. Eventually the business decline may be accompanied by a contraction in the money supply.

Consumer spending is more stable than investment spending, and it is also much larger. In 1977, when gross private domestic investment was $297 billion, personal consumption expenditures were $1,206 billion, over four times as large as investment expenditures. Personal consumption expenditures tend to remain more stable than investment outlays, but occasionally, under the stress of war or other emergencies, they may also change quickly. It will be useful therefore to look into the factors that influence this largest source of aggregate demand.

Personal consumption expenditures are determined primarily by income, but they are also subject to a variety of influences that are not completely understood. This is particularly true of spending on durable goods like houses, refrigerators, and automobiles. Unlike food and basic services such as gas or electricity, the purchase of these durables can usually be postponed. If millions of persons, for example, decide to make the family car "do" for another year, their decisions can have a tremendous effect on the business situation. The surveys of consumer spending plans made in recent years by the Board of Governors of the Federal Reserve System and the University of Michigan reveal that we have much to learn about consumer motivations. More than once we have been surprised by unexpected shifts in their behavior.

Sometimes consumers' expectations cause people to act in such a way that what they expected actually does happen. One example occurred right after the outbreak of the Korean War, in the summer of 1950. With memories of the shortages of the Second World War still vivid, consumers rushed out to buy certain items "before the hoarders got them." This wave of consumer buying created some scarcities that might not have developed during a normal buying period and certainly helped push up the level of consumer prices. Businessmen reacted in the same way and decided to increase their inventories of raw materials, with the result that the prices of these also rose. A more recent example was the decline in consumer spending in 1974, which contributed substantially to the deep recession of that year. The higher rate of inflation and increasing unemployment created so much uncertainty about the future in the minds of consumers that they saved more and spent less, thus contributing to the decline in aggregate demand. Recurring waves of consumer expectations about the future thus can play an important part in economic fluctuations.

Normally, however, consumption expenditures tend to be strongly influenced by the level of disposable personal income. In the quarter century 1952–77, yearly consumption expenditures were between 92 and 95 per cent of disposable income. At times, they have gone as low as 75 per cent and as high as 101 per cent. Consumption declined to 75 per cent during the Second World War, when goods were scarce and the government was discouraging consumer spending. It was over 100 per cent of disposable income in 1932–33, when income and employment were so low that millions of people lived beyond their incomes for several years. However, these extremes occurred in unusual periods—in war and depression. Under more normal conditions, consumption expenditures are more closely related to the flow of income—although the relationship is by no means a fixed percentage.

Government spending, which is also part of aggregate demand, is influenced in the short run by special occurrences such as wars and recessions. Over the years, however, the amount of government spending is most influenced by prevailing philosophies of what the economic role of government should be in our society. For many years, in the 1950s and 1960s, national-defense considerations tended to dominate the federal budget as the nation waged a "cold war" with the Soviet Union and "hot wars" in Korea and Vietnam. In the 1970s, however, these expenditures have diminished in relative importance. The dominant items of expenditure now are for such programs as "income security" (which embraces social security benefits, welfare, food stamps, etc.), health, education and training, community and regional development, the environment, energy, and aid to states and cities, all of which together accounted for almost 60 per cent of total federal spending in the 1978 budget, with national defense accounting for 23 per cent. These figures reflect the current priorities of the American people, who are concerned today about such social matters as helping the aged, the poor, the unemployed youth, and the sick, cleaning up the environment, increasing our energy supplies, and trying to restore our cities to economic health.

Because private spending by consumers and business is so changeable, public spending has a special significance. The amount of private spending results from the individual decisions of millions of households and business firms, but public spending can be planned and directly controlled by the federal government. It can be deliberately increased or decreased by specific amounts. Thus it may be possible, through changes in the federal budget, to attempt to fashion government spending into a sort of economic "balance wheel." Government spending can be deliberately increased in an effort to boost aggregate demand and deliberately decreased to reduce demand, though it is difficult to alter in the short run. This is the "fiscal policy" instrument which will be discussed in the next chapter. As we saw, the motivations underlying private spending are varied and complex. They are not fully understood, and we certainly have not reached the point where we can either accurately predict or precisely control private spending. Nevertheless, a large part of governmental policy today is concerned with efforts to influence private demand by means of monetary and fiscal policies.

WHY ARE SOME FLUCTUATIONS "CUMULATIVE"?

As we noted earlier, neither recessions nor inflations follow a uniform pattern. Some recessions are deeper than others; some last longer than others. Similarly, an inflation may develop slowly, or it may become a "runaway." Severe fluctuations in business activity generally are the result of the tendency of small changes in spending to gain momentum as they are transmitted through the economy.

One aspect of the cumulative effect is what economists call the "multiplier principle." Let us say there has been a decision to build another large atomic energy plant. The payments made to the workers, to the suppliers of concrete, to the owners of the land needed, and so on, will increase income in the community nearby. Presumably private spending will be increased, too. The workers, for example, will spend more money in the grocery and clothing stores, at the local taverns and gas stations, and on renting houses and apartments. The grocery and clothing store proprietors, the tavern keepers and gas station operators, and the landlords and builders of the community can be expected to increase their spending, too, as they receive larger incomes. Thus the increase in total spending is likely to be several times the initial amount invested and to result in an expansion not only of income but also of output and employment in many communities.

The original investment sets up a chain of consumer spending, which could go on indefinitely if people always spent their entire income. But they do not. People save a portion of their income. Consequently, the multiplier is not infinite; unless new investments are made, the chain of added consumption will gradually peter out.

The multiplier can also work in reverse. It can contribute to a shrinkage in national income since a decline in investment spending will be followed by a chain of reductions in consumer spending. Without going deeper into multiplier analysis, the basic point to remember is that increases or decreases in investment or government spending may initiate relatively larger increases or decreases in income, output, and employment.

Cumulative changes in spending may also occur in accordance with the "acceleration principle." This means that changes in the rate of growth in the demand for consumer goods can lead to changes in the level of production of the capital goods needed to make the consumer items.

For example, assume that there is a steady consumer demand for 1,000 widgets per year, and that production for this level of demand requires the use of 10 machines, each of which produces 100 widgets. Assume further, as is reasonable, that one widget-making machine wears out and has to be replaced each year. As long as consumer demand stays the same, the demand for widget-making machines will be for one machine per year.

But suppose that for some reason the consumer demand for widgets increases from 1,000 to 1,100 per year, an increase in consumer demand of 10 per cent. To produce the additional 100 widgets, the manufacturer will not only have to replace one widget-making machine as scheduled for that year but will also have to buy another one as well. The demand of the manufacturer for widget-producing machines has thus doubled whereas the consumer demand for widgets has increased only 10 per cent.

Now, if consumer demand fails to increase further and stabilizes itself at 1,100, the demand for machines will actually *decrease*—to 1.1 a year. Thus capital goods industries may expand sharply when consumer demand increases, but they may also contract as a result of the failure of consumer demand to maintain a rate of increase. If consumers merely buy as much as they did before, the capital goods industry will go into a slump. It is as though we have to keep running faster and faster to stay where we are.

On the other hand, if consumer demand for widgets should fall by 10 per cent—that is, from 1,000 to 900—the producer would need only 9 machines for the coming year instead of 10. He would not need to buy any new widget-making machine at all. So a 10 per cent decline in consumer demand would have reduced the demand for machines to zero. This simple example helps explain why the capital goods industries experience the greatest fluctuations.

The acceleration principle applies also to inventories. Suppose again that consumer demand for widgets is 1,000 per year and that the retailer maintains an inventory equal to sales, that is, an inventory of 1,000. Plainly, then, he must buy 1,000 widgets a year from the manufacturer. But suppose consumer demand increases by 20 per cent (that is, from 1,000 to 1,200). In the year of that increase, the retailer would have to buy 1,400 widgets, an increase of 40 per cent in his purchasing. He would have to increase his purchasing by that much in order to satisfy the increased consumer demand (200) and to bring his inventory up to the new sales level (up, that is, by 200). Thus a small increase in consumer demand may bring about a much larger increase in production. If demand later stabilizes at 1,200, he will *cut* his orders from 1,400 to 1,200. The "acceleration principle" builds up the force of an expansion, but it also provides a cause for the downturn; thus when consumer demand is stable or growing slowly, producers of capital goods or inventory may suffer.

Because people expect a continuation of what is happening, the role of expectations is another source of cumulative economic change. Earlier we noted the effect of expectations of consumers and businessmen in periods of rising or falling incomes or prices. If, for instance, the public interprets a slight rise in unemployment as an indication that the economy is headed for a major decline, it may curtail spending for all but the essentials of life. Similarly, if bankers and other creditors interpret a small decline as an indication of worse days ahead, they may reduce their volume of loans, causing a shrinkage in the money supply and forcing sales of goods at a loss.

However, a change in the level of spending need not become cumulative. Many downturns in incomes and spending have reversed themselves without any new outside stimulus to spending. For example, if incomes fall because of a decrease in business purchasing for inventory, the decline may be "automatically self-correcting." That is, if other spending holds up fairly well, the depletion of inventories will eventually force businesses to order more goods. Or, if some production stops because prices are not moving up as rapidly as costs and some firms are losing money, employment will tend to fall. If the decline in employment leads to lower costs for such items as labor and raw materials, it may enable idle firms to resume production. In these examples, the stimulus to recovery is caused by forces that the contraction itself generates.

The key to such "automatic correction" lies in the continuation of "other" spending. As we have seen, there are reasons to suspect that a decline in one part of the economy will be transmitted to another part, but this may happen only gradually and in the meantime the contraction may come to a halt. "Minor cycles" of this sort occur repeatedly in our economic

GROSS NATIONAL PRODUCT, 1969–70

	1969-III	1970-I	1970-III
GNP (Total Spending)	730.9	723.8	727.4
Personal Consumption Expenditures	468.7	474.0	479.6
Durable goods	84.1	82.7	83.6
Nondurable goods	201.9	205.6	208.2
Services	182.7	185.8	187.8
Gross Private Domestic Investment	114.1	102.9	104.1
Business fixed investment	81.9	80.9	79.6
Residential construction	22.3	20.7	20.0
Changes in business inventories	9.9	1.3	4.6
Net Exports of Goods and Services	0.8	1.9	3.1
Government Purchases of Goods and Services	147.3	145.0	140.6
Federal	75.2	71.1	66.2
State and local	72.1	73.8	74.4

Notes: Details will not necessarily add to totals, because of rounding. Roman numerals indicate quarters of year. Figures are annual rates for the quarter.
Source: *Economic Report of the President, 1971.*

system, and they only become a matter of major public concern when the period of readjustment is unduly prolonged.

The 1969–70 recession is an instructive illustration of a "minor cycle." From prosperity to the trough of the recession to recovery took about one year. The table below shows the changes in the components of the GNP between the high point in the third quarter of 1969 (July–September), the low point in the first quarter of 1970 (January–March), and the third quarter of 1970, when the GNP almost reached its pre-recession high. From the peak to the trough the real GNP fell by 1.0 per cent. The figures are in billions of constant 1958 dollars to eliminate the effect of price changes.

These figures show that the major elements in the slowing down of the economy between the third quarter of 1969 and the first quarter of 1970 were in four categories of demand: federal government spending, changes in business inventories, residential construction, and business fixed investment. As shown in the following table, the total decline of these four was $15.3 billion. But these declines were partially

CHANGES IN TOTAL SPENDING, 1969–70

	1969-III to 1970-I	1970-I to 1970-III
GNP (Total Spending)	−7.1	+3.6
Personal Consumption Expenditures	+5.3	+5.6
Durable goods	−1.4	+0.9
Nondurable goods	+3.7	+2.6
Services	+3.1	+2.0
Gross Private Domestic Investment	−11.2	+1.2
Business fixed investment	−1.0	−1.3
Residential construction	−1.6	−0.7
Changes in business inventories	−8.6	+3.3
Net Exports of Goods and Services	+1.1	+1.2
Government Purchases of Goods and Services	−2.3	−4.4
Federal	−4.7	−4.9
State and local	+2.4	+0.6

offset by increases in personal consumption expenditures, net exports, and state and local government spending, which kept the net decline in total spending to a relatively moderate $7.1 billion, or 1 per cent of the GNP.

From the first to the third quarter of 1970, federal government spending, residential construction, and business fixed investment continued to decline, but business demand for goods to restock depleted inventories rose sharply and, together with a continued expansion of consumer spending and smaller increases in net exports and state and local government spending, this was enough to bring the economy back close to the pre-recession level.

These figures tell us *what* happened, but further analysis is necessary to understand *why* it happened. We cannot here give a full analysis of all the factors influencing demand, but one or two will suffice to illustrate how the various sectors of our economy function over the years.

Perhaps the most important factor in 1969–70 was the determination of the federal government to reduce its spending on the Vietnam War and on various social programs and thus to curtail the rate of inflation, which had been gathering force since 1966. In 1969, the Federal Reserve tightened up on the money supply, raising interest rates to very high levels. This discouraged business investment by raising the costs of borrowed funds. Higher interest rates for home mortgages were particularly important in reducing spending on residential construction. Indeed, one might say that a sharp application of the monetary and fiscal brakes was a major reason for the 1969–70 "mini-recession."

A secondary effect of these government decisions was that many business executives concluded it would be wise to be cautious in the accumulation of inventories; indeed, they ended up by shrinking their inventories. This was an important factor in the decline of gross private domestic investment.

In spite of these developments, however, the recession did not snowball into a full-scale depression. Consumer demand remained strong, and personal income lost through unemployment was offset by a reduced tax "take" by the government, by a rise in unemployment compensation payments, and by increases in social security benefits, among other things. Our principal customers in Europe and Japan continued to buy our goods. State and local governments continued to expand their activities in such fields as education and health.

The experiences of 1969–70 illustrate some of the inherent strengths of our economy as well as some of its weaknesses. The performance of such an economy depends not only on the policies of the federal government, which are important, but also on the independent decisions of millions of households and business firms.

Other Causes of Inflation and Unemployment

The level of aggregate demand, important though it is, is not the only factor to be considered when analyzing inflation and unemployment. In recent years, we have become more aware of certain so-called "structural" relationships in our economy that have an important impact on its performance. In 1974, for example, the price level rose by 9.7 per cent and in 1975 by 8.7 per cent. Yet this inflation did not stem from excess aggregate demand, since both years were years of severe recession, when total spending dropped and unemployment rose—as high as 9.0 per cent of the labor force in May 1975, for example. Clearly some other inflationary factor or factors must have been at work. One of these was what economists now call "cost-push" pressures on the price level.

Let us consider for a moment the relationship between costs, productivity, and prices. Wages are an important cost of production. An increase in wage costs can be absorbed by business if it is accompanied by an increase in productivity— that is, if there is an increase in output per hour by workers. In such a case, "unit labor costs"—that is, the labor cost of each unit of the product produced—remain the same. But what happens if wages rise more than productivity? If, for example, productivity in an industry rises by 2 per cent and wages by 8 per cent, then unit labor costs will rise by 6 per cent and business will try to compensate itself for this by raising prices.

In some industries, it is not the rising cost of labor but, rather, the rising cost of capital (buildings, machines, tools) or the rising cost of raw materials that pushes prices up. Whatever the cause—labor, capital, or materials—higher costs must be met either by producing and selling more output or by cutting down on other costs or by raising prices.

"Cost-push" inflation is made easier today by the fact that wages and prices in many key industries are not determined by impersonal market forces but, rather, by the decisions of those who have economic power in the market place, such as strong unions and large businesses in industries where price competition is limited. When unions and business—and government, too—have such power, the process is called "administered pricing."

Experience has shown that wages and prices in key industries such as steel, automobiles, aluminum, or coal can be pushed up even during a recession. Unions have often won substantial wage increases when unemployment was high, and large companies have raised prices even when they have had substantial idle productive capacity. To make matters worse, such increases tend to spread through the economy. For example, if steel prices rise, then the cost of making automobiles and refrigerators and construction costs go up and producers in these fields have to raise their prices too. And if the steelworkers' union wins a favorable contract, other unions are likely to demand at least as much.

Clearly, "cost-push" inflation is not a function of excessive aggregate demand and cannot be combated by monetary and fiscal policies. Unfortunately, as we shall see in the next chapter, no one has yet come up with a satisfactory answer to the problem.

In the 1970s, Americans have become aware that inflation and recession can also be "imported" from abroad. Following the quadrupling of oil prices by OPEC, the foreign oil cartel, in the fall of 1973, inflation accelerated sharply not only in the United States but in all the advanced industrial nations that consume foreign oil. Not only the price of gasoline at the filling station but also the cost of making petrochemicals, of running airlines and electric utilities, of heating houses, and of fueling many industries rose sharply. One estimate is that half the increase in the rate of inflation in 1974 was due to this one factor alone. One might think of the oil price increase as a special kind of imported "cost-push" inflation.

Ironically, however, the oil price increase also helped turn what might otherwise have been a mild recession into the worst one since the 1930s. In 1973, the American people paid $7 billion for foreign oil; in 1974, they paid $25 billion. Thus an additional $18 billion of purchasing power was transferred from the United States to the oil producers, a substantial reduction in aggregate demand for our domestic product.

Inflation was also worsened in the United States in 1974 by a series of bad harvests around the world, including in the Soviet Union. This led to massive foreign purchases of American agricultural products, which pushed up food prices in this country.

Finally, it must be noted that the government itself, in spite of its avowed goal of fighting inflation, follows numerous policies that raise particular prices. One example is the tariff and other import restrictions, which raise the prices of imported goods. Another is the farm price support program, which keeps some food prices higher than they would otherwise be. Still another is the activities of some regulatory agencies, particularly in the transportation field, which prevent the forces of competition from working to keep down certain prices. Environmental and safety requirements, imposed by such agencies as the Environmental Protection Agency and the Occupational Safety and Health Administration, also impose additional costs on industry which must be covered by higher prices. A recent estimate is that there is now about five hundred dollars of federally mandated antipollution and safety equipment on each automobile in the United States. Finally, periodic increases in the minimum wage and in social security taxes constitute another cost-push pressure on prices.

Unemployment also results from other causes than declines in aggregate demand. One reason for unemployment today is the existence of many persons, particularly minorities and young people, who lack the education and training for today's jobs. Even in periods of full employment, such persons are unlikely to be hired.

Temporary cutbacks in demand, such as the cancellation of a defense contract, can also create unemployment in a particular area. For example, several thousand persons were laid off in the Southern California aerospace industry following President Carter's decision in 1977 to cancel the B-1 bomber program.

In the mid-1970s, two groups of workers—women and teenagers—were becoming increasingly important in the labor force, the former because of social changes and the latter because of the high birth rate back in the 1950s. Unemployment among such groups is traditionally higher than among, say, married men in their thirties, and this has pushed up the over-all unemployment rates.

Other factors that can keep people out of work are the long-run loss of an industry's competitive position (e.g., the U.S. shoe industry finds it hard to compete with foreign producers), the exhaustion of natural resources in an area (remember the "ghost towns" in mining areas), discrimination in employment, technological change (self-operating elevators put elevator operators out of work), and seasonal changes (the closing down of summer-resort hotels in the winter). One other controversial source of unemployment is the minimum wage law, which many economists now believe prevents unskilled teenagers from finding jobs, since they are not worth what the law says employers must pay them. Clearly, while the maintenance of aggregate demand is important, other factors must also be considered if full employment is to be achieved.

We will now explore the problem of unemployment further, using the methods we have followed in previous chapters.

The Problem and the Issues

In May 1975, 8,314,000 persons were recorded as being unemployed in the United States. This amounted to 9.0 per cent of the civilian labor force. Regardless of how one might define "full employment," this level of unemployment was universally regarded as too high. A major objective of public policy was to put people back to work.

The first step is to analyze the unemployment figures in

more detail. Only in this way can the true dimensions of the problem be understood. Unemployment can be broken down into various categories, including age, sex, race, type of work performed, and the length of time the person has been out of work. The following table shows the unemployment figures for each of these categories in May 1975, a month selected because the second quarter of 1975 happened to be the bottom of a deep recession and national unemployment was at its highest level since before World War II.

The figures in the table show that unemployment was worse among women than among men, much worse among teenagers than among adults, much worse among nonwhites

UNEMPLOYMENT, MAY 1975 AND MAY 1979
(AS PER CENT OF EACH GROUP)

	May 1975	May 1979
Total: Civilian Labor Force	9.0	5.8
By Sex and Age		
Males, 20 years and over	7.3	3.9
Females, 20 years and over	8.5	5.8
Both sexes, 16–19 years	20.8	16.8
By Race		
White	8.1	5.0
Black and other	14.1	11.6
By Type of Work		
White-collar	5.3	3.2
Blue-collar	12.3	6.7

DURATION OF UNEMPLOYMENT, MAY 1975
(AS PER CENT OF THE UNEMPLOYED WHO ARE
16 YEARS OF AGE AND OVER)

Less than 5 weeks	37
5–14 weeks	32
15–26 weeks	18.5
27 weeks and over	12.5

Source: U. S. Department of Labor, *Monthly Labor Review.*

than among whites, and worse among blue-collar, or factory, workers than among white-collar, or service, workers. About 37 per cent of the unemployed had been out of work for less than five weeks, but about one eighth had been unemployed for about seven months or longer.

One can also break down unemployment geographically. In the spring of 1975, for example, unemployment in Detroit was around 17 per cent but in Houston less than 3 per cent. Clearly, unemployment is a complex problem with multiple causes.

The Objectives

The over-all objective in 1975 was, of course, to provide jobs for the unemployed who were able and willing to work. Unemployment is costly in many ways. The nation loses the output the unemployed could be producing, and those who are working have to support those who are not. But the most costly consequence is the damage that persistent unemployment does to its victims. In particular, the special plight of the younger and minority unemployed workers demands attention. Clearly, getting these people back to work is a major objective of our society.

Another national objective is to keep the economy as free as possible from additional government controls. In addition, we want to solve the unemployment problem without resorting to policies that are likely to make inflation worse. The over-all issue, then, is whether full employment, economic freedom, and price stability are compatible goals.

The Alternatives

A number of policies are available to the nation for reducing unemployment. One is to stimulate the economy by increasing the money supply, cutting taxes, and stepping up government spending on public works. These policies would stimulate total spending on goods and services, and this would lead to expanded production and lower unemployment.

A second approach, if private business cannot provide enough jobs to the unemployed, is for the government to become the "employer of last resort" and provide so-called "public service jobs" to the unemployed. A third approach, if nonwhites are barred from jobs because of their race, is to enforce civil rights legislation and "affirmative action" programs. An example of this is the placing of government pressure on some of the white-dominated construction-trades unions to force them to admit more nonwhites into the unions.

A fourth approach, if people are out of work because they lack the education and skill needed to hold a job, is to develop special educational and training programs funded by the government and conducted by business and unions. Fifth, if Americans are out of work in certain industries such as shoes, clothing, and steel because of foreign competition, as some believe, then imports of these products could be restricted by raising the tariff or by imposing quotas. Another approach to unemployment caused by imports would be for the government to provide what is called "adjustment assistance" to the affected workers—that is, aid in the form of training programs to convert them to new skills.

Finally, unemployed workers can be put to work more easily if we have more information available on job vacancies and can match the unemployed to these.

Appraising the Alternatives

Most of these approaches to unemployment have been used in recent years. Monetary and fiscal policies are used to stimulate the economy in times of recession. We do have a federally funded public service jobs program, civil rights legislation, an Equal Employment Opportunities Commission, "affirmative action" programs, and retraining programs such as those authorized by the Comprehensive Employment and Training Act. We have from time to time restricted imports in order to preserve the jobs of American workers, and the Trade Act of 1974 does authorize "adjustment assistance" to such workers. State employment services have developed computerized job banks to match job seekers with job vacancies. The question to be considered, however, is the compatibility of all these approaches with the three goals we have identified: full employment, economic freedom, and price stability.

For example, in 1975, would not increasing the money

supply, cutting taxes, and increasing government spending on public works and other programs have aggravated inflation, which was then running at an annual rate in excess of 8 per cent?

It could be argued that it was safe to stimulate the economy in 1975, since production had been falling and unemployment rising for eighteen months. With so much idle manpower and industrial capacity, there seemed little immediate danger of excessive demand worsening inflationary pressures. The inflation at that time was of the cost-push variety and also due to higher oil and food prices.

Other approaches, such as pressuring unions to admit more nonwhite members, requiring businesses to develop "affirmative action" programs, and pressuring workers in industries affected by imports to move to new jobs all have laudable intentions. But all give the government a larger role to play in the economy and restrict the freedom of individuals and organizations. Finally, if the United States restricts imports from other nations to preserve jobs here, might this not lead to such nations' retaliating against our exports, in which case unemployment is likely to increase in those industries? Clearly, dealing with unemployment involves many conflicts and requires many trade-offs.

What actually happened to unemployment after May 1975? The economy turned up from the bottom of the recession and continued to expand—although not at a steady rate—into 1978. By May 1979 (see table on page 165), unemployment had dropped to 6,193,000, or 5.8 per cent of the civilian labor force. What was perhaps more significant than the drop in unemployment, however, was the rise in employment. Total employment rose by almost 10 million in the four-year period. Looking at these employment figures, one might conclude that the economy did a better job of providing jobs—almost 10 million of them in four years—than is perhaps generally realized. The reason unemployment stayed up near the 6 million mark was due to the rapid growth of the labor force through a great influx of women and teenagers. These two groups, for various reasons, experience higher unemployment rates than adult males; hence their swelling numbers keep up the total unemployment rate. In short, the growth of the economy—6.2 per cent in 1976 and 4.9 per cent in 1977—was enough to provide jobs for millions of new entrants into the labor force and also to bring down unemployment. But unemployment did not come down as much as one would have wished, because the number of new entrants into the labor force was so great.

In summary, we can see that the unemployment problem combines the basic elements of the market system and the problem of economic instability. People are more likely to find jobs if they can move easily from one labor market to another in response to changes in technology and the demand for goods and services. Such things as racial and sex discrimination, lack of knowledge of job opportunities, and above all lack of education and training, prevent the market mechanism from operating smoothly and increase unemployment. In addition, there will not be jobs for all who wish to work unless aggregate demand is kept at the right level. Recessions and slow growth are the great destroyers of jobs.

This chapter has stressed the following ideas:

1. Economic fluctuations do not occur at regular intervals. Their severity varies from cycle to cycle and their impact on each industry may be different each time. The causes of fluctuations are equally varied—they may begin with any series of events that causes total spending to change. Explanations of cycles that rely on psychology can help us understand why some cycles are severe and others are mild, but psychology cannot explain why cycles begin.

2. We can analyze cycles by using the breakdown of the gross national product. By these measures we can see where spending, or aggregate demand, changed—and then we can try to find out why they changed. Consumers, businessmen, and government spend for different purposes so we must try to understand the conditions that influence all three groups.

3. Consumer spending is the largest and most stable part of aggregate demand. The relationship between outlays of consumers and their income is close, although at times consumers have upset predictions of their spending. Investment spending is more unstable and depends heavily on the expectations of businessmen for profitable investment opportu-

nities. It is influenced by the flow of technological developments, the cost of borrowing money, and a host of other considerations involved in managing a modern business. Government spending reflects a number of social objectives: national defense, public works, aid for the underprivileged, and the needs of stabilizing aggregate demand, to mention a few.

4. Some fluctuations are cumulative. The multiplier effect of investment can increase the flow of consumption. The acceleration principle may lead to large changes in outlays for investment. But not all fluctuations need be cumulative. Some will correct themselves.

5. Inflation can result from other causes than excess demand. The most important of these is cost-push pressures stemming from administered pricing by those who have power in the market place. Inflation may also be imported from abroad, as happened when oil prices were raised.

6. Finally, unemployment can also result from other causes than a low level of aggregate demand. These can include lack of education and training, racial and sex discrimination, technological change, import competition, seasonal factors, and demographic and social changes of the kind that in recent years have led to such an increase in the number of teenagers and women in the work force.

Suggested Reading

Paul A. Samuelson, *Economics*, Chaps. 13 and 14, pp. 234–68. George L. Bach, *Economics: An Introduction to Analysis and Policy*, Chaps. 9, 11, 15, and 19. These readings deal with some of the theories used to understand business cycles. Some of them may be a little difficult for beginners but, if mastered, will be highly rewarding, as these theories are very useful tools for understanding why we have fluctuations in the level of economic activity.

The Economic Report of the President. Published annually in January, these reports give the official view of the President's Council of Economic Advisers on the current state of the economy. They review the previous year, forecast the upcoming year, and discuss the various economic policies that might be pursued.

Chapter 7

STABILIZING THE ECONOMY

During the depression of the 1930s, the federal government borrowed money and launched a public works program in an effort to stimulate the economy. In both 1964 and 1975, taxes were lowered to increase private spending at a time when the economy was sluggish. During World War II and in 1968, Congress raised taxes to drain off spending power that might otherwise have been used to bid up prices for consumer goods. From time to time, the government has also influenced private spending by changing the cost of borrowing and the ease with which consumers and businesses can obtain borrowed funds. In this chapter we shall look at these and other measures that the government has used or may use to smooth out fluctuations in income and employment. We shall see that our economy has a number of methods of pursuing one of its foremost objectives—economic stability.

Economic stability means, first, full employment of our productive resources. But what does "full employment" mean? How full is "full"? Must there be no more than transitional unemployment among those who are able and willing to work and no idle industrial capacity at all? Or should the limit of tolerable unemployment be defined as a percentage of the civilian labor force, such as the 4 per cent target established by the Kennedy administration in 1962? Should full employment of our fixed capital be defined as a particular capacity utilization rate, such as 90 per cent of industrial capacity?

In recent years the term "full employment GNP" has come to signify a level of output that is consistent with full use of our productive resources—however "full" is defined—and there has been growing discussion of ways to eliminate the "gap" between what the economy can produce, "potential GNP," and what it produced, "actual GNP." Clearly "full employment" is not a precise term, but in a general sense, it is undoubtedly one of our objectives.

Economic stability also means that the average price level changes slightly or not at all. Certainly, we want to avoid the kind of price collapse we had in 1929–33 and the kind of inflation we had in 1946–48 and in 1974–75. On the other hand, we do not want to introduce so many rigidities into the price structure that prices cannot perform their proper function as indicators of what goods people want produced. In general, we might say that we want flexibility in individual prices with reasonable stability in the average price level. Historical experience suggests that 2 per cent is a reasonable target, since the best performance since World War II was the 1955–65 decade, when the annual increase in the price level (as measured by the GNP deflator) averaged 1.9 per cent.

Let us take a look at the formal commitment the United States has assumed in this field and see what light it throws on our objective of economic stability. The Employment Act of 1946, Section 2 of which is entitled "Declaration of Policy," states:

> The Congress declares that it is the continuing policy and responsibility of the Federal Government to use all practicable means consistent with its needs and obligations and other essential considerations of national policy, with the assistance and cooperation of industry, agriculture, labor, and state and local government, to coordinate and utilize all its plans, functions, and resources for the purposes of creating and maintaining, in a manner calculated to foster and promote free competitive enterprise and the general welfare, conditions under which there will be afforded useful employment opportunities, including self-employment, for those able, willing, and seeking to work, and to promote maximum employment, production, and purchasing power.

In less formal language, the meaning of the Employment Act can be stated as follows:

The United States Government will follow policies designed to promote maximum employment and production and to avoid serious depression. The act has also been interpreted to mean that the government should use its power to prevent disruptive changes in the price level. These objectives are to be achieved within the framework of a system of competitive private enterprise.

There are many ways in which the government can promote a steady rise in income and employment. But we are concerned here primarily with those that operate through their effect on total spending in the economy. The foremost of these controls involve the monetary and fiscal powers of our government.

Most of the following discussion of economic policy concerns monetary and fiscal policy because the most influential economic powers of the government are its power to control the money system and its power to collect money from the public and to spend it. Occasionally, the government has taken more drastic action, such as rationing goods, fixing prices, and allocating raw materials and labor. But, in a free economy, these compulsory measures are generally measures of desperation, introduced in emergencies such as wartime. Except in such emergencies, the nation rejects direct controls and relies mainly on indirect instruments of economic management.

MONETARY POLICY

Monetary policy is the policy of the central bank—in the United States the Federal Reserve—toward the supply of money and the level of interest rates. The task of the Federal Reserve is to try to manage the money supply in a way that will contribute to over-all economic stability and to the steady growth of aggregate demand.

In carrying out monetary policy, the Federal Reserve—or the "Fed," as it is often called for short—deals primarily with the commercial banks, since it is these which, as we saw in Chapter 5, create money by making loans and investments.

In the nineteenth and early-twentieth centuries, the banking system was a major source of instability in the economy. It tended to exaggerate booms by overlending and creating too much purchasing power and to deepen depressions by calling in loans and destroying purchasing power. Since the 1930s, the Federal Reserve has tried to prevent this. Monetary management by the Fed now reflects the statement by Walter Bagehot, nineteenth-century British banker and editor of *The Economist*, that "money will not manage itself."

The Federal Reserve System, consisting of twelve banks located around the country, is under the central direction of a Board of Governors. This board has the primary responsibility for formulating and executing monetary policy. Although not all commercial banks are members of the Federal Reserve System, member banks hold over three quarters of our checking accounts; therefore the Federal Reserve System is in a strong position to influence the entire money and banking system of the United States.

All member banks must have deposits at the Federal Reserve Banks. These deposits, or "reserves," must equal a designated percentage of deposits held by the public at the member bank.[1] The portion of the reserve account of the member bank with the Federal Reserve that exceeds the required minimum is called "excess reserves" and may be used as a basis for the expansion of bank loans or the purchase of securities. Without excess reserves, a commercial bank cannot create credit.

The crucial power of the monetary authorities is their control over the total reserves of the member banks. When a Federal Reserve Bank buys something, a bond or some other type of IOU, it gives the seller a claim on the Federal Reserve Bank. When these claims are held by commercial banks, in the form of deposits in the Federal Reserve Bank, they are called bank reserves. Total reserves change, therefore, when the total deposits (debts) *owed* by the Federal Reserve Banks and *held* by the commercial banks change. Let us see how some of these changes take place.

[1] "Vault cash" (currency) kept by banks in their own vaults is also counted as part of their legally required "reserves."

Total reserves change when the public decides to hold more or less cash. At Christmastime, for example, consumers and business firms may want to have more cash in hand than usual. To meet such demands for currency, banks probably will turn to their Federal Reserve Banks, which will give them the currency, deducting the amount from the reserve accounts of the member banks. The total reserves of the commercial banking system are reduced by the amount of currency withdrawn by the public. When the currency finds its way back into the banks after Christmas, it is deposited in the Reserve Banks, and reserves will be increased again. Thus changes in the amount of currency in circulation change total reserves of commercial banks.

Total bank reserves frequently change when the public sends money to the United States Treasury or receives money from it. The change occurs when the money is deposited by the government or withdrawn from the deposit of the government in one of the Federal Reserve Banks. The procedure is as follows. An individual sends a check to the Treasury in payment of taxes. The Treasury deposits it in its account at the Federal Reserve Bank. Then the Reserve Bank will deduct the amount of the check from the account of the bank of the individual and credit it to the account of the Treasury. The individual's bank will, in turn, deduct the amount of the check from the individual's account. But the important effect is that the amount of the check has been withdrawn from the total reserves of the commercial banking system. Later, if the Treasury should write a check payable to an individual, the reverse process would occur. The account of his bank at the Federal Reserve Bank would be increased, the account of the Treasury reduced, and the total reserves of the commercial banking system enlarged.

Commercial banks can also borrow reserves from the Federal Reserve Bank. When they do so, they increase the total reserves of the whole banking system. When member banks borrow from the Federal Reserve, deposits to their credit are created—by the same process that private deposits are created when individuals borrow at commercial banks. Banks borrow by putting up collateral, as do private citizens. As a matter of fact, among the securities that they might pledge are the notes that firms have given when they borrowed from the commercial banks. Most of the time, however, the banks use government securities as collateral.

The volume of bank reserves, therefore, is dependent on a number of things. We have seen that the public, the United States Treasury, the banks themselves, and the Federal Reserve Banks all influence the amount of bank reserves. However, as the Federal Reserve System has the duty to control the volume of commercial bank credit, its effects on reserves are deliberate and planned. Its tools for controlling commercial bank reserves are called "quantitative controls."

The most flexible quantitative tool is called open-market operations.[2] When the Federal Reserve sells some of its holdings of government securities on the open market, it reduces total bank reserves. The reduction comes about in the following way. The purchaser of the securities pays the Federal Reserve by writing a check on his bank. The Federal Reserve collects the payment from the bank of the purchaser by reducing its reserve account. The bank, in turn, reduces the purchaser's account. Thus at the end of the transaction, the purchaser has the bond formerly held by the Federal Reserve and his bank account is lower. But most important, the account of his bank—or reserve—at the Federal Reserve Bank is lower. A lower reserve reduces the volume of deposits that the bank can create by lending to the public.

The process is reversed when the Federal Reserve authorities want to increase total bank reserves. The Federal Reserve buys government securities on the market, giving their checks, which ultimately are deposited by commercial banks in their reserve accounts. If the Federal Reserve buys $1 million of government bonds, it creates a like amount of reserves for commercial banks. Such an increase in reserves is capable of supporting an expansion of commercial bank credit.

The Federal Reserve Banks can also influence the amount of reserves by controlling the conditions under which they

[2] Here the "open market" means simply the place where United States government securities are regularly bought and sold. The Open Market Committee, consisting of members of the Board of Governors and representatives of the Federal Reserve Banks, has primary control over open market operations.

will lend to commercial banks. Commercial banks can build up their reserves at the Federal Reserve Banks by "rediscounting" loans—that is, by borrowing from the Reserve Bank and putting up some of the assets they own as collateral. An obvious means of control, then, is to change the *rediscount* rate, the rate of interest that the Federal Reserve Bank charges the commercial bank that wants to borrow money. The Federal Reserve authorities can raise the rediscount rate and thereby discourage member banks from borrowing to build up their reserve accounts, or can reduce the rediscount rate and make it cheaper for banks to borrow reserves.

Because moderate changes in interest rates are seldom enough to encourage or discourage banks from borrowing reserves to make loans, such changes in the rediscount rate are only a mild means of control compared with open market operations. However, when they are combined with open market sales, the rates can be raised to put "the squeeze" on banks that need to borrow reserves. Changing the rediscount rate also has psychological value. When bankers encounter higher rediscount rates, they know that the monetary authorities believe that credit is expanding too rapidly. They will expect other, more stringent steps if the expansion continues.

Within a range set by Congress, the Federal Reserve System also has the power to set the legal ratio of bank reserves to deposits. This power gives the Federal Reserve System a third quantitative control: a control over the amount of credit that a given amount of reserves will support. When the Federal Reserve authorities want to restrain credit creation, they can raise requirements, say, from 18 to 20 per cent of commercial bank deposits. This action changes "excess" reserves into "required" reserves, leaving less room for credit expansion. In order to contract credit, the authorities could even increase reserve requirements beyond the point where banks have excess reserves, forcing them to reduce their deposits to bring their reserve ratios back into line.

As frequent changes in reserve requirements would complicate the banking business, the Reserve System does not readily use this method of contracting credit. It is used mainly when the Federal Reserve wishes to have a prompt, over-all effect on reserves. For the most part, it raises reserve requirements to "sop up" excess reserves and make the banks more sensitive to other controls. When credit expansion is desired, it is, of course, a quick way to give the commercial banks excess reserves.

Other tools of monetary policy are the so-called "selective controls." Selective controls, unlike quantitative controls, apply to particular types of commercial bank credit and do not affect bank reserves. Selective controls affect some sort of down-payment arrangement. They say, in effect, that if people are going to buy something on credit, they cannot borrow more than a certain portion of the total price—they must pay cash for the rest. Regulation "U," for example, gives the Federal Reserve System the power to say how much down payment, or margin, must be made in order to borrow money to buy stocks. Regulations "W" and "X" were two other selective controls that were authorized by Congress for short inflationary periods. Although the authority to use them has now expired, they could be re-enacted if needed again. Regulation "W" stated the down payment necessary in order to borrow money for consumers' durables, and Regulation "X" did the same thing for houses. Regulations "W" and "X" also gave the Federal Reserve authorities the right to determine how much time will be granted the borrower to pay off his loan. These selective controls were not designed to attack monetary problems by changing the reserves of banks. Their purpose was to make credit more or less available for the customers of the banks and thus influence aggregate demand.

A further tool of the Federal Reserve System has been called "moral suasion." This is the power of the Federal Reserve System to make suggestions to bankers. Such suggestions are given some force by the fact that the Reserve authorities can restrict certain privileges that members ordinarily enjoy at Reserve Banks, and in extreme cases, the Federal Reserve can expel member banks from the system. The Voluntary Credit Restraint Program used during the Korean War illustrates one application of moral suasion. In this program, the Federal Reserve System joined the American Bankers Association and other lending institutions to restrain credit that might add to inflation. The Reserve Banks and lending institutions got together and decided what types of loans would be most appropriate in the tight wartime situation, and everyone agreed to do his part to see that only the proper financing was done. The same thing might have been accomplished by the more convincing means of taking away the reserves of the banks, but the voluntary approach was tried so that banks might curtail some unnecessary borrowing at the same time as they were permitting war industries to borrow.

The Federal Reserve System can use its controls one at a time or in unison. From time to time, it has combined open market operations and rediscount rate changes in a "scissors operation." When it felt banks were expanding credit too rapidly, it sold government securities in the open market and raised its rediscount rate at the same time. Thus as bank reserves were drawn down by the open market operations, the banks were forced to borrow new reserves at the higher discount rate. Then when bank expansion was desired, the Federal Reserve reversed these two tools; it bought government securities and lowered the rediscount rate.

In general, economists believe that monetary policy can be helpful in correcting a moderate business decline. We should recognize, however, that monetary policy cannot invent new products or new technology. Alone, it cannot make people borrow and spend when they are in the midst of a major depression and strongly pessimistic about the prospects for the future. It may, however, create a monetary environment that encourages business. This in turn may help hasten recovery.

How can monetary policy encourage recovery? First, excess reserves encourage commercial banks to search for good loans. Excess reserves are "idle funds"; they do not earn interest and to make a profit with them new loans must be made. Excess reserves can therefore heighten competition among banks for the better (less risky) loans and thus can lead to a decline in interest rates on these loans.

Lower interest rates are a stimulus to greater production and employment. Business executives may have an opportunity to produce and sell a product, but they may not be willing to do so because the profit is too small to compensate for the time and the risk. However, if they can reduce their interest payments to the bank, they may go ahead. For example, a $50,000 inventory loan would cost $4,000 per year if the interest rate is 8 per cent, but if the interest rate falls to 6 per cent, their interest costs will be cut by one fourth—the saving of $1,000 may be enough to persuade them to borrow and expand production.

During a recession many individuals and businesses want to convert assets into cash—in time of uncertainty they would rather be holding money than holding goods or the IOU's of other people. Monetary policy, by increasing the supply of money, can help to satisfy this desire for liquidity. By increasing banks' excess reserves and the cash holdings of the public, an expansive monetary policy will hasten the day when people would rather use (spend or lend) money than merely hold it.

Economists are also generally agreed that the Federal Reserve has the power to pull the economy up short during inflation. It can do this by using its existing tools to contract the supply of bank reserves. To combat inflation, the Federal Reserve authorities need to contract the supply of reserves enough to raise interest rates; they need to contract credit until spending shrinks enough to stabilize the price level.

The traditional view of monetary policy is clear. The Fed should "lean against the wind," as the saying goes. When aggregate demand is too low, a policy of increasing the money supply and reducing interest rates will make it easier for banks to lend and cheaper for consumers and businesses to borrow. Thus aggregate demand will be stimulated. When aggregate demand is too high, a policy of holding down the money supply and raising interest rates will make it harder for banks to lend and more expensive for consumers and businesses to borrow. Thus aggregate demand will be damped and inflation combated.

In recent years, however, this traditional view has been challenged by the so-called "monetarist" school of thought, and today economists are strongly divided on the subject of monetary policy. Much more research needs to be done before we can be certain of the impact of monetary policy on the economy.

The traditional view says that the inherent instabilities in our economy can be lessened by wisely timed changes in the money supply and interest rates. The monetarists believe that the instability of our economy is largely a *result* of the Federal Reserve's constantly pushing the money supply up and down in order to influence interest rates. In their view, for example, it was the great increase in the money supply engineered by the Fed in 1971–72 that led the nation into the high inflation of 1973–75. The monetarists recommend that the Fed abandon its efforts to "lean against the wind" in the short run and concentrate on allowing the money supply to increase gradually in the long run at approximately the same rate as the potential growth rate of the economy. In short, financing long-run growth should replace promoting short-run stability as the main objective of Federal Reserve policy.

Critics of the traditional view stress the following obstacles to successful management of the economy by the Federal Reserve. The first two are equally applicable to fiscal policy.

First, there is the problem of "timing." How does the Fed know when the time has come to "shift gears"—to move from monetary ease to monetary tightness or vice versa? It can rely in part on the so-called "leading indicators" published by the U. S. Department of Commerce, which are supposed to give an indication of where the economy is going. It can examine the various surveys that are regularly made of consumer expectations and of planned business investment. It can rely on its own econometric forecasts. But experience has shown that it can be wrong as well as right in its estimates of future economic trends.

Many feel that in 1959, for example, recovery from the 1957–58 recession was aborted and the recession of 1960–61 precipitated in part by the fact that the Fed, incorrectly fearing inflation, applied the monetary brakes too soon and too fast. On the other hand, most feel that, in 1965, the Fed correctly anticipated that inflation, rather than recession, was the principal threat and correctly moved toward a tighter monetary policy.

A second problem is that there is a considerable time lag between the implementation of a particular monetary policy and some of its results. Some monetarists believe indeed that the full effect of an increase in the money supply on the price level may not be realized for more than a year. But, by the time the effects are felt, economic conditions may have changed and the policy may be inappropriate.

Thirdly, the monetarists deny that increasing the money supply will necessarily bring down interest rates except in the very short run. If lenders believe that increasing the money supply will lead to inflation, they will want to charge higher interest rates to compensate themselves for the loss of purchasing power of their dollars when they are repaid later. Higher interest rates discourage borrowing in the housing industry and sow the seeds of the recession that will follow the inflation.

Fourthly, there is the complicated question of what money supply the Federal Reserve is trying to manage: M-1, M-2, or M-3. The Fed currently has targets for all three. But the velocity of circulation of money—the rate at which it changes hands—must also be considered. In 1977 the Fed responded to critics who said that it was not increasing the money supply fast enough to bring down unemployment by saying that the velocity of circulation had been high and thus less money was needed to stimulate noninflationary growth than if velocity had been lower.

Finally, as we will see later in this chapter, monetary policy has to be integrated with fiscal policy. The nation cannot achieve its economic goals if the two principal policies of economic management are not co-ordinated. Yet sometimes this is difficult.

The Federal Reserve has made a bow in the monetarist direction in recent years by making quarterly reports of a desirable growth-rate range for the money supply. This range represents the Fed's projection of the needed growth of the money supply, based on its evaluation of economic conditions. For example, for the period from the fourth quarter of 1976 to the fourth quarter of 1977 the targeted growth rate for M-1 was 4½–6½ per cent. The actual growth rate turned out to be 7.8 per cent, which tells us something about the Fed's ability to manage the money supply precisely in the short run.

Most economists would probably agree that monetary policy is a useful tool in spite of its limitations. In the first place, it is indirect and impersonal. In using monetary management, the government does not directly intrude into individual transactions, incentives, or goals. Instead it changes the economic environment in which people transact their business. It creates an environment in which credit is easier or more difficult to obtain.

In the second place, monetary policy is useful because it can be changed quickly. It is controlled mainly by an administrative group, the Board of Governors of the Federal Reserve System, and is therefore more flexible than controls that are imposed by congressional action. Because a business decline can spread quickly, the rapidity with which controls can be applied is extremely important. Mild action early in a business decline may be far more effective than drastic action later on.

Supporters of traditional monetary policy can point to those occasions when it has made a useful contribution to economic stability. Critics can point to those occasions when it seems to have failed. Most would probably agree that it is not an instrument of "fine tuning"—that is, it cannot compensate for every small change in the price level and the level of income and employment. Nevertheless, it remains one of the principal instruments at our disposal for influencing aggregate demand and thus the performance of our economy.

FISCAL POLICY

Fiscal policy is the use of federal taxing and spending powers to change the level of income and employment. When the federal government was small and accounted for only a minor part of the total spending of the economy, its ability to influence national income was limited. In 1978, however, it purchased almost 8 per cent of our gross national product, collected over $400 billion in taxes, and spent over $450 billion. Consequently it can exercise a substantial influence over national income and employment. It may use its fiscal powers to moderate inflation or recession, as explained below, or to influence the rate of economic growth.

The focal point of fiscal policy is the federal budget, which records the total tax revenues and expenditures of the federal government. Taxes take money away from people and business and reduce demand. Government spending puts money into circulation and increases demand. When the federal government collects more in taxes than it spends (a budget surplus), the net effect is to reduce aggregate demand. When it spends more than it receives in taxes (a budget deficit), the net effect is to increase aggregate demand. To some extent also, the government may stimulate or depress national income by merely altering its rate of taxing and spending, even though the budget is kept in balance.

There are two ways in which fiscal policy can be implemented: through the *automatic stabilizers* and by means of *discretionary* fiscal policy. Of the automatic, or "built in," stabilizers, the federal corporation income tax and the individual income tax are most important. Without any change in their rates, they draw in more revenue as national income rises and less when income falls. On the spending side, unemployment compensation, farm subsidies, and payments on the many types of loan insurance sponsored by the federal government have automatic stabilizing effects. Such payments decrease in times of prosperity and increase during depression without any changes in the laws. Taken together, the various programs tend to increase government spending and reduce government receipts as national income falls; they tend to do the opposite as national income rises. This helps us understand one reason for the large budget deficits in the fiscal years 1975–79. Increases in government spending were one important factor, of course, but in addition, tax receipts were held down by the fact that the economy was operating at substantially less than full employment.

Because automatic stabilizers operate without any new action by Congress, they quietly go to work as soon as income and employment change. Even if a depression becomes so severe that the government must pass additional laws to stabilize national income, the task is easier because the automatic stabilizers are operating while the lawmakers debate the issues.

Discretionary fiscal action occurs when Congress changes tax and spending laws. Thus during a period of declining income, the government can stimulate the economy not only by spending money on existing programs (automatic), but also by spending more money on new programs (discretionary). It can further stimulate the economy by reducing tax rates or eliminating some taxes altogether. But changing taxes and spending presents many difficulties. The process is not a simple one of pumping money in and out of the economy at will. First of all, policy makers must decide which of three alternative approaches to use.

The government can hold spending constant and change taxes, hold taxes constant and change spending, or change both taxes and spending. Considerable difference of opinion has existed among economists over which of these methods is most desirable. However, most will agree that in any serious decline, the program probably should involve changes in both taxing *and* spending.

A reduction in taxes tends to increase private spending and an increase in taxes tends to contract private spending. The relationship between consumption and "after tax income" is fairly stable, although not constant. Hence an increase in taxes that cuts disposable income will have a depressing effect on the volume of consumer spending. A decrease in taxes will tend to stimulate consumption. The effect of tax changes on investment is less certain. Lower taxes, like lower interest rates, encourage investment, but they will not bring it forth unless other conditions and expectations of businessmen are favorable. Yet, there are usually some investment opportunities that will attract investment if the returns are less heavily taxed. In other words, tax reduction tends to stimulate investment, although the degree to which it does is less predictable than it is for consumption.

Of course, all taxes do not affect income in the same way. Sales or excise taxes fall heavily on those who spend their money for consumption. Progressive income taxes or estate taxes fall more heavily on the higher-income groups that tend to save or invest a larger portion of their income. Corporation income taxes, special tax exemptions and deductions, social security taxes, and excess profits taxes affect spending in different ways. The following discussion deals with taxes as a whole, but it is important to remember that the final effect of tax changes depends partly on which taxes are changed.

Tax reduction leaves more income in the hands of spenders, therefore it stimulates demand. But it has limitations in a stabilization program. In the first place, it is sometimes difficult to determine when a recession has started or, for that matter, when it is over. In the fall of 1974, for example, the Ford administration's "WIN" program ("Whip Inflation Now") had to be hurriedly scrapped when it was realized that the nation was going into a deep recession. Similarly, in 1977, the Carter administration had to abandon its plan for a fifty-dollar tax rebate to each citizen when it appeared that the economy was recovering nicely on its own and did not need as large a tax-reduction stimulus as had been planned.

Second, needed tax action may be delayed by public resistance or for political reasons. Most economists felt a tax increase was needed in 1966, for example, when inflation started to heat up. But tax increases are never popular with voters. Hence the tax increase did not come until 1968, by which time the inflationary forces had intensified.

Third, changing taxes is generally a slow process. The nation could have benefited from a substantial tax cut in 1961 in view of the state of the economy at that time. It did not actually get it until 1964. In 1962, President Kennedy asked Congress to approve a measure that would shorten the time lag for tax reduction to combat recession. His request for standby authority to make temporary across-the-board tax cuts reflected growing awareness among economists of the need for more timely action if this anti-recession tool is to be fully effective. However, the political obstacles to this idea are numerous, and a search has continued for acceptable alternatives.

The effectiveness of tax reduction may be reduced, critics point out, because a portion of the cut will not be spent. A dollar of tax reduction may result in, say, only ninety cents of new spending, whereas an extra dollar of Government spending will add a dollar to aggregate demand. Supporters of tax changes argue, however, that tax reduction has a great effect on investment incentives and therefore may foster additional spending for investment. The potency of tax reduction and of government spending as a fiscal tool was amply demonstrated by the events of the 1960s. Under the Revenue Act of 1964, Congress cut taxes by approximately $11 billion in an effort to reduce the gap between what the country could produce and what it was producing. An increase in private spending followed that led to a reduction in unemployment from 5.7 per cent in 1963 to 4.5 per cent in mid-1965. (By 1969 unemployment had fallen further, to 3.5 per cent as a result of the increasing expenditures for the Vietnam War and the "Great Society" social programs of the Johnson administration.)

If the government decides to alter expenditures rather than taxes to correct cycles in income and employment, it must decide how to spend varying amounts of money. During the 1930s, the government spent large sums for relief payments and so-called make-work projects. But now these are not generally considered a basic part of a fiscal program for economic recovery. Relief spending is an emergency program designed to alleviate the acute suffering of the unemployed and to get the economy moving again. Although it reduced distress, the fabled "leaf-raking" of the 1930s was a slow way to restore public confidence in the ability of the nation to regain prosperity. The necessity for this "stop-gap" spending has been reduced by our present-day programs of unemployment compensation, farm subsidies, and aids to other groups.

Some economists have pointed out that, if the government wants to stimulate the economy, it could even build pyramids as a way of putting funds into the hands of those who will spend. They say this to point out that the income effect of government spending should not be confused with the usefulness of the things it buys. Even building a pyramid can be useful if it is the only way to get money into circulation and put people back to work on farms and in factories.

Most people prefer that the government produce useful facilities and services by its spending. A great deal can be done to build schools, roads, dams, and other public works while combating depression. But it is well to recognize that when the nation is threatened with a recession it is important to stimulate private *spending*. At such a time, the most important goal may be to put funds into the hands of those who will revive spending and thereby generate normal production and employment. This can usually be done more effectively through expanded unemployment compensation benefits and the provision of public service jobs than through programs of public works.

Two major objections have been raised to the use of spending for public works to smooth out cycles. One objection is that it is difficult to turn some spending programs off when the depression emergency has come to an end. A dam started in the midst of a depression cannot be left unfinished. Thus some of the projects begun in the 1930s continued over into the 1940s, when the depression was far behind us. A comprehensive program of public works for the future should therefore have some short-range and some long-range projects. Of course, the difficulty is that the government may be unable to determine whether a short-range or a long-range program is needed. The second objection is that public spending might discourage some private spending. If, in building a dam, the government gives the impression that it wants to build all hydroelectric facilities, it may retard private spending for power development. Public spending for recovery should clearly raise the level of total spending, and not merely take the place of private investment.

An even more difficult problem arises when it becomes necessary to cut government spending to combat inflation. Most people are in favor of cutting government spending "in general." But government spending cannot be cut "in general"; only specific budget items can be cut. But powerful organized groups usually try to block cuts in programs that benefit them, whether they be veterans, defense industries, farmers, the poor, the elderly, or the big-city mayors.

In the late 1970s, strong public pressures developed to cut federal government spending and reduce the size of the budget deficit, which many conceived to be a significant source of inflation. It proved difficult, however, for the government to change its spending plans. Moreover, according to the Office of Management and Budget, almost three quarters of federal expenditures are "relatively uncontrollable items."[3] This means that they are either outlays that contractually must be met, such as interest on the national debt, or they are for programs, such as social security, medicare, and welfare, in which anyone who qualifies under the law is entitled to a payment.

We may conclude therefore that, in general, government spending is a relatively inflexible instrument for influencing the performance of the economy in the short run.

In certain circumstances the level of income and employment might be changed by programs of taxing and spending, even though the total budget is balanced. For instance, if the government starts with a balanced budget and then increases *both* its taxes and spending by, say, $10 billion, gross national product will rise by some amount up to $10 billion, since total private spending may not decline, or may decline by less than $10 billion. On the other hand, if the government cuts both its taxes and spending by an equal amount, total spending may fall. The actual effect, of course, would depend on what happens to private spending for consumption and investment.

Fiscal policies designed to stabilize the economy require surpluses in some years and deficits in others. Some economists suggest that our goal should be to balance the budget over the whole business cycle, so that the surpluses accumulated during the boom would offset the deficits of the depression. A more sophisticated version of this is that we should establish a level of taxes and spending that would result in the budget being balanced if the nation is at full employment. Then, if a recession set in, the automatic stabilizers would push the budget into deficit. If inflation threatened, they would produce a surplus. But even a cyclically balanced budget may be difficult to obtain. New emergencies and new requirements for public services arise at all stages of the cycle. Moreover, there is no assurance that the cycles that fiscal policy seeks to correct will be neatly balanced cycles of

[3] Executive Office of the President, Office of Management and Budget, *Fiscal Year 1978 Budget Revisions*, February 1977, pp. 90–91.

inflation and deflation. In fact, the federal budget has been in surplus only twice (in 1960 and 1969) in the past twenty years and only eight times since 1930.

Continued deficits can result from continued high defense requirements, a chronic tendency for the nation to slide into recession, or from a growing demand for public services and benefits by a politically organized electorate. Whatever the causes, budget deficits have continued and the national debt has continued to rise.

Much has been learned about the national debt in recent years. The economic effects of debt are now better understood, and it is not regarded with the horror that it once was. Today, a major depression is seldom thought to be preferable to an increase in the public debt. Moreover, public debt management is now considered a tool for stabilizing income and employment.

Public debt management is a meeting ground for fiscal and monetary policy. The debt, which results from an excess of expenditures over taxes, requiring the government to borrow, exerts strong influences on our credit system. When the government redeems securities held by the public, it puts money in the hands of the public. When the government borrows from people, it takes money away from them—as it does when it taxes. But government borrowing is not as strong a restraint as taxation, because people acquire bonds, which are income-bearing assets. An increase in the debt, then, is only a partial substitute for an increase in taxes when the desire is to restrain public spending.

An increase in the national debt is a restraint on total spending as long as the government only takes money away from people. But if the government spends what it borrows, the effect is to increase expenditures. In other words, to determine the impact of a debt increase, it is necessary to know what the government does with the borrowed funds.

Moreover, it is necessary to know where the government borrowed the money. Government borrowing from the commercial banks is likely to be more expansionist than borrowing from people. This is because the Federal Reserve Banks often supply the banks with excess reserves so they can loan to the government without curtailing their loans to private borrowers. When this is done, the government can spend without drawing funds from private spending. If the government spends $50 billion, which it obtains through an "easy money" policy of the Federal Reserve, the result will certainly be a greater stimulus to the economy than if the whole $50 billion had been raised through taxation. In general, it will also be a greater stimulus than if the $50 billion had been borrowed from individuals and businesses.

In recent years, concern has been expressed that the federal government might "crowd out" private borrowers as it seeks to finance its deficits by tapping the savings of the nation and borrowing from the banks. If public and private demands together put pressure on a limited supply of loanable funds, interest rates will be pushed up. This will pose a dilemma for the Federal Reserve. If it increases the money supply to accommodate both the government and private borrowers, we run the risk of more inflation. If the Federal Reserve refuses to increase the money supply, the government's competition with private borrowers in the capital markets could push up interest rates, which in turn could slow down economic growth or even bring on a recession.

A final concern that has been expressed in recent years is that the federal government's fiscal activities might be encouraging consumption at the expense of saving and investment. If government tax collections are primarily from those who work and from business, i.e., the savers and investors in our economy, but government spending is primarily on such programs as "income security," i.e., benefiting those who consume rather than save, then the fear is that the long-run growth of the nation might eventually slow down because of a shortage of investment.

HOW EFFECTIVE ARE MONETARY AND FISCAL POLICIES?

Experiences to date do not tell us conclusively how effective these policies have been. The evidence that must be used to prove or disprove the validity of monetary and fiscal theories is inadequate. Because the effects of monetary and fiscal actions cannot be isolated from the influence of other factors in the economy, it is always difficult to determine what a given policy may have accomplished.

What can be said of these devices is that they appear to work reasonably well *when they are properly applied*. The effective use of monetary and fiscal policies depends on: (1) a prompt recognition of the need for corrective action, (2) an understanding of the consequences of various monetary and fiscal measures, and (3) the political feasibility of carrying them out.

We do not have precise indicators of danger points in the changing flow of income. Therefore, it is frequently difficult for public officials to decide when to use new policies. Without clear-cut indicators of future conditions, the use of public policy must depend on discretion based on an accumulation of incomplete evidence. Perhaps it is only when enough indicators of economic activity show signs of a harmful trend that policy changes can be justified; and by then some damage may have been done. However, our statistical data have improved, and our forecasting skills have become better over the years. Thus even though the timing of fiscal action cannot always be unerringly correct, it has been improved. Nevertheless, the choice of proper timing and the choice of proper methods will always be major problems in economic stabilization.

Our limited knowledge of the full effects of particular policies also hampers our ability to control business fluctuations. Economists are not completely certain about the effects of different programs on private spending. As a result, the selection and timing of various monetary and fiscal policies cannot be precisely scheduled. For instance, we do not know how much stabilizing action is derived from the automatic fiscal devices, and therefore we cannot be sure how far inflation or deflation should be permitted to continue before new tax and spending programs are inaugurated. Similarly, if the monetary authorities are not entirely clear on how well monetary policy can bring about an upturn in business, they may be reluctant to use their powers to curtail and possibly reverse a developing boom. However, these limitations are most apparent in the selection and timing of action for moderate fluctuations; in the event of major economic fluctuations, precise measures of the effects of particular policies are less necessary.

Political considerations also limit the application of monetary and fiscal controls. American economic policy is generally responsive to popular demands. If, for various reasons, the people are opposed to a change in public policy, the government tends to reflect their wishes. The government generally cannot raise taxes during inflation if the public strongly disapproves of higher taxes. Similarly, if the public fears larger government spending or a growing public debt more than it fears a decline in income and employment, then various anti-depression policies cannot be used. These limitations on the use of monetary and fiscal controls diminish, however, as the need for stabilization grows. When conditions get bad enough, the public usually demands action.

In spite of these limitations, monetary and fiscal policy combined can contribute greatly to stability of income and employment. Monetary policy, we have seen, may operate quickly in a mild dip, but it may be handicapped in a period of deep depression. Expanding bank reserves and declining interest rates can stimulate private spending under most conditions; but in a depression crisis, the response may be slow. Fiscal policy, however, can probably provide a more definite boost in either a major or a minor decline. By facilitating new spending, fiscal policy can act directly as the prime mover. Then if the upturn occurs, monetary policy can make a major contribution to the revival.

In curtailing inflationary pressures, the two can also be co-ordinated. Generally, monetary policy can act quickly and unobtrusively without creating fears of a subsequent collapse. The automatic fiscal devices also move quietly into action as spending rises. Finally, if a major inflation appears to be under way, Congress may undertake major changes in taxing and spending programs to shrink private spending.

A major characteristic of monetary and fiscal programs is that they tend to be over-all or aggregate controls. Thus they tend to influence the total volume of spending instead of a particular situation that may be causing trouble.

But, as we saw in Chapter 6, other factors influence the performance of the economy besides changes in aggregate demand. If we want a more stable economy, we have to find some answers to these other problems. One of the most difficult is "cost-push" inflation, which occurs when wages and other costs rise faster than is warranted by productivity increases. What is needed here is an effective "incomes policy." However, various efforts to develop this in recent years have not been very successful.

In 1962, the government issued the so-called "wage-price guideposts" which linked wage and price increases to productivity. President Johnson in particular tried a combination of "jawboning," publicity, and the mobilization of public opinion to keep unions and business in line. This approach had limited success. In 1978, President Carter launched a new effort along these lines.

Between 1971 and 1974, formal wage and price controls were imposed. Wage increases had to be approved by the Pay Board in Washington and price increases by the Price Commission. But the eventual conclusion reached by most observers was that wage-price controls during this period created more problems than they solved, and they were abandoned. The problem of cost-push inflation remains unsolved.

Finally, there are steps that can be taken to improve the precision of our stabilization program. These include farm price supports to maintain the incomes of farmers in times of recession, altering the interest rates on government-insured mortgage loans to influence home construction, varying margin requirements to influence the stock market, and relaxing import restrictions on certain products—for example, beef in 1978—to increase supply and hold down prices. Such specific policies enable the government to influence the economy in a *selective* manner by correcting specific danger spots, rather than waiting until the *over-all* weapons of monetary and fiscal policy can be brought into play.

In the fourth quarter of 1973, the American economy started downhill into a severe recession. The bottom of the recession was reached in the first quarter of 1975, after which a recovery began that continued into 1978. We will use this recession as our case study for this chapter, using the same approach as before.

The real GNP of the United States (measured in constant

The Problem and the Issues

1972 dollars to eliminate the effect of price changes) fell from an annual rate of $1,243 billion in the fourth quarter of 1973 to an annual rate of $1,172 billion in the first quarter of 1975, a drop of 5.7 per cent in what turned out to be the deepest recession since the great depression of the thirties. Unemployment, which averaged 4.9 per cent of the civilian labor force in 1973, reached a peak of over 9.0 per cent in the spring of 1975. By the first quarter of 1976, the real GNP had recovered to $1,255 billion, or more than its pre-reces-

GROSS NATIONAL PRODUCT OF UNITED STATES, 1973–76
—BY QUARTER

(ANNUAL RATES, IN BILLIONS OF CONSTANT 1972 DOLLARS)

	1973 4th Quarter	1975 1st Quarter	1976 1st Quarter
Gross National Product	1,242.6	1,171.6	1,255.5
Personal Consumption Expenditures	765.9	757.2	806.3
Durable goods	118.1	106.4	124.8
Nondurable goods	308.0	302.0	314.6
Services	339.7	348.8	366.9
Gross Private Domestic Investment	211.8	134.6	168.5
Business fixed investment	132.4	117.7	115.5
Residential construction	54.0	36.3	45.5
Change in inventories	25.4	−19.4	7.5
Net Exports of Goods and Services	12.9	20.5	16.5
Government Purchases of Goods and Services	252.0	259.3	264.3
Federal	94.3	95.9	96.2
State and local	157.7	163.4	168.1

(Figures will not necessarily add to totals because of rounding.)

Source: U. S. Department of Commerce, *Survey of Current Business*, July 1977.

sion level. At the same time that the nation was experiencing this sharp recession and recovery, it was also experiencing one of its worst periods of inflation. The price level (as measured by the GNP deflator) rose 5.6 per cent in 1973, 9.7 per cent in 1974, 8.7 per cent in 1975, and 5.2 per cent in 1976.

As can be seen in the table on page 195, the principal factor in the substantial decline of the real GNP between the fourth quarter of 1973 and the first quarter of 1975 was a 36 per cent drop in gross private domestic investment. Business moved from accumulating inventories at an annual rate of $25.4 billion to *reducing* them at an annual rate of $19.4 billion. In addition, there were sharp drops in business fixed investment and residential construction. Personal consumption expenditures declined very slightly and spending on services actually increased. Federal government spending hardly changed, though state and local spending increased slightly. Only an increase in net exports prevented the decline from being even greater than it was.

The problem we must consider, then, is: What kinds of public policies, particularly monetary and fiscal policies, are appropriate during a period of severe recession accompanied by inflation?

The Objectives

The most important objectives of public policy were, of course, to halt the decline in the economy and put it back on the path of economic growth, bring down unemployment, and at the same time bring down the rate of inflation. The achievement of these objectives promised to be extraordinarily difficult, partly because the policy makers had had little experience in dealing with recession and inflation simultaneously. Conventional economic theory told us that, if stimulative monetary and fiscal policies were used to fight the recession, we ran the risk of making the inflation worse, whereas if restrictive monetary and fiscal policies were used to fight inflation, we ran the risk of making the recession worse.

To complicate matters, some important elements in the picture were largely outside our control. Oil prices, which contributed to both recession and inflation, were determined by a foreign cartel. Our exports were affected by economic conditions in other countries, many of which were also experiencing a recession. Finally, other domestic objectives were being pushed by various groups. Environmentalists, for example, were pushing for tighter environmental protection laws. Most of these resulted in higher prices for such products as steel, chemicals, and automobiles. Conservative groups wanted to reduce the economic role of government and balance the budget. More liberal groups sought expanded government programs for the aged, the poor, and the sick, and for aid to our cities. Monetarists pushed for a reduction in the growth of the money supply to fight inflation. Keynesians pushed for increases in government spending to fight recession. Somehow, despite all these economic and political crosscurrents, policies had to be formulated and put into effect.

The Alternatives

What alternative policies are available when the nation is confronted by such a complex situation?

One is in the area of monetary policy. Depending on its evaluation of what constitutes the greater problem—recession or inflation—the Federal Reserve could follow a policy of monetary ease designed to encourage consumer and business spending or it could tighten up on the money supply and get interest rates up in order to combat inflation. Or it could postpone a decision for a month or two, hoping that it would become clearer which was the major threat.

A second is in the area of fiscal policy. If the federal government decided recession was the greater of the two problems, it could cut taxes on consumers and business to try to stimulate private spending. In particular, it could, by means of tax cuts, try to "replace" the $18 billion of purchasing power siphoned out of the American economy by the oil price increase. The federal government could also step up its spending by increasing the duration and coverage of unemployment compensation benefits, providing more public service jobs, and embarking on a public works program. Or it could take the view that tax cuts and increases in spending were risky when inflation was so high, and do nothing, relying on the automatic stabilizers to make their contribution to stability.

The third area for decision-making is incomes policy. The dramatic rise in prices apparently was not caused by excess demand, since aggregate demand was dropping. Cost-push pressures seemed to be the problem. Insofar as wages and prices were concerned, the administration could ask Congress for authority to impose wage and price controls. Or it could rely on presidential "jawboning," backed up by publicity and the mobilization of public opinion, to persuade unions and business to keep wages and prices within certain limits.

Also in the area of cost-push pressures, the government could relax environmental and safety requirements so that these added less to the costs of production and thus to price increases. It could try to remove teenagers from the jurisdiction of the minimum-wage law in the hope that this would both reduce teenage unemployment and hold down business costs. It could relax restrictions on imports of foreign goods in the hope that more competition for domestic producers would hold prices down. On the other hand, it could put people back to work in domestic industries hit by import competition by raising the tariff or restricting imports in other ways.

Appraising the Alternatives

Which of these various policies would actually be followed would depend on three things. The first would be the government's evaluation of the relative importance of the nation's goals. Were recession and unemployment so pressing a problem that stimulating the economy was more important than following anti-inflationary policies that might make the recession worse? Or should fighting inflation take top priority, in which case the price paid for success might be a further slowing down of the economy? What is the relative importance in the total picture of preserving the environment, of promoting social justice, of promoting freer trade in the world, and so on? In short, decisions needed to reflect a ranking of our national priorities.

The second consideration would be the determination of trade-off points among conflicting policies. Obviously, the government would not go all out to fight inflation regardless of the possible cost in terms of slowing down the economy. Nor would it ignore the possible inflationary consequences if it decided that economic stimulus should have top priority. Somewhere there would be a trade-off point where the costs of a particular policy would not be excessively high in terms of the benefits received. Similarly, the government, in its efforts to hold down business costs, presumably would not abandon its environmental and safety goals completely by scrapping all its regulations in those areas. Again, some satisfactory trade-off point would have to be determined.

Third, the government would have to evaluate the relative effectiveness of various policies in given situations. As it did this, it would have to keep in mind that we do not always know all we would like to know about the results of particular policies, nor are economists always in agreement on what is the right thing to do. For example, if the government decided to give top priority to stimulating the economy, should it put primary emphasis on cutting taxes or on increasing government spending—or should it do both? If it is to be tax cuts, should they mainly benefit middle- and low-income households to stimulate consumer spending or should they mainly benefit business to stimulate investment? If the emphasis is to be on increases in spending, should it be on projects designed to inject purchasing power into the economy as quickly as possible, such as more generous unemployment compensation payments, or should it be on long-range public works projects, which add to the nation's stock of fixed capital? The field of monetary policy also poses a problem. Should the Federal Reserve continue its traditional policy of "leaning against the wind" or should it edge closer to the monetarist position of emphasizing the long-run growth rate of the money supply?

We have only identified a few of the highlights of public policy problems that faced the nation during the years 1973–75. The annual *Economic Report of the President* spells out all that happened in much detail. But we have said enough to show, first, that it is extraordinarily difficult to predict the course of a complicated economy like that of the United States and, second, that hard choices have to be made among alternatives. The hardest choice of all involves the trade-off between anti-inflationary and anti-recession policies. Looking back over the period, it is apparent that the Ford administration clearly regarded inflation as the main threat to the nation and was willing to go slow on anti-recession policies for fear of making inflation worse. This clearly was the view of the Board of Governors of the Federal Reserve System, too. By the first quarter of 1976, as the table on p. 195 shows, recovery from the recession finally pushed the GNP above the pre-recession level.

This chapter has stressed these basic ideas:

1. The federal government has assumed the responsibility for smoothing out the fluctuations in income, employment, and the average price level that occur in our economy. Its goal is not to prevent change; rather it is to provide a steady and stable growth of spending and jobs.

2. Monetary policy is one of the tools that may be used for this purpose. By working primarily through the commercial banking system, the Federal Reserve System influences the level of interest rates and the volume of lending in the whole economy. Fiscal policy is another tool that can be used by the federal government. By changing the flow of taxes and spending, the government can influence the flow of private spending.

3. These policies are not precise instruments of control that can eliminate every ripple in the level of income or employment. To some extent, all of them require decisions based on the judgment of government officials, and these decisions must sometimes be based on inadequate information. There are a number of administrative problems in using monetary and fiscal controls—nevertheless, they offer a means of positive action to curb harmful fluctuations in economic activity.

Suggested Reading

Paul A. Samuelson, *Economics*, Chap. 17, pp. 314–34, and Chap. 19, pp. 355–78. George L. Bach, *Economics: An Introduction to Analysis and Policy*, Chap. 16, pp. 191–201, and Chap. 18. Current problems of monetary and fiscal policy are discussed in the annual *Economic Report of the President*. A useful summary and analysis of the federal budget for the layman is published each year by the Office of Management and Budget, entitled *The United States Budget in Brief*.

Chapter 8

ECONOMIC GROWTH, NATURAL RESOURCES, AND THE ENVIRONMENT

The United States has had a growing economy through most of its history. Population has increased, new industries and new urban centers have been developed, and living conditions have improved. In good times this expansion has been taken for granted, as something natural and desirable. But, as studies of other nations indicate, the experience of the United States is not typical of the entire world. Nor has U.S. growth been uninterrupted. Looking back, we are reminded that four decades ago the outlook for economic progress was dark indeed. The economic catchword of the 1930s was "stagnation." Then there seemed to be no new frontiers to develop, unemployment was high, investment in new equipment was negligible, and the nation seemed more preoccupied with just "hanging on" than with visions of great economic advances.

After World War II the economy surged ahead again. Despite unevenness in economic performance from year to year, both unemployment and inflation were generally kept in check for two decades. Economic growth was widely accepted as a key target of economic policy—the means of achieving full employment and a rising level of living.

Since the late 1960s, new challenges to economic growth have arisen, however. The cost of the Vietnam War and the legacy of inflation reduced the rate of improvement in real income. Unemployment rates hovered at levels far above those of the earlier postwar period. The oil embargo of 1973 rekindled concerns not only about energy costs but also about the adequacy of the nation's resources for the long run. Also during the 1970s, increases in the levels of air and water pollution and local conflicts over land use raised questions about the desirability of all-out economic growth. By the late 1970s, economic growth was no longer either taken for granted or universally accepted as the nation's all-important goal. The quest for growth was tempered. Americans wanted growth without inflation, growth without endangering the long-run availability of resources, and growth without endangering the environment. There was even some talk about the desirability and feasibility of a "no-growth" policy.

Let us now take a "long-run" view of our economy. We shall explore the sources of economic growth and try to identify the reasons for our expanding production. With this background, we shall then try to show how concerns about natural resources and the environment are likely to influence our future growth.

MEASURING ECONOMIC GROWTH

One common measure of economic growth is the increase in real gross national product. This is the figure that economists usually have in mind when discussing the question: How fast is the economy growing and how fast should it grow? Real gross national product measures the economy's total output in dollars of the same purchasing power—thus it is not affected by changes in the price level.

Historically, the average annual rate of growth, by this yardstick, has been about 3 per cent for the period since 1910, and closer to 4 per cent for three decades after World War II. From year to year during this century, the rate has varied with changes in the business cycle. It also has varied geographically: while it has lagged in recent years in New England it has surged in the Southwest, for example. And, in addition, it has varied by sector. The chart on page 204 shows the trend of the nation's growth rate and how widely it has varied over the past half century.

An important measure of our advancing economic well-being is the growth of real income per capita. As we noted in Chapter 2, this measurement is useful because it is not distorted by changes in the price level or by changes in population. Before using it, however, we must recognize that it is not a complete measure of economic welfare. It does not tell us about the many improvements in the quality of living conditions, such as the improved health of the American people, better recreational and cultural facilities, or the greater leisure for enjoying them. Nor does it reflect increases in congestion and pollution, which lower the quality of life.

Per-capita income is an *average* figure computed by divid-

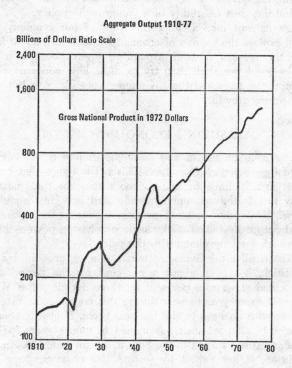

Aggregate Output 1910-77

Billions of Dollars Ratio Scale

Gross National Product in 1972 Dollars

Source: *Economic Report of the President,* January 1979, p. 184. This data is shown on a "ratio scale" chart that shows at a glance what the growth *rate* is at any time. On this type chart an increase of $5 billion in a year when GNP is $50 billion would show the same slope as an increase of $50 billion when GNP is $500 billion. The slope would be the same because each of these is a 10 per cent increase.

ing the total income of the nation by the total population. Thus it obscures regional differences, occupational differences, and individual differences in income. Furthermore, it does not show what products were produced, and how these products were distributed.

The level of living is particularly difficult to measure in a growing economy in which new products are constantly being introduced and old ones improved. Today our level of living includes television, jet airplane transportation, synthetic fibers, and life-saving antibiotic drugs—none of which could have been purchased by a millionaire in 1900. If we recognize these limitations, we can use changes in real income per capita as an approximate measure of the trend in our level of economic life.

The chart on page 206 shows the growth in the income per capita after payment of taxes. The figures cover the period 1929–78, during which the government's share of income has grown sharply, yet per-capita disposable income has also increased. In other words, in spite of a rising population, inflation, and higher taxes, our personal level of living is almost twice as high as it was twenty-six years ago, in 1952.

In the years since 1929, per-capita income grew, but not steadily. During the depression of the 1930s, the flow of income declined sharply; then it slowly began to rise. By 1939, total income was higher than it had been in 1929, but as population also increased during the same period, per-capita income remained below its 1929 level until the 1940s. The marked rise in per-capita income by 1944 reflected the intense wartime production effort. By putting more people to work and by lengthening the work week, the American economy increased its flow of income by over 40 per cent in five years. Much of this income could not be used for civilian consumption, however, so although per-capita income rose, there was not a corresponding increase in consumption. Instead there was a sharp increase in personal saving. After the Second World War, production declined during reconversion, and then resumed a gradual growth. Over the next twenty-six years, wars in Korea and in Vietnam and recessions altered the pace of economic growth but did not change the long-run upward trend.

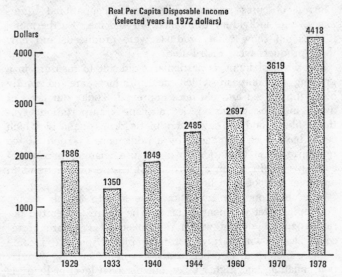

Real Per Capita Disposable Income
(selected years in 1972 dollars)

Source: *Economic Report of the President,* 1979, p. 209. Disposable income excludes not only taxes but also the income retained by corporations.

The advance in the level of living has been even greater than these income figures show because the work week has been shortened. That is, people have preferred to take some of the benefits of economic growth in the form of leisure rather than in income. The table on page 207 illustrates the decline of the average hours worked over a century. In the 1970s, the scheduled length of the work week continued to average about forty hours and the number of hours actually worked by employees in the manufacturing sector continued to be about forty hours. But in the financial sector and other service businesses the work week was shorter. Thus taking into account the shorter work week in these areas and the schedules of part-time workers, the number of hours actually worked averaged thirty-six hours.

AVERAGE WEEKLY HOURS WORKED, 1850–1950

Year	Nonagriculture	Agriculture	All Private Employment
1850	66	72	70
1900	56	67	60
1920	45	60	50
1930	43	55	46
1940	41	55	44
1950	39	47	40

Source: J. Frederic Dewhurst and Associates, *America's Needs and Resources* (1955), p. 1073. Figures are rounded.

THE INGREDIENTS OF GROWTH

The United States was blessed with an abundant supply of natural resources. It has fertile fields, vast forests, and extensive grazing land. It has been able to draw on rich deposits of coal, petroleum, iron, copper, and other minerals. Rivers crisscross the land, offering potentials for navigation, irrigation, and generation of power. The climate is predominantly temperate yet varied enough to nurture the growth of many kinds of useful plants.

But natural resources offer only the raw material for economic activity. Many nations with abundant resources have failed to develop them effectively. The potential usefulness of resources must be recognized; techniques for developing them must be devised. In short, putting resources to work productively requires manpower, knowledge, research, managerial talents, tools, and capital.

In the United States, the labor to develop resources has been provided by a continually increasing population. Immigration brought millions of people to our shores. The birth rate has varied considerably, but always has been large enough to bring about an annual net increase in population. The life span has lengthened. As a result, the population of the United States increased by about one third every decade from 1700 to 1860. Since the turn of the century, the population growth rate has varied considerably, as the following table indicates:

Year	Total Population (in millions)	Percentage Increase Over Preceding Decade
1900	76	26
1910	92	21
1920	106	15
1930	123	16
1940	132	7
1950	152	15
1960	181	19
1970	205	13
1980 (est.)	222	8

These population figures tell us that the nation had a growing supply of labor and more mouths to feed, but they do not explain the growth in the level of living. If population were the only requirement for a high level of living, people in areas such as China, India, or Puerto Rico would be living much better than they do.

An expanding population can help raise the level of living only if the additional people deliver a *more than proportionate* increase in production. Thus if population increases 10 per cent, the total production of the society must increase by 10 per cent merely to stay even. If the level of living is to grow, production must increase faster than population. Over the years, that is what has happened. The American economy has provided an increasing population with a rising level of living. In brief, the keys to economic growth are the conditions that enable the nation to produce goods and services faster than it produces new consumers.

The task of producing goods and services for a growing population is complicated by the fact that not everyone works. Some people are not part of the "civilian labor force" —that is, they either are unable to work or choose not to work—and some who are in the labor force (that is, they want to work) are unemployed. The civilian labor force, for example, does not include children, the incapacitated, the aged, or members of the armed forces. It includes a smaller number of women than of men, though the proportion of women at work has increased substantially in recent years. Thus the ratio of men to women, the age composition of the population, the drain on manpower for military service, and the traditions of the people—such as their attitude toward child labor and retirement—help determine the size of the labor force. In the United States, the civilian labor force in mid-1979 was about 46 per cent of the population—102 million out of a population of about 220 million. For per-capita income to grow, the employed workers must produce more—not only for themselves but for the rest of the population as well—or a substantial number of the unemployed must find jobs.

The major reason for our increased level of living has been the growth in the productivity of the work force.

The most common measure of productivity is *output per employee hour.* A growth in output per employee hour indicates the growing efficiency with which labor is used. Let us take an example to see how we measure the growth of productivity. Suppose an appliance factory with 10 employees working an 8-hour shift can produce 160 washing machines a day with the help of a mechanized production line. In this case, the input of labor is 80 employee-hours (10 employees × 8 hours), and the output is 2 washing machines per hour (160 machines ÷ 80 employee-hours). Now let us assume that the engineering department of the factory develops and installs a faster punch press to form the tubs and installs new handling equipment that enables the workers to keep up with the new punch press with ease. The 10 employees are now able to produce 200 washing machines each day. Output is now 2.5 washing machines per hour (200 washing machines ÷ 80 employee-hours). Productivity in this factory has increased 25 per cent.

Although it is easy enough to figure productivity in a factory that produces just washing machines, it becomes quite difficult to figure productivity in a plant that produces half a dozen different products with the same workers and machines. It becomes even more complicated when statisticians attempt to measure output per employee-hour for manufacturing as a whole or for the economy as a whole. In general, economists believe that productivity figures are more reliable for measuring long-term trends than for measuring short-term improvements from year to year.

Estimates by the U. S. Bureau of Labor Statistics, covering the period since 1909, indicate that output per employee-hour has increased at a long-run rate of about 2.5 per cent a year for the entire private economy. This increase in output per employee-hour is an average over a long period, and it masks considerable variation from year to year. The evidence suggests, for instance, that in the period immediately following World War II, output per employee-hour fell. The decline in productivity was probably due to the fact that old equipment was used to supply the unusually high demand for consumer goods and because rather poorly trained wartime workers were being shifted into new jobs. From 1947 to 1966 (when Vietnam-War expenditures began to affect the economy) productivity rose at an annual rate of 3.2 per cent. From 1967 to 1976 the annual rate of increase was 1.6 per cent. This slowdown reflected the impact of two recessions and the continuing shift of employment to the services sector.

Not only is there a good deal of variation in growth of productivity from one year to the next, depending on economic conditions, but there is also a great deal of difference among industries. Agriculture, for instance, probably lagged behind nonagricultural industries before the Second World War, but after the war the use of mechanization, improved fertilizers, and insecticides caused output per hour of farm work to increase faster than the long-run trend. On the other hand, manufacturing productivity has apparently grown faster than the trend for the economy as a whole.

As the chart on page 211 shows, in some industries, productivity soars. In others, little or no progress is made. Even within a single industry, changes in the productivity of labor vary from firm to firm. However, for our inquiry the important fact is that the measurements show a long-run growth in productivity for the economy as a whole.

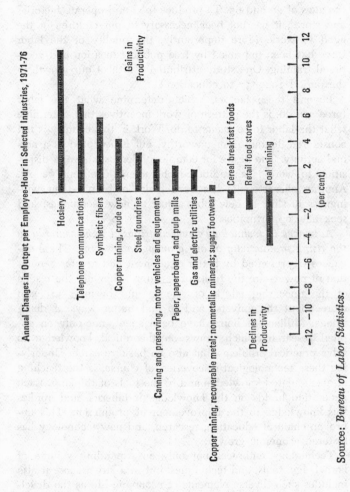

Annual Changes in Output per Employee-Hour in Selected Industries, 1971-76

Gains in Productivity

Hosiery
Telephone communications
Synthetic fibers
Copper mining, crude ore
Steel foundries
Canning and preserving, motor vehicles and equipment
Paper, paperboard, and pulp mills
Gas and electric utilities
Copper mining, recoverable metal; nonmetallic minerals; sugar; footwear

Cereal breakfast foods
Retail food stores
Coal mining

Declines in Productivity

(per cent)

Source: Bureau of Labor Statistics.

SOURCES OF INCREASED PRODUCTIVITY

Output per employee-hour depends in part on the quality of the labor force—its age distribution and its level of skills and education. The quality of the American labor force is partly a reflection of the fact that most workers are between the ages of 20 and 65. To produce food and operate factories and stores, it has not been necessary to put children or the aged to work. More importantly, the quality of the labor force has been improved by free public education and vocational training. One study attributed a fifth of our growth in the period 1929–57 to education.[1]

Beyond these factors, which determine what the labor force *can* do, is the pattern of work incentives that determine what the labor force *wants* to do. Work in this country is not considered degrading or unworthy, but is accepted as a normal activity. The desire for complete idleness is rare; a disposition to work is a traditional characteristic of our people. Another characteristic has been their "mobility"—their willingness to shift to new jobs, adjust to new techniques, and seek new opportunities.

Advances in technology have contributed immeasurably to the rising productivity of our growing labor force. These advances—represented by better equipment and greater generation of power—are the fruits of research. They are the results of the unceasing efforts of science and business to learn more about the universe and to find better ways of doing things. Millions of hours have been spent, not only on applied research, which draws on theoretical knowledge to solve practical problems, but also on basic research. Underlying these technological discoveries, of course, is the teaching of accumulated knowledge and of the tools of thinking. Each generation builds on the knowledge it inherits, and applies this knowledge to the improvement of production. This unbroken chain of education, research, and new technology has fostered economic growth.

Technology embraces not only an expanding volume of knowledge, tools, and techniques, but in a larger sense it also includes such diverse elements of economic life as the development of industrial engineering and labor unions and fiscal policy and accounting techniques—these "new ways" have all

---

[1] Edward F. Denison, *The Sources of Economic Growth in the United States and the Alternatives Before Us.* (Committee for Economic Development, 1962.)

had an impact on the performance of the economy. However, we shall concentrate here on the role of technology as it is generally understood. In this sense, technology refers to the industrial "arts"—the processes by which we produce our material goods and services.

Technological innovation has its main impact on productivity through the building of new plants and machinery. As we pointed out in Chapter 1, "capital" is the economist's name for productive equipment, and "capital formation" is the name for the process of creating capital.

Since the end of World War II, about 8 per cent of the GNP has been invested annually in new plant and equipment. Part of this investment has been used to replace worn-out or outmoded facilities and part of it has been used to increase the nation's total stock of plant and equipment. From 1950 to 1975, for example, the nation's manufacturing plant and equipment nearly doubled (rising from $103 billion to $202 billion in 1972 dollars). Not only has the total stock grown, but the amount for each manufacturing worker has also increased. In a sense we have become more "capitalistic"—that is, we are using more and better capital per worker now than we used to.

We cannot catalogue all the types of capital equipment of the nation, but it will be useful to stress the importance of energy-producing facilities. All of the productive equipment of the nation requires the use of energy. The leading sources of energy used in the United States are petroleum, coal, natural gas, hydroelectric power, and nuclear energy. (See accompanying chart.) In 1850, about two thirds of the work in this country was done by animal power and human power; little more than 10 per cent was done by fuel combustion. By 1950, the situation was reversed; about 90 per cent of the work was done by fuel combustion and less than 2 per cent by human beings and animals.[2] In 1950, the United States used more electric power in one week than it produced during the entire year 1902, and since that time the consumption of electricity has continued to rise. The development of

[2] Dewhurst and Associates, *America's Needs and Resources,* p. 1116.

The Shift from Coal to Petroleum and Natural Gas

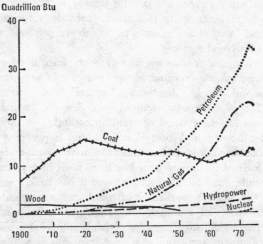

Source: *Resources*, No. 51. (Washington: Resources for the Future, Winter 1976)

How Petroleum Is Used

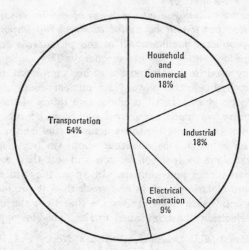

Source: *Resources*, No. 51.

the techniques and equipment to provide a growing volume of safe and efficient sources of power is a basic requirement for an expanding industrial economy.

Capital formation is not automatic, something that just happens as a result of increased technological knowledge. Someone has to decide to make tools and build factories, and the resources to build them must be available. This brings us to the process by which the economy creates capital.

The nation must save to create capital. We saw in Chapter 2 that a society can add to its stock of capital only if it produces more than it consumes—that is, if it saves. Capital formation is possible only when some money income is not used for consumption and, instead, is made available for investment. This also means that some portion of our total production must be capital goods—things that are to be used to expand our capacity to produce in the future instead of things to be used for current consumption.

The rate of saving from income varies from one society to another, and within any society, it varies from one time to another. In some societies, most of the national income must be used to keep the people fed and sheltered; consumption is high and saving low. In more productive societies, the rate of saving can be higher. Wealthy nations therefore may set aside a larger part of their national income for investment—which further increases their wealth.

In the United States, custom and tradition, the distribution of personal income, and economic institutions have encouraged saving and investment. An attitude of self-reliance required individuals to save in preparation for possible future "rainy days." The determination of parents to give their children a better start in life also required saving.

Another reason for our willingness to save is that the rewards for saving and investing have been large. For years our nation had vast unused land resources, but the labor to develop them was scarce. Labor was therefore the relatively expensive resource. Tools and equipment that could increase the work that men could do cut this expense by reducing the labor time necessary to produce a given product. The desire to save was therefore partly a result of the desire to get tools to reduce labor costs and expand production.

The unequal distribution of income also played a role in the high rate of saving in this country. More can be saved by the wealthy few than would be saved if income were distributed more equally. Of course, some other countries that have unequal distributions of income have not saved as large a share of their income. In any society, the wealthy people at the top of the income scale have the capacity to save—in our society they have been rewarded for doing so.

Another important reason for the relatively high share of income being used for investment is that businesses save and invest a major portion of their earnings instead of distributing their entire net profit to their owners. Because corporation executives may want to expand the operations of their companies, they may save and invest, even though some of the owners prefer to receive dividends they could use for consumption. When this happens, the corporation functions as a device to induce the group to save more than they would as individuals.

Banks and other financial institutions have also played a part in the saving-investing process. As we noted in Chapter 5, financial institutions make saving more attractive to many people by providing them with liquid assets to hold (insurance policies, savings accounts, or demand deposits). For the many people who do not want to own a direct share of the capital of industry, these assets provide another method to accumulate savings. If many of these people could not hold an insurance policy or a savings account, they would save less, or perhaps they would save nothing at all.

But the role of financial institutions in the saving-investing process goes deeper than this. Banks can help encourage the economy to invest. If business wants to borrow and spend a greater proportion of national income than savers want to lend, the banks can meet the needs of business by creating demand deposits. And if businessmen can borrow enough, they can bid the necessary labor and resources away from consumers. The banks can, in other words, generate a process that is similar to saving—they can cause some of our production to be used for investment instead of consumption. Thus even the "wildcat" banks of the 1800s aided the growth of capital for a while. Although many such banks were on shaky financial footing and later failed, the money they created and loaned to businessmen kept men at work building factories and railroads rather than working on consumption goods.

The main catalyst that turns savings into investment is the business firm working under the profit motive. Although consumers and governments are users of savings, it is the business firm that makes most of the decisions to put the savings of the economy to work. The willingness to try new methods and to expand production is an intangible but crucial aspect of our process of capital formation. Investment decisions must be made in the face of many uncertainties—uncertainties about government tax and monetary policies, uncertainties about the supply of labor, uncertainties about consumer tastes, and uncertainties about what competitors will do. Because of these uncertainties, the decision to invest involves risk. That is the reason risk taking is said to be a key factor in economic growth.

The American economy has generally encouraged risk taking. As a result, there has usually been a strong demand by business for funds to invest. Although from time to time we hear the view that the government or unions have destroyed risk taking in our economy, the fact that business continues to invest record sums of money indicates that investment motives remain strong and active. In a sense, the economy forces investment by business. Because the economy is largely competitive, each firm must expand and improve with the others in its industry. Like a squirrel in a wheel, the business firm in a competitive economy must run to keep up; as long as someone tries to get ahead, there is pressure on everyone to invest and improve.

An expanding market for the increased production of the economy is a requirement of economic growth. If the economy is to continue to pour out goods, there must be a demand for the products—people must be willing to buy them at a price that covers the cost of their production. Over the broad sweep of our history, there has been an adequate demand. The same population that supplied the growing labor force has also expanded the market for the things produced; and the same characteristics that have caused Americans to look for new ways to improve their ability to produce have also caused them to seek higher and higher levels of economic welfare.

But the demand for goods has not always paralleled the growth in productive capacity. From time to time, the demand for goods and services has fallen behind or moved ahead of our ability to produce. These fluctuations in purchases have made our rate of growth unstable and occasionally have brought severe hardship to some people. They were discussed in Chapter 6, on "Inflation and Recession," so we will not go into further detail here.

Before examining the outlook for future economic growth and the role of resources and environmental policy, let us summarize briefly the basic factors that have been responsible for the past growth of the American economy:

First, the United States has had abundant resources—land, raw materials, and sources of power.

Second, its growing population has supplied the labor force needed to put these resources to use.

Third, the labor force has been mobile and willing to work for greater output.

Fourth, the productivity of labor has increased because workers have become better trained and educated and because research and technological improvements have fostered the development of new productive equipment.

Fifth, the capacity and willingness of the American people to save and invest has provided the funds for new machines and factories.

Sixth, the prospect of profits and the pressures of competition have induced business firms to take risks in order to improve and expand their output. In addition, the federal, state, and local governments have taken steps to encourage the development of new lands and new industries.

Seventh, a gradual, although unsteady, growth in the demand for goods and services has encouraged producers and workers to continue to expand production.

RESOURCES, ENERGY, AND ECONOMIC GROWTH

Questions of resources, energy, and environmental policy have assumed greater importance in the analysis of economic growth. The possibility that the supply of natural resources will be exhausted by the needs of a growing population has been a recurrent specter for nearly two centuries, but in the advanced nations of the world the pessimists have so far been proved wrong. Improvements in technology have more than kept pace with population growth and the demand for better living standards. Fertilizers, insecticides, and better agricultural machinery and methods have vastly increased the output per acre of land. New technology has made it possible to utilize lower-grade ores. Continuing investment in research—estimated at $47 billion, or about 4.5 per cent of total gross national product in 1978—is intended to maintain this rate of technological improvement. Optimists say that technology can do as well in the future.

Pessimists argue, however, that technological gains merely postpone the inevitable. Timber, metals, petroleum, and other resources are being consumed at an accelerating rate. Less developed countries, aspiring to levels of living comparable to those achieved by the advanced nations, have contributed substantially to the rising demand. The widely discussed report of the Club of Rome in 1972 envisioned the world running out of resources in a hundred years if trends continued. Although the specifics of the study, *Limits to Growth,* were sharply attacked and indeed later restated in less of a doomsday tone, the study served to rally those who were particularly concerned about the rate at which resources are being used up. Certainly there was no gainsaying the fact that greater efficiency in the use of resources would be a continuing requirement for growing economies.

Natural-resource scarcities can be viewed largely as economic events. As a resource becomes more scarce, the prospect of greater shortages will tend to drive up the price of that resource. The price will rise more rapidly than the prices of other goods or services. The rise in the relative price will encourage conservation and greater efficiency in the use of the more expensive resource, as well as a search for less expensive substitutes. Moreover, the higher price will make possible the use of lower-grade ores. So goes the line of reasoning expounded by many economists.

Underlying this argument is the view that the availability of a resource is greatly affected by its price. Thus if one asks how much iron ore or copper ore can be obtained from the earth, the economist would answer: It depends on the price of copper or steel. At the present price and with the present state of technology, we can probably extract a certain tonnage and make enough money to cover the cost. If the price were twice as high (in comparison with other commodities), the supply would be much greater, because mining companies could afford to mine ore in inaccessible places or to make use of rock with smaller concentrations of metal. For example, at one time it was not economical to mine copper ore that did not contain at least 2 or 3 per cent copper. Now companies can make a profit mining lower-grade ores, containing less than 1 per cent copper.

The implication of this view is that long before we are in danger of actually running out of any resource, we will be warned of the impending crisis by a period of rising prices for that resource. Such sharply rising prices will force changes in production and consumption that will enable society to adjust to the change. The nature of this adjustment process can be illustrated by the example of energy, which is one of the key ingredients of economic growth.

The world's energy problem has been long in the making. Between 1950 and 1975, the world consumption of energy more than tripled, and consumption per capita more than doubled. During the same period, the industrial nations gradually shifted from coal to oil as the principal source of energy. Use of natural gas also increased. Although the United States continued to be the greatest user of energy, the annual rate of growth in energy use was more rapid in Japan and Western Europe.

Up to mid-century, the United States was the world's largest producer of petroleum, as well as its greatest user, but during the 1950s its rate of output began to level off. As a result, the United States began to turn to foreign sources of supply. By the end of the decade there was sufficient concern about the military security implications of the nation's growing dependence on foreign oil to cause the government to invoke a system of quotas to limit oil imports. The quotas continued for fifteen years.

Thus though it was the oil embargo of 1973–74 that alerted the general public to the dangers of dependence on foreign oil and the inevitability of higher energy prices in the future, the energy crisis had been foreshadowed by the trends mentioned earlier: the world's increasing consumption of energy and the shift from coal to oil. Within the United States two other developments exacerbated the problem. One was the decline in exploration and drilling in the United States, a decline that occurred when oil companies found it more profitable to exploit huge oil reserves of the Middle East. At the same time, the development of alternative sources of power lagged. Technical problems, rising costs, and rising public opposition combined to slow down the adoption of nuclear power, for example, and efforts to put greater reliance on coal also ran into difficulty.

One of the great uncertainties is how much oil and gas will be available during the next half century. Some studies have suggested that real prices will begin to rise sharply in the late 1980s, in recognition of a growing scarcity, and that by about 2025 oil will no longer be readily available at reasonable prices. But no one really knows how much oil is in the ground. It was doubted that there was any likelihood of discovering any great new fields comparable to those in the Middle East until Mexico's announcement of huge new reserves in late 1978. Other major oil strikes cannot be ruled out. Nor does anyone know how much success the petroleum industry will have in increasing the proportion of oil that is recovered from a well. Under present methods, only about one third has been recovered. So-called secondary and tertiary methods of recovery can increase this percentage, but by how much and at what cost is not clear.

One line of analysis suggests that more than half of all the oil that will ever be recovered has probably already been recovered, and that while conservation, new fields, and greater recovery will all help stretch out available supplies, the era of oil as the dominant source of energy is coming to an end and that oil may no longer be even a major source of energy midway in the next century.

Others argue that we have only begun to explore technologies for extracting oil from shale or for developing synthetic fuels from coal. They believe that oil and gas and synthetic fuels could continue to be major sources of energy for another century or more—although at higher prices than today.

In 1979 the sensitivity of the world's supply of oil to political disturbances was demonstrated for the second time in the decade by the Iranian revolution. To long-term uncertainties was added a reminder of the vulnerability of the United States to short-term disruptions of supply. In the five years since the embargo of 1973–74, the United States had increased its imports of oil and had made little progress in assuring itself of a secure source of supply.

By the late 1970s, the role of nuclear power had also become very uncertain in the United States, though its use was increasing in other countries. The seventy-odd plants operating in the United States were providing about 13 per cent of the nation's electric power (and about 1 to 2 per cent of its total energy needs). At one time more than one hundred additional plants were planned or under construction, but they were making little headway because of public concern over several issues:

> *Nuclear waste*—Could highly radioactive spent fuel be disposed of safely and permanently so that it would not pose a hazard to human health? *Radiation*—Could plants be operated safely, as proponents insisted, or were leaks of radiation and other kinds of accidents reasonable probabilities? *Weapons proliferation*—Would the operation of nuclear plants for peaceful energy purposes (particularly the so-called breeder reactor) make it easier for additional nations to develop nuclear weapons, and could nuclear plants be adequately protected against sabotage? These issues of safety and war have led to deep divisions of opinion throughout the nation.

The safety issue captured the headlines and dominated policy discussions following the accident in 1979 at the Three Mile Island nuclear plant in Pennsylvania. Although a catastrophe was averted, confidence in the performance of nuclear reactors was shaken. Questions were raised about the design and equipment of the Three Mile Island plant, about the training and qualifications of plant management and personnel, about the location of nuclear plants near urban centers, and about the reliability of earlier estimates that had led to reassuring statements about the probability of serious nuclear accidents. The government's response, initially at least, was to explore ways to make nuclear power more reliable, rather than to abandon it, a position supported by adherents, and attacked anew by critics, of nuclear power.

On one grim fact, however, there seems to be almost unanimous agreement: All forms of energy now available pose risk. Oil spills and blowouts of drilling rigs in the ocean, as well as explosions of storage tanks, are reminders that oil is not without its dangers, though they may be smaller on balance than those associated with nuclear power and coal. Coal, which was proposed as the most economical supplement to oil, poses health threats to miners, damage to land through strip-mining or subsidence of underground mines, heavy air pollution, and a possible change in the earth's climate that might come about because the increased discharge of carbon dioxide into the atmosphere could create a so-called greenhouse effect, trapping heat and raising the earth's temperature.

For the long run, the most appealing source of energy is probably solar energy. It is clean, safe, and abundant. It needs only to be made economical as well. The fourfold increase in crude oil prices in 1973–74 helped reduce the gap between the costs of solar and conventional sources of energy. In some areas solar is being used for space heating in homes, offices, and industry, often with a supplementary back-up system. Research on the development of a reliable and inexpensive solar battery was greatly increased. There were experiments in the United States and other countries in the use of mirrors to concentrate the sun's rays on huge boilers that could be used in the generation of electricity. At selected sites, windmills of new experimental design were tried out, and research was conducted on the rapid growth of vegetation (biomass) that could be converted into useful forms of energy.

The crucial question is whether solar energy can be developed rapidly enough so that it will be available before oil and gas become excessively costly, before the increased use of coal imposes heavy environmental costs, and before the world has to increase greatly the use of nuclear plants.

A central issue in the energy timetable is the role of conservation. Can an effective conservation program buy the time necessary to ease the transition to other forms of energy? Supporters of a vigorous conservation effort point to the lower use of energy in other countries, such as Sweden. In the transportation sector, they can point convincingly to automobile fuel economy. U.S. consumption of gasoline could be greatly reduced by the shift to smaller, more fuel-efficient cars. More emphasis on proper insulation and energy-efficient machinery would also help cut consumption. But beyond such measures, the case is not so clear-cut. The much greater size of the United States requires Americans to make greater expenditures for transportation than are made by Europeans, for example. More important is the mix of products. The United States uses more energy not because it is wasteful in the way it produces goods but because it produces proportionately more goods of a type that require a great deal of energy. Clearly, there are opportunities for energy conservation, but we should not allow comparisons with foreign countries to lead us to exaggerated expectations about what can be achieved in the United States.

ENVIRONMENTAL POLICY AND GROWTH

One of the consequences of the increasing public preoccupation with environmental protection has been the enactment of regulations to reduce pollution. During the 1970s, there was a spate of environmental legislation that went far beyond the provisions of the federal air and water pollution control acts of two and three decades earlier.

The purpose of these regulations has been to require firms

and government agencies to reduce the pollution of the nation's air, water, land, and places of work. The focus has been on reaching certain targets such as the reduction of sulphur oxides in the air to a certain level of concentration or to reduce the discharge of nitrogen oxides from automobiles to a prescribed level, or to achieve "fishable and swimmable water" by a certain date. The efforts required to meet these goals are costly. Economists have sought to answer the question, among others: What will be the impact on the nation's rate of economic growth of such expenditures?

Environmental control measures do not necessarily lead to a decline in productivity. Improvements in worker health, for example, are reflected in less absenteeism, more sustained effort, and fewer accidents and errors—all of which enhance productivity. Such benefits may in the long run exceed the cost of improvements in the workplace. Similarly, experiments in ways to reduce pollution may lead to new ways of production that may increase efficiency in the long run. Nevertheless, the immediate and observable impact of environmental legislation has been to increase greatly the costs of production in many industries.

Trying to measure the costs and benefits of expenditures for environmental improvement is exceedingly difficult, especially the benefits. Sharp differences can be expected for some time in the estimates of the economic impact of environmental expenditures. But the problem of measurement can be clarified by drawing on a recent study that tries to measure the impact of pollution abatement costs.[3] It begins by distinguishing between two kinds of pollution control costs: those that directly reduce national output as measured in the National Income and Product Accounts, and those that do not.

The study is concerned with the former, that is, the amount of money that is spent on pollution abatement, rather than on investment that would increase output. For example,

[3] See Edward F. Denison, "Effects of Selected Changes in the Institutional and Human Environment upon Output per Unit of Input," *Survey of Current Business*, January 1978. The article also includes estimates of the impact of costs to protect safety and health of workers and costs of dishonesty and crime.

if a firm spending $100,000 a year to produce 100 widgets has to spend $2,000 in pollution control activity to meet a government standard, the cost of widgets will increase by 2 per cent. That is, as a result of regulation it costs $102,000 to produce 100 widgets. Presumably, without the regulation, the firm could have produced two more widgets for the same expenditure or could have invested in new equipment that would lead to a reduction in the unit cost of widgets. This is the kind of loss that results if pollution control activities merely increase the cost of production.

Over the period beginning in 1967, when pollution abatement expenditures were virtually nonexistent, and ending in 1975, the study estimated that money spent on pollution abatement rose to $10 billion a year. The amount increased each year by a steadily growing percentage.

In a trillion-dollar economy, this amount might not seem great at first glance, but when expressed as a proportion of the annual rate of economic growth, the impact is seen to be quite significant. By 1975, according to this study, the annual rate of increase in the productivity of the nation's businesses (excluding construction) had been cut by about one fourth of a percentage point (.25 per cent), equivalent to about 10 per cent of the long-term growth rate of 2.5 per cent.

This estimate of the reduction in the rate of economic growth is not intended by itself to answer the broader questions about the desirability of pollution control expenditures or the wisdom of the government's environmental policies. It deals only with the costs that show up in the national income accounts; whereas the benefits often do not show up in the way output is currently measured. Benefits such as a reduction in illnesses, an increase in longevity, or the restoration of degraded recreation areas simply are not reflected in the accounts. Whether, on balance, benefits are greater or less than costs, it can be said that they are now being obtained at the cost of a reduction in the rate of economic growth as it has been conventionally measured.

From an environmentalist position, however, the historical record can be interpreted with a different emphasis. If environmental expenditures are required today to deal with the degradation resulting from industrial growth, it can also be said that past economic growth was overstated, since the external costs borne by people and the environment were not taken into account.

OTHER INFLUENCES ON GROWTH

Economic instability could cause serious dislocations. Inflation, recessions, and depressions are constant hazards to expansion. Mild fluctuations are to be expected in a changing economy, but severe fluctuations resulting in widespread unemployment and stagnation of investment are not consistent with continued economic development. Moreover, economic growth itself may be disruptive. As old obstacles are overcome, new ones emerge. For example, technological changes, while increasing productivity, may displace workers and even render industries obsolete.

Less tangible and more difficult to assess is the possibility of a long-run change in the attitude and temper of the American people. Perhaps the incentive for greater economic advancement will diminish. We may succeed so well in satisfying wants that the philosophy of the nation will change. Will the wage earner who works so hard today to give his family a new house, a new car, and the latest appliances continue to strive as hard after he has provided these goods? This is a great imponderable.

Conceivably, the preoccupation with economic growth may diminish and preoccupation with spiritual, intellectual, and leisure pursuits increase. Certainly, there will be an opportunity to choose among alternative uses of time and effort. It is not within the scope of this book to examine the psychological, religious, and philosophical issues underlying our assumptions that economic growth is desirable, but the fact that we have made this assumption needs to be reiterated. If a major change in popular attitudes does take place gradually, it will require a major change in the assumptions on which much economic reasoning rests. Such a change, though widely debated, is not yet in prospect for the foreseeable future.

Because the objective of economic expansion is a part of

our national culture, we frequently hear proposals advocated or criticized because of their possible effects on our long-run economic growth. The arguments often stress one or two aspects of the problem, although, as we have seen, economic growth has many ingredients. One of the functions of economic reasoning is to help us keep track of a many-sided problem of this sort so that we can understand the problem as a whole. The problem discussed below will illustrate some of the complexities in tracing the effect of governmental policy on economic expansion.

The Problem and the Issues

The effectiveness of the environmental legislation of the 1970s has been widely debated. Some critics have charged that the regulations have not been adequately enforced and that polluters have been able to use delaying tactics to avoid compliance. Other critics have charged, however, that environmental improvements have cost too much and that the trade-offs between costs and benefits have not been properly evaluated; they say that environmental goals need to be balanced against other economic and social goals.

In part, the criticisms expressed by both those for and those against existing environmental regulations reflect the same dissatisfaction with federal regulatory policies in general. This dissatisfaction is based on (1) the establishment of detailed rules about what can and cannot be done and (2) the enforcement of these rules by government agencies or by the courts.

Setting standards of legal and illegal behavior is always difficult, and it has seemed especially difficult for environmental regulators. What kinds of standards should be set: limits on the amount of pollutant that can be discharged into the water or into the air by each business firm or household (effluent standards) or limits on the amount of pollution in a specified body of water or in the air of a particular region (ambient standards)? What pollutants should be controlled? How much pollution and what kinds can be tolerated without destroying the recreational attractiveness of park and wilderness areas and the livability of our cities?

Enforcement of standards is at least equally difficult. How

can government monitor the discharges from industrial plants, households, publicly operated institutions, and sewage plants? What procedures should be established to impose penalties and to provide for examination of controversial decisions so that the public will be protected against arbitrary government action?

Historical evidence suggests that such difficulties have led to periodic attacks on regulatory agencies for arbitrariness, inefficiency, and delay. Moreover, regulations tend to get progressively more complicated. As loopholes are discovered, government agencies respond by enacting new rulings in an attempt to close them. And so the regulatory process becomes increasingly cumbersome.

Environmental legislation has also included the use of subsidies to encourage construction of municipal sewage-disposal facilities. Critics often charge that these subsidy programs are excessively costly and not very effective.

As a result of these various criticisms, there have been calls for a new approach. What is missing in the traditional regulatory process, according to its detractors, is an incentive that will encourage firms to stop polluting and to use their resources more efficiently. Various kinds of incentives have been suggested to improve environmental regulation. Most of them would utilize a system of charges to be levied against those polluting the air, water, or land.

The Objectives

The broad objectives of federal environmental protection policy are to reduce the discharge of harmful and unsightly wastes into the environment, to preserve selected recreational and wilderness areas, and to repair some of the damage that has already been done to the ecological system. At the same time, policy makers need to keep in mind other goals, such as the goal of sufficient economic growth to provide jobs for an increasing population, the goal of reasonable price stability, and the efficient use of natural resources.

The Alternatives

One alternative is simply to concentrate legislative and administrative efforts on improving the kinds of regulatory programs that have been developed during the past decade. Despite their shortcomings, they have had some beneficial effects. Perhaps not all of the progress made in recent years in improving air and water quality and in reducing health hazards can be attributed to the government's environmental programs, but nevertheless substantial gains have been made. Better educational efforts and public exposure of violators can help encourage greater voluntary compliance. Study of past experience can lead to the establishment of better and more realistic standards and improved techniques of monitoring behavior by potential polluters. Increased expenditures for enforcement might pay off. Many of the difficulties of the current regulatory program would probably crop up in any alternative approach. No panacea should be expected, and rather than looking for one, we should simply try to improve our present system step by step.

An alternative to the present system has been called a "charges" system. An "effluent charge," for example, would require a firm to pay a specified amount for each unit of a pollutant that it discharged. The charge should be sufficient to encourage the polluter to seek ways to reduce the volume of discharge. For example, rather than pay the charge, some firms might find it advantageous to treat wastes before discharging them. Others might find it desirable to change their production processes to reduce the volume of waste produced. The purpose of the legislation would be to encourage each firm to reduce the amount of pollution that it generates. The less pollution a plant discharges, the lower the charge it has to pay. Depending on the special conditions under which each firm operates, some firms would find it profitable to reduce output of wastes by 97 per cent, others by 90 per cent, and others by only 80 per cent.

The major advantages of this approach, from an economic standpoint, are twofold. First, each firm is encouraged to search for the best way to reduce its discharge of wastes—to find out which pays off best: use of different materials in the production process, modification of the production process, or installation of waste-treatment equipment. Second, each firm will be encouraged to pursue the reduction of pollution up to the point where the cost of further improvement would be greater than paying the tax.

In such a system great attention must be given to the setting of the proper charges. If the charge is too low, firms may prefer to continue polluting, rather than to pay the costs of reducing their pollution. If the charge is too high, firms may cut back on production or even shut down. While critics of a charges system stress the difficulty of determining the proper charges, defendants of the approach believe that a trial-and-error approach would work.

From an enforcement standpoint, an important advantage of a charges approach is that it would reduce the incentive to postpone compliance. Under this system, so long as a plant is not in compliance with the law—that is, as long as it is discharging more than an acceptable level of wastes—it will accumulate an increasingly large bill.

Appraising the Alternatives

A system of charges such as the one described here in a highly simplified sketch has not been tried in the United States, and opponents say that it hasn't been tried because it isn't workable. But supporters of the charges approach have gathered examples of a wide variety of similar systems put into operation by foreign countries and by state and local agencies in the United States. These various schemes offer flexibility in the way firms go about reducing pollution and in the amount of improvement that could be achieved. Probably none would meet the ideal formulation of the approach, but all reflect an effort to provide incentives, rather than regulations, to alter behavior. Some systems have been imposed and enforced by governments, and some, like one in operation in the Ruhr Valley of Germany, have been established by the co-operation of private firms. Collectively they suggest the possibility that pollution control systems other than those embodied in the legislation of the 1970–77 period may be useful.

But even proponents of a new approach recognize the continuing need for direct regulation. Certain toxic substances, such as those that are clearly destructive of wildlife or demonstrably dangerous to human health, may have to be outlawed entirely. For cancer-causing substances, the question is not what is the most economical way to reduce their use but, rather, how to ban them; cost in such circumstances is a minor consideration.

Environmental-protection policy must cope with a variety of hazards. Some are hazards to human health, causing respiratory disorders, loss of fertility, cancer, and so on. It has been estimated that 60 to 90 per cent of all cancer is of environmental origin, including the environment of the workplace. Other environmental threats, such as strip-mining, may damage land, or, like the excessive discharge of carbon dioxide, modify the climate. Others may simply make the world a less pleasant place to live in. The variety of these hazards and the diversity in sources of pollution suggest that the government may need an array of policies. Thus there is a search not only for ways to improve the traditional regulatory approach but also to seek novel approaches, such as the charges approach, that may be useful in some circumstances.

This chapter has stressed these basic ideas:

1. Economic growth can be measured roughly by the growth of per-capita income. Although this measure does not take into account the many changes in the quality of the things produced in our society, it does show that the average level of living of the American people has tended to rise from decade to decade. We now tend to take this trend for granted, but a look at our depression experience and at many other societies shows that economic growth does not always occur.

2. The essence of economic growth is the expansion of production faster than the increase of population. A number of diverse ingredients must be brought together to bring this about; natural resources, skilled labor, knowledge, tools, managerial ability, and a desire for a higher level of living.

3. At the present time, it appears that the basic ingredients for continued economic growth are still present in the American economy. However, we have become increasingly aware that rapid economic growth may be accompanied by undesirable by-products, such as inflation, depletion of resources, and pollution. As a result, economic growth policy

must take into account the need for price stabilization, efficient use of resources in the long run, and environmental protection.

Suggested Reading

Paul A. Samuelson, *Economics*, Chap. 37, pp. 725–46. George L. Bach, *Economics: An Introduction to Analysis and Policy*, Chaps. 15–17. For a systematic analysis of the factors responsible for our past growth and a summary of the choices available to increase the rate of growth, see Edward F. Denison, *Accounting for United States Economic Growth, 1929–1969* (Washington: The Brookings Institution, 1974). See also "Is Growth Obsolete," by William Nordhaus and James Tobin, in *Readings*, pp. 293–97, and "The Limits to Growth," by Donella H. Meadows and others, in *Readings*, pp. 298–302. For a succinct analysis of economics and environmental policy see *Pollution, Prices, and Public Policy*, by Allen V. Kneese and Charles L. Schultze (Washington: The Brookings Institution, 1975), especially pp. 1–29. For a comprehensive account of the energy problem and prospects, see *Energy in America's Future: The Choices Before Us*, by Sam H. Schurr, Joel Darmstadter, Harry Perry, William Ramsay and Milton Russell (Baltimore: published for Resources for the Future by the Johns Hopkins University Press, 1979).

Chapter 9

THE WORLD ECONOMY

Three familiar issues keep recurring as we consider the economic problems of the United States. These are economic stability, economic growth, and the workings of the market system. Up to now, we have examined them within a national context. They are equally important, however, in an international setting. One might wonder, therefore, why there should be a special field called international economics. The answer is that certain features of international economic relations are distinctive. They stem from the political fact that the world is divided into a large number of independent nation-states, each of which is capable of autonomous economic action.

In the first place, governments can and do erect a number of obstacles to the free flow of goods and services between countries. In contrast to the generally unrestricted flow of American products from state to state, the international flow of goods is obstructed by tariffs, quotas, and administrative restrictions of various kinds. There are restrictions, too, on the free movement of labor between nations. For example, in contrast to the great migration of Americans to the Sunbelt states in recent years, there are immigration regulations that restrict the movement of Japanese workers into Australia and of foreign workers into the United States. There are also barriers to the flow of savings between countries. For a variety of reasons, American savings do not flow into Egypt or Indonesia as easily as they do into Texas or Tennessee. These trade barriers are reinforced, of course, by differences in language, commercial customs, laws, and trading practices.

Another complicating factor is that each country has its

own monetary system and pursues its own independent monetary policy. This frequently obstructs international payments and creates a barrier to international trade and investment. There is a striking contrast between the smoothness with which we are able to make contracts and pay for goods and services within the United States, and the instability and uncertainty encountered in making contracts and payments abroad.

Finally, special mention should be made of an important noneconomic factor that strongly influences international economic relations; that is, political friction between nations and the subordination of economic goals to the needs of foreign policy. Thus many countries support, by subsidies or other means, uneconomic industries that are regarded as vital to national defense. They also restrict or prohibit the export of certain goods to unfriendly nations.

This chapter will consider several aspects of international economics: why international trade is important, how it is organized, and how it is financed, what the consequences are of barriers to international trade, and how the problem of economic growth and the business cycle are related to international economics.

WHY IS INTERNATIONAL TRADE IMPORTANT?

A nation gains by producing what it is best fitted to produce and exchanging its products for those of other nations. The economic reason for trade between nations is, therefore, no different from that for trade between different parts of the same country.

What a region is best fitted to produce depends on its relative supply and quality of the factors of production—natural resources, labor, capital, and entrepreneurial skills. For example, location, the relative abundance of skilled labor and capital equipment, and the relative scarcity of land, make Rhode Island unsuitable for ranching but most suitable for manufacturing. Similarly, Wyoming—with its abundance of land, its relative scarcity of labor, and its remoteness from heavily populated areas—is unsuitable for heavy industry but most suitable for sheep raising. Florida has a special advantage in oranges, Iowa in corn, the Pittsburgh area in steel, and Oregon in lumber. These special advantages provide the bases of trade among cities, states, and regions.

Similarly, their relative endowments of productive resources make the United States notably efficient in producing airplanes and in growing tobacco, Brazil in growing coffee, Australia in raising sheep, and France in making perfume. The way to maximize real income internationally would therefore seem to be to specialize and to trade.

Trade takes place because of price differences arising from the uneven distribution of productive resources. Prices are the basis of trade. When new sources of raw materials are discovered, when skilled labor becomes available, or when new modes of production are developed, these changes will be reflected in changing prices and in a different pattern of trade. Thus the price mechanism works internationally to decide what shall be produced, how it shall be produced, and who shall get it, in a manner similar to the way it works within a country.

International (or interregional) trade is beneficial because it helps us to use scarce resources efficiently, to maximize output, and to satisfy wants on a larger scale. The reasoning behind this statement is contained in what economists call the theories of absolute and comparative advantage. These theories hold that a country (or region) will do better to concentrate on producing those things in which it has the greatest cost advantage over other areas, or those in which its competitive disadvantage is least.

The term "comparative advantage" may be unfamiliar, but the principle it describes is not. We all recognize that a busy executive who is a fast and accurate typist finds it advantageous to hire a stenographer who may not be as skilled. It is advantageous because it permits the executive to specialize in affairs in which administrative skill is much more scarce and more valuable than typing skill. Such specialization helps maximize output within the limits set by the available resources. Similarly, in a larger sense, the United States is better off if it specializes and trades than if it tries to produce every commodity in which it has a competitive advantage.

International trade not only provides goods at lower costs, it also widens the range of available products. There are many things, such as tin and nickel, which we need but do not have within our boundaries. We have copper, newsprint, petroleum, and bauxite (for aluminum), but not in sufficient quantities. We also import many highly specialized products because their quality is superior or their prices lower—for example, Scotch whisky, Belgian lace, Brazilian shoes, Japanese cameras.

Specialization has been carried to such lengths that we export and import different qualities of the same product—we export American Fords and import German Fords. These imports help contribute to our high living standards, and, in addition, they help make our exports possible. In the long run, trade is a two-way proposition, for a nation cannot continue to sell unless it is also willing to buy.

International trade helps sustain high levels of income and employment. In agriculture and in the mass production industries, foreign markets are of particular importance. In some years, we have exported as much as 40 per cent of our total annual production of cotton, tobacco, and wheat; indeed the prosperity of farmers has been linked with foreign trade since colonial days. Jobs and profits in any manufacturing industries depend in large part on foreign demand for machinery, trucks, tractors, and electrical equipment. A decline in foreign sales of farm or manufactured products can lead to a decline in income and employment for the entire economy. Thus aside from its effect on long-run economic efficiency, international trade also affects our short-run stability.

Benefits are maximized when international trade is multilateral. Exports and imports of any two countries do not need to be in balance. For example, we normally buy more from Malaysia than we sell to Malaysia, and we usually sell more to Britain than we buy from it. Britain, for its part, sells more to Malaysia than it buys from Malaysia. In this simplified triangular example, we can think of Malaysia's surplus earnings from exports to the United States as being spent on British goods, and of Britain financing some of its imports from the United States with the proceeds of its exports to Malaysia.

Each country is buying its imports from the cheapest source and selling its exports in the most profitable market, with the result that trade is multilateral and all nations benefit.

BARRIERS TO INTERNATIONAL TRADE

If international trade is beneficial, why are tariffs, quotas, embargoes, licensing systems, exchange controls, and other protective devices used by almost all nations? Why is the argument over "protectionism" a perennial one in the United States? In order to find the answers to these questions, we must examine the arguments and the assumptions involved in the issue of free trade versus protectionism.

Traditionally, free traders have not paid much attention to particular situations and to problems of adjustment in the short run, although they are doing so more today. They have presented an *economic* argument, which assumes that the most efficient use of resources and maximization of real income are the primary objectives of society. The argument for the maximum freedom of trade considers the world or the nation as a whole and the benefits to be derived in the long run by all nations and all people. The arguments for protectionism are usually special or local in nature, are based on short-run considerations, and often are noneconomic in nature.

A strong noneconomic argument for the use of controls over international trade is based on foreign-policy considerations. The possibility of armed conflict intermittently fosters trade restrictions and embargoes among many nations. The purpose is to withhold strategically important goods from others and to protect industries that may be militarily important.

A further argument that has always carried great weight in the world, and still does today, concerns economic development or, to use the old-fashioned term, "infant industries." Industrialized countries tend to favor more liberal trade policies because they wish to buy raw materials and foodstuffs from the cheapest sources and sell their manufactured products in the most profitable markets without restriction. This was the position of Britain in the nineteenth century. In advocating free trade, the great economists of the "Classical School"—Adam Smith, David Ricardo, John Stuart Mill, and others—were reflecting the interests of Britain as an advanced industrial nation.

People in less developed countries, however, were often less enthusiastic about the free trade doctrine. They saw themselves doomed by it to remain specialists in agriculture and raw materials, dependent on Britain for manufactures. They therefore advocated protectionism in order to enable their "infant industries" to get established or, as we say today, to promote economic development. Alexander Hamilton was one of the earliest advocates of this point of view in the United States.

Today, the arguments are similar, but the cast is different. It is the United States that now, as the most advanced industrial nation of the world, tends to advocate a relaxation of trade barriers in the free world as Britain did one hundred years ago. And as one hundred years ago we practiced protectionism to promote our economic development, so today India, Egypt, Brazil, Mexico, Indonesia, Spain, and many other countries seek to promote their economic development by protectionism. They believe that in the long run this policy will foster economic growth as it did in the United States in the nineteenth century.

This argument has much validity, but it also has limitations. It is difficult to know in advance what industries will be able to stand on their own feet eventually and, in view of the vested interests that tend to grow up, it is even more difficult to remove the protection when the "infants" have become "adults." Thus underdeveloped countries run the risk of developing uneconomic industries that can never survive in competitive markets. The gains of specialization and trade are still available to most nations; hence it may be highly wasteful for many of them to attempt to imitate the industrial pattern of the United States.

Some American protectionists also argue that imports made by cheap foreign labor represent unfair competition. They contend that the jobs and high wage scales of American workers will be undermined unless they are protected. One might ask, then: If low wages mean low costs and high wages high costs, how can the United States export anything? Actually, our mass production industries, such as the automobile industry, pay the highest wages in the world and yet they usually undersell the whole world. Mexico, on the other hand, whose auto workers receive considerably less than is paid in Detroit, levies a high duty on "cheap" American cars in order to preserve the home market for their domestic production.

It is not wage rates alone, but wage rates in combination with labor productivity that determine labor costs. If, for example, a pencil maker in a less developed country getting $1.00 an hour and using hand methods turns out 5 pencils, the labor cost per pencil is $.20. If an American worker getting $5.00 an hour and using modern machinery turns out 100 pencils, the labor cost per pencil is $.05. As we have seen in earlier chapters, labor is only one factor of production, so we cannot determine production costs by looking at wages alone.

Some foreign countries tend to have an advantage over the United States in the production of goods that require relatively large amounts of skilled labor, of which they have plenty, and relatively small amounts of capital, in which they are deficient. This is simply the counterpart of our specialization in goods that require large amounts of capital, of which we have plenty and which is relatively cheap, and small amounts of labor, which is relatively high-priced. Trade takes place largely because of this difference in productive resources.

Protectionists have also argued that a reduction in tariffs will create unemployment and that an increase in tariffs will diminish unemployment. Obviously, if an industry is exposed to increased competition from cheaper imports, the result may be an immediate increase in unemployment in that industry. Certainly, if the American tariff were abolished overnight, chaotic conditions would result in particular industries. But there are few today who believe that "free trade" is an immediate practical objective. What is advocated by a large number of persons is "*freer* trade." Their argument calls for a gradual, selective, and moderate program of reducing trade barriers, so that attention can be given to the short-run problems of adjustment that arise in particular industries. This is the process being followed by the more than eighty countries that are signatories of the General Agreement on Tariffs and Trade (GATT). These countries periodically negotiate with one another to achieve mutual reductions in trade barriers.

It is difficult to defend the argument that raising the tariff is a satisfactory cure for unemployment. A higher tariff will not appreciably reduce unemployment that is due to technological or cyclical causes. Raising the tariff will not alleviate unemployment in such export industries as automobiles, machinery, or wheat; indeed, it will tend to harm export industries. And the harm will be even greater if foreign countries retaliate with additional barriers against our exports. Actually, keeping out imports may increase employment in a protected industry, but it may lead to layoffs in other industries. When the United States excluded Danish cheese, Denmark switched its coal purchases to Poland. What may have been gained in Wisconsin, therefore, was probably lost in Pennsylvania and West Virginia. Even if, in such cases, total employment should be increased, there would still tend to be a loss because labor would have moved out of areas where it was more productive into areas where it was less productive.

Nevertheless, when unemployment is high, as it has been in most industrial countries in the late 1970s, the demand for protection from "unfair" foreign competition always increases. In fact, some of the advanced industrial countries may have to face up to the fact that some of their older industries, such as textiles, cannot compete with newer producers in some of the developing countries overseas. If such a structural change in the pattern of world production is indeed taking place, the answer to the problem of some of the "older" industries of the United States is not protectionism but the transfer of productive resources into the "newer," high-technology industries, where we are competitive in world markets, and into service occupations.

There are, of course, other arguments for and against protectionism. Some are naive; some are sophisticated. The most important requirement in examining any of them is this: to set forth carefully the assumptions on which the argument is based and to consider their broad, long-run consequences as well as their narrow, immediate effects.

The tariff has traditionally been an important problem of public policy in the United States. Before the Civil War, northern manufacturing interests used the "infant industry" argument to demand a high tariff, while the South, whose interests lay in exporting agricultural products to world markets and importing manufactured goods from the cheapest sources, favored more liberal trade policies. After the Civil War, the protectionist influences triumphed and gradually the tariff was raised. By 1930, when the Hawley-Smoot Tariff Act was passed, American trade policy was one of the most restrictive in the world.

Since 1934, a reversal has taken place. The Reciprocal Trade Agreements Act, originally passed in 1934 and extended periodically since then, gave the President the power to negotiate trade agreements with foreign countries. These agreements provided that the United States would lower the tariff on selected imports in return for reciprocal concessions from the other country. Between 1934 and 1947, numerous trade agreements were concluded. Since 1947, the process has been broadened under the General Agreement on Tariffs and Trade (GATT) to cover multilateral negotiations by a large group of nations, all of which reduce duties on one another's imports. In addition, the general rise in prices since World War II has reduced the protective effect of many so-called "specific duties"—those expressed as a specific amount of money per unit of quantity. As a result of these two developments, the United States tariff is now in general a relatively moderate one, although some individual duties are still very high. The Trade Act of 1974 gave the President renewed powers to lower the U.S. tariff in return for reciprocal concessions by other nations.

Many other trade practices are more restrictive than the tariff. For example, the United States imposes quantitative restrictions (quotas) and even embargoes on many agricultural imports. When procuring supplies for itself, the United States Government, under the "Buy American" legislation, sometimes gives preference to domestic goods over foreign goods even when foreign goods are cheaper. A great deal of red tape is involved in importing goods into this country, and the process of classifying imports for duty purposes, valuation procedures, sanitary regulations, and so on all hamper the free flow of goods. In addition, the "escape clause" in our trade agreements with other countries permits the United States to cancel concessions already granted if the imports of such commodities harm or threaten to harm domestic industries. Other nations also restrict imports in the same way. These barriers are known as "non-tariff barriers to trade," or N-T-B's for short.

The question of trade barriers continues to be a major problem of American foreign economic policy. Those who favor removing or scaling down many of the restrictions on imports argue as follows: (1) The United States can more easily sell if it also buys; international trade, therefore, can help maintain high levels of employment and income as well as promote efficiency in the use of scarce resources. When the nation is running a deficit in its Balance of Payments, it is particularly important to stimulate our efficient export industries in order to increase our international receipts. (2) Both the government and private firms have made large investments abroad; the logic of our creditor position requires that we permit other countries to earn the dollars to service and repay these debts by selling goods to us. (3) The Soviet economic challenge to the West requires that we do everything possible to promote the economic strength and unity of the free world; this means working with friendly nations to strengthen trade ties, rather than creating divisions among them by maintaining trade barriers. (4) The United States lives in an increasingly competitive world. Its exports can have access to such expanding markets as those of the European Economic Community only if it is prepared to cooperate with other nations in measures to promote mutual trade. (5) A flow of cheaper foreign goods helps hold down prices in the United States and benefits consumers at a time when we are concerned over inflation.

The arguments against liberalizing import restrictions stem mostly from concern over the problems of such industries as textiles, steel, shoes, pottery, and dairy products, which are confronted by the need for painful and serious adjustments when they are subjected to the competition of more imports.

An interesting change in political orientation has occurred in the field of the tariff over the years. As already stated, it used to be the northern industrialists who wanted a high tariff, and the farmers of the South who wanted a low one. But today the liberal trade group is spearheaded by many of the leading businessmen of the nation, representing such industries as automobiles, business machines, and petroleum. Their interest in more liberal trade policies is, of course, related to their interest as exporters in expanding world markets and as importers in getting cheap foreign raw materials. In this respect, the wheel has turned full cycle, and the United States is using an argument put forward by British industrialists one hundred years ago. On the other hand, certain agricultural groups—producers of sugar, dairy products, and meat—have turned protectionist.

One of the most important single issues faced by the United States in the field of trade policy concerns its relationship to the European Economic Community (EEC), popularly known as the Common Market.

The EEC, which came into being on January 1, 1958, is an association of nine countries—France, West Germany, Britain, Ireland, Denmark, Italy, Belgium, the Netherlands, and Luxembourg—which is designed to gradually merge the nine individual economies into an integrated market. The members have abolished all tariffs on each other's goods and have established one common external tariff with respect to the rest of the world. They have established free movement of labor and capital, common agricultural policies, a common anti-trust policy, and certain supranational governmental institutions including a parliament, an executive, and a court of justice.

The significance of this development is that there is now emerging in Europe a new economic power, comparable to the United States in population and resources. Its per-capita income is the highest in the world after the United States and Canada, and its rate of economic growth has been rapid. As the world's largest trader, the EEC will play a major role in determining whether the world will become more protectionist or more liberal in trade policies.

The Common Market constitutes both a challenge and an opportunity to the United States. It constitutes a challenge because its rapidly growing and increasingly efficient industries are providing increasing competition for American firms not only in Europe and in areas such as Latin America and Asia, but even here at home. It constitutes an opportunity because the expanding purchasing power and rising living standards of the West Europeans make them important customers for our exports and create new opportunities for profitable investment by American business. The greatest volume of trade in the world is between nations with high national incomes.

THE BALANCE OF PAYMENTS

A nation's total exports of goods do not usually balance its total imports. Until recently, the United States, for example, each year exported more goods than it imported. Mexico, on the other hand, normally has an import surplus. But, although imports and exports of goods need not be equal, a nation's total international debits and credits must be equal in an accounting sense. International transactions are all listed in a statistical table usually called the balance of payments (B.O.P.), which records all the transactions of the citizens, businesses, and government of a country with the rest of the world. It includes not only exports and imports of goods but also the expenditures of tourists, government foreign-aid grants, private international capital flows, payments for shipping services, and other items, including gold movements and other flows of funds to settle outstanding balances.

A commonly heard term is "balance of payments deficit" or "balance of payments surplus." This has traditionally suggested either an excess of certain payments over certain receipts or an excess of certain receipts over certain payments, respectively. However, in 1976 the U. S. Government accepted the recommendation of a special advisory committee that these terms be avoided, partly because of conceptual difficulties and partly because they were frequently interpreted as "bad" or "good" developments, when in fact this was not necessarily the case. Official U. S. Government figures now show the "Balance of Trade," which is a clear concept showing whether the nation had an export surplus or an import surplus; the "Balance of Goods and Services," which includes services as well as trade; and the "Balance on Current Account," which shows whether total receipts on current account are in excess of total payments or vice versa.

The accompanying table shows an abbreviated version of what the U. S. Department of Commerce now officially calls

UNITED STATES INTERNATIONAL TRANSACTIONS, 1978
(IN BILLIONS OF DOLLARS)

Current Account		
Exports of goods		141.8
Imports of goods		175.9
BALANCE OF TRADE		−34.1
U.S. military sales contracts		7.7
Direct defense expenditures		−7.2
Receipts of income from U.S. assets abroad		41.5
Payment of income from foreign assets in U.S.A.		−21.6
Receipts from other services (travel, transportation, etc.)		26.9
Payment for other services		−24.1
BALANCE OF GOODS AND SERVICES		−10.9
Unilateral transfers		−5.0
BALANCE ON CURRENT ACCOUNT		−15.9
Capital Account		
U.S. capital outflow		−58.7
Government	−3.8	
Private	−54.9	
Foreign capital inflow		63.2
Government	33.9	
Private	29.3	
Statistical discrepancy		11.4
		15.9

Source: U. S. Department of Commerce, *Survey of Current Business*, May 1979, p. S-3. The table shows only the basic arithmetic of the nation's international economic transactions. To find out *why* a given item is what it is—and is larger or smaller than in previous years—requires further analysis.

"United States International Transactions" for 1978. The full table lists eighty-one items. It shows that, in 1978, the United States imported $34.1 billion worth of goods more than it exported and therefore had a "trade deficit." When services are taken into account, however, the "Balance of Goods and Services" showed a deficit of $10.9 billion. The largest service items are "Receipts of income on U.S. assets abroad" and "Payments of income on foreign assets in U.S.A." "Receipts of income" represents the inflow of interest and dividend payments, royalties, and profits earned by American businesses and investors from their overseas operations. Examples would be an American bringing home the interest earned on bonds issued by the government of Norway, and Sears, Roebuck bringing home some of the profits earned by its stores in Spain. "Payment of income" represents the amount foreigners earned on their investments in this country and took home; for example, a Swiss investor who transfers his General Motors dividends back to Switzerland or Sony taking some of the profits earned by its San Diego plant back to Japan. Because U.S. investments abroad greatly exceed foreign investments in the United States, our net earnings for these items were $19.9 billion.

Receipts and payments for "other services" cover tourist expenditures, transportation expenditures, insurance payments, book and motion picture royalties, and, on the payments side, direct defense expenditures, which are the expenses of supporting U.S. military forces and bases abroad in such countries as South Korea, Spain, and the Philippines.

To the excess of payments over receipts of $10.9 billion we add one final item: "Unilateral transfers." Part of this consists of social security and private pension payments to elderly Americans living abroad and of charitable contributions. But the largest part is what is popularly called "foreign aid" —mostly U. S. Government grants to poor countries and contributions to international organizations such as the World Bank. Thus, the final figure for "Balance on Current Account" is −$15.9 billion—a substantial deficit.

Turning to the "Capital Account," "U.S. capital outflow" embraces such items as U. S. Government loans to foreign countries, private U.S. citizens buying foreign stocks and bonds, American businesses building factories abroad, and the movement of bank accounts out of the United States. "Foreign capital inflow" embraces such items as foreigners buying U.S. stocks and bonds, foreign businesses building factories here (for example, Volkswagen's new plant in Pennsylvania), foreign money moving into U.S. banks, and foreign governments placing some of their reserves in the United States (for example, Saudi Arabia using some of its oil earnings to buy U. S. Government securities).

The "Statistical discrepancy" item reflects the difficulty of collecting precise statistics on international transactions, particularly on money moving through banks and on tourist expenditures. Allowing for this discrepancy, the B.O.P. statement balances, as it must, since the whole table is an exercise in double-entry bookkeeping; for example, the "foreign aid" item is balanced by the exports of goods made possible by foreign aid.

Looking at the B.O.P. tells us a great deal about a country's international economic position. It tells us, of course, whether the country is, on balance, a debtor or a creditor. But the most important thing about the B.O.P. is that it can be used as a tool of analysis for understanding the reasons for changes in the nation's trade and payments, the relationship of these changes to the domestic economy, and their impact on the foreign exchange market.

One important influence on the trade items is the rate of economic growth in the United States and its principal trading partners. One of the major reasons for the U.S. trade deficit in 1977 was that the United States recovered from the world-wide recession of 1974–75 faster than Western Europe and Japan. As our industrial production and national income rose, we bought an increasing quantity of imports from abroad—18 per cent more than in 1976, in fact. But, because the economies of our principal trading partners were still sluggish, they were not expanding their purchases of our goods as rapidly. So our exports lagged and increased by only 4.9 per cent over 1976.

Another influence on trade is the price structure of internationally traded commodities. Oil is an important example. The quadrupling of oil prices by the OPEC countries in

1973, with further increases in subsequent years, pushed up the price of a key import into the United States and helped enlarge our trade deficit. Movements in the price level will also influence trade. If the United States has more inflation than, say, Germany, U.S. goods will be relatively less attractive to Germans and our exports to Germany will lag. But German goods will seem relatively more attractive to Americans and our imports from Germany will rise.

Still another influence on the B.O.P. is the flow of short-term funds, such as bank accounts, from country to country. This is a highly volatile item which can reverse itself in a short period of time. The two main factors influencing the movement of short-term funds are interest rates and the desire for security. If interest rates are higher in Zurich or London than in New York, short-term funds will tend to move to Europe in search of higher earnings. But, if the holders of short-term funds feel their money is not safe in a country, they will move it somewhere else, regardless of interest rates.

The perceived threat may be political—for example, Italian money leaving Italy in anticipation of a possible Communist victory in the parliamentary elections. Or the perceived threat may be economic—a fear of devaluation. If you were a Swiss company holding dollars in a New York bank account when the rate of exchange was $1.00 = 2 Swiss francs, as it was in 1977, but you thought the dollar was likely to drop in value, you would want to get your money out of the United States before the rate did drop—as it did in 1978 to $1.00 = 1.5 Swiss francs.

Finally, a very important influence on U.S. trade and payments is the rate of exchange between the dollar and foreign currencies. Monetary problems are especially difficult to cope with in the international arena, because each country has its own currency and pursues its own monetary and fiscal policies independently. Those engaged in international trade and finance must thus convert their money into the money of other countries. If they are to do this, there must be a properly functioning "linkage mechanism" between the monetary systems of various countries. This "linkage mechanism" is the network of foreign-exchange markets in which foreign currencies are bought and sold. As in any market, they are bought and sold at a price determined by demand and supply. This price is the "rate of exchange."

When people "buy foreign exchange," they buy claims for foreign money. These claims are usually obtained from people who sell goods abroad and want to convert the payment into the money of their own country. Thus an American exporter might sell the British pounds he has earned to an American importer who wants to buy goods from Britain. The exporter will end with dollars and the importer will get the pounds he needs to buy in Britain. Both the importer and the exporter are therefore concerned with the rate of exchange, the price at which dollars can be converted to pounds.

The principal objective of an international monetary system is to establish reasonably stable exchange rates while maintaining a reasonably free foreign exchange market. "Stability" in exchange rates does not mean that rates cannot change slightly from day to day or even considerably in the long run. It means only that rates will not fluctuate so widely in the short run that foreign buyers and sellers cannot make plans for the future. If rates change rapidly from day to day, trade is harmed, for it is like buying or selling a product without knowing the delivery price. Stable exchange rates encourage international trade by providing more certainty in the terms of trade.

Before the First World War, this objective was achieved fairly well by the international gold standard. Under the gold standard, the nations defined their currency units as equal to so much gold. Different currencies were thus all related to one another in a network of exchange rates established by reference to this common gold content and known as the "mint pars of exchange." For example, as a British pound contained the same amount of gold as 4.8665 American dollars, the "mint par" between them was $4.8665 = £1. Citizens had complete freedom to convert their cash or bank accounts into gold and to send this gold to foreign countries if they wished. There were thus two alternatives for settling a debt in a foreign country—to buy the currency of that country in the foreign exchange market at the current rate of exchange, or to obtain gold and ship it abroad. The existence of the alternative of shipping gold abroad meant that the market rate did not change materially from the mint par of exchange.

The reasons for the successful operation of the gold standard in the nineteenth century cannot be explored here, but we should realize that the system was based on a set of circumstances that were in many respects probably unique in history and that most certainly have vanished today. They included relatively free trade, flexible prices and wages, a peaceful capitalistic world living in an atmosphere of confidence and believing in the inevitability of progress, and the dominance of Britain in world trade and finance.

The breakdown of the gold standard began with the First World War. Since that time, international monetary affairs have been unsettled. Following the war, exchange rates fluctuated widely, and although many nations later returned to the gold standard, prewar conditions were not restored. The twenty years between the First and Second World Wars was a period of recuperation from the dislocations of the First World War. It was also a period of economic instability and political uncertainty, with recurring threats of a renewed outbreak of war. In this setting, the gold standard system of international monetary co-operation was discarded. By 1939, international monetary relations had been put into a strait jacket of government controls over the prices and uses of foreign exchange (exchange control).

After World War II, a new international monetary system was established. It was called the Bretton Woods system, because it was devised at an international conference held at Bretton Woods, New Hampshire, in 1944. The main goal of the Bretton Woods system, which was established in 1946, was to provide a network of stable exchange rates and free foreign-exchange markets so that international trade and investment could expand, which they did in an unparalleled way for the next twenty-five years. Countries pegged their currencies to the U.S. dollar and committed themselves to keeping this rate stable within a narrow band of 1 per cent on either side of the declared par value. The rate could be changed only in the most exceptional circumstances and then only after international consultation.

One might ask if there is not a theoretical inconsistency in what has just been said. Does not a free market imply that the price—in this case the rate of exchange—will fluctuate in response to changing market forces? Conversely, does not a fixed rate imply government control of the market? Under Bretton Woods, this dilemma was resolved by having governments intervene in the market in order to keep the rates stable. If market forces appeared to be pushing down the value of the British pound, for example, the British authorities would buy up pounds in sufficient amounts to prevent their price from dropping more than 1 per cent. If on the other hand market forces appeared to be pushing up the value of the German mark, the German authorities would supply more marks in sufficient quantities to prevent their price from rising more than 1 per cent. During all this, private buyers and sellers would be free to carry out their market transactions at the prevailing price.

In order to be able to intervene in the market and buy up their own currencies, as in the British example above, governments had to have foreign-exchange reserves. These were primarily gold and the U.S. dollar. The key role of the U.S. dollar in the Bretton Woods system can now be appreciated. It was the "numéraire," or benchmark, for determining exchange rates. It was the principal reserve asset held by other nations. And it was the "intervention currency" that countries used when they had to support their own currencies and that they acquired in exchange if they had to supply their own currency, as in the German example above.

Another important feature of the Bretton Woods system was the International Monetary Fund, a specialized agency of the United Nations that now has over one hundred thirty countries as members. The Fund is a pool of foreign currencies and gold contributed by more than a hundred nations, which can be drawn on by a member who is temporarily short of a particular foreign currency needed to buy imports or to meet debts. A member can "borrow" from the Fund only under certain conditions, and not indefinitely. As a short-run aid in stabilizing foreign exchange rates, the Fund is very useful. In any event, it is the principal medium for dealing with some of the international monetary problems in existence today.

In the early 1970s, the Bretton Woods system broke down and the system of fixed exchange rates was abandoned. The reasons for this are complex and need not be explained in detail here. They relate in part to the problems encountered by the U.S. dollar, which was the keystone of the system, and in part to the reluctance of nations to adjust exchange rates when they were no longer appropriate in light of changed economic conditions.

Efforts to establish a new international monetary system have been stalled by the severe and continuing problems facing the world economy in the late 1970s, including the high price of oil, high inflation, and the failure of the advanced industrial nations to recover fully from the recession of 1974–75, which was the worst economic setback for these countries since the great depression of the 1930s.

Many important exchange rates were "floating"—that is to say, moving up and down in response to market forces. Thus, in mid-1978, the U.S. dollar was "floating" down in terms of the German mark, the Swiss franc, and the Japanese yen, while the British pound was "floating" up in terms of the U.S. dollar. In most cases, these were not completely free floats, however, but what are called "managed floats." This means that, periodically, governments intervened in foreign-exchange markets to influence the rate of exchange, even though they did not peg it to a fixed rate as under Bretton Woods. Other countries have attached their currencies to the currency of a country that is a particularly important trading partner. Denmark, Belgium, and the Netherlands, for example, for some years pegged their currencies to the German mark.

World monetary reform—the establishment of a new international monetary system—is still in the future and must await both an improvement in world economic conditions and the achievement of agreement on a number of controversial issues, such as whether fixed or floating rates of exchange are preferable.

INTERNATIONAL TRADE AND
ECONOMIC GROWTH

The desire for economic development is now worldwide. It is characteristic of almost all countries today. It is much in evidence, for example, in the Soviet Union and China, where the communist authorities are bending every effort to promote increased output and industrial development. It is particularly intense in the countries of Latin America, Southeast Asia, and the Middle East. The basic needs of such countries as India, Brazil, and Turkey are capital, the development of technical and managerial skills among the population, and the development of stable political and economic institutions that will facilitate growth.

One way to acquire productive capital for economic development is to encourage domestic saving. The processes of domestic saving and investing can be helped by modern financial institutions, particularly a sound system of banking and credit. Many underdeveloped countries lack these. A more serious obstacle to domestic saving is poverty. The millions of people in India, for example, who are already living at the margin of subsistence can hardly abstain from consumption in order to save. The irony of the situation is that countries are poor because they lack capital, and they are unable to accumulate much capital because they are poor. A rich country like the United States, on the other hand, can devote a sizable part of its annual production to capital accumulation without any hardship.

Another way to acquire capital is to borrow it from more advanced countries. During the nineteenth century, the United States borrowed large amounts of capital from Great Britain. The *money capital* borrowed by selling bonds and stock to British investors was used in part to buy *capital goods,* such as railroad equipment and machinery, from abroad. Later, in the twentieth century, the United States not only became independent of foreign capital, but became able to lend capital to others.

What is the nature of the problem today? Why does not capital flow from the United States to the underdeveloped countries of Asia, the Middle East, and Latin America in the same adequate quantities that it once flowed from Europe to this country?

First, the political and social upheavals of the world today stand in the way of international investment. Countries that are politically unstable are not attractive for investors, because they must live with the constant threat of property expropriation or nationalization or, at the very least, rigid controls over its use. Second, there is no smoothly functioning mechanism for international payments comparable to the gold standard. Investors are reluctant to risk their money in a country with exchange control because they fear they may be unable to convert their earnings into the currency of their own country, or will suffer losses in doing so. It is hardly surprising, therefore, that capital does not flow freely. Most American capital investment abroad today goes either to countries that have oil, or raw materials such as iron ore and bauxite, or to countries that are already well developed, such as the Common Market and Canada. At the beginning of 1978, 24 per cent of the direct investments overseas of United States business were in Canada and 41 per cent in Western Europe. Only 3 per cent were in Africa.

The principal international investment institution is the International Bank for Reconstruction and Development, known as the World Bank. As one of the specialized agencies of the United Nations, the World Bank has a capital fund of $31 billion, subscribed by the more than one hundred thirty members. It makes loans out of this capital and also out of the proceeds from the sale of its bonds. These loans are designed to promote the long-run economic growth of the borrowing country. They are usually obtained for such purposes as improving transportation and communication, power facilities, and industrial equipment.

Several international investment institutions have been formed to accomplish specific development objectives. The International Finance Corporation, for example, was established in 1956 to channel "risk capital" into medium-sized manufacturing firms in the less developed countries.

The International Development Association (IDA) was started in 1960 to make long-term loans to the less developed countries on more liberal terms than the World Bank. Its loans have been interest-free and repayable over fifty years with no payments at all for the first ten years. The IDA was established as an affiliate of the World Bank to meet the criticism that the World Bank was too conservative in its lending policies.

The Inter-American Development Bank was established in 1960 by the Organization of American States to finance developmental projects in Latin America. Its members at present are the United States, all the Latin American republics except Cuba, and some European countries. In addition to its lending activities, the Inter-American Development Bank manages the Social Progress Trust Fund established by the United States in 1960 to channel funds into the development of housing and health and education facilities in Latin America. In 1966, an Asian Development Bank was established to help finance the economic development of that continent.

A foremost example of government lending abroad is the Export-Import Bank, which was established by the United States in 1934. Its original purpose was to make loans to finance American exports during the depression, but it has since become the principal medium for foreign lending by the United States Government to promote the national interest.

The United States has also concluded a number of "investment treaties" with foreign countries. It has tried to persuade those who need capital of the importance of creating an atmosphere favorable to private enterprise. The United States Government has encouraged foreign governments to guarantee that foreign property will not be expropriated, that the earnings of foreign investors will be convertible into the currency of their country, that foreign technicians will be allowed access to the country and so on. Turkey is an example of a country that has done this and has benefited accordingly. For its part, the United States is willing, under certain circumstances, to insure prospective American investors against loss of their property through expropriation and against loss of their earnings through inability to convert them into dollars.

Underdeveloped countries also seek the accumulation of

technical skills that have been acquired in advanced countries over the years. It is useless to provide complicated pieces of capital equipment to people who lack the technical skill to operate them efficiently. Consequently, one of the most significant developments of recent years has been the initiation of programs to give technical assistance to underdeveloped areas. These programs are now being carried out by the United Nations, by the United States Government, and by several other countries.

The United Nations Development Program (UNDP) is a joint venture participated in by most of the UN's member nations. Under this program, experts of all nationalities in agriculture, public health, elementary education, public administration, and industrial development are sent to underdeveloped areas to survey local problems and to help the local people deal with them. Fellowships are provided so that persons from underdeveloped areas may go abroad and study to acquire the skills their homelands need. The United States program of technical assistance is carried out through agreements with the countries concerned.

These investment and technical assistance programs can benefit both the underdeveloped countries and the advanced countries. In the underdeveloped country, resources can be developed, production increased, national income increased, and the inhabitants can enjoy rising living standards. An advanced country such as the United States—which provides the capital and technical assistance—may obtain new sources of supply for needed raw materials, and the creation of a more prosperous market for exports. For example, United States investments in Jamaica are opening bauxite mines the output of which is increasingly needed for our aluminum industry; the rising Jamaican national income means not only a better life for the Jamaican people but also a growing demand for American exports.

It is sometimes suggested that the United States will be harmed if its investments help create competitive industries in foreign countries. If the United States helps establish a textile industry in South Korea, for example, the South Koreans may stop buying American textiles. In the short run, of course, such problems of adjustment will arise. Usually the first industries to become established are those producing light consumer goods such as processed food, clothing, and furniture. As these become established, the immediate market for American food and clothing may be temporarily reduced. But the market for textile machinery, tools, and other American-made capital equipment will increase and, ultimately, economic development will lead to a growth in the total volume of trade. The greatest volume of trade and the most profitable economic relations today are between advanced countries with highly specialized production and high levels of income. For example, Canada, with 23 million people, is far more important to us as a trading partner than is Mexico, with its 60 million.

Economic development abroad will require adjustments in the structure of production in the country that is exporting capital. But these adjustments cannot necessarily be considered "harmful" in the long run, even though they can be exceedingly painful in the short run, as the shoe manufacturers, for example, are finding today. They are similar to the adjustments that must constantly be made as economic change occurs *inside* the United States. The railroads have had to adjust to the competition of automobiles, truck lines, and air lines; the motion picture industry to television; the silk manufacturers to nylon; the downtown department stores to suburban shopping centers; New England to the textile mills in the South; and hotels to motels. Economic growth and expansion are characterized by continual change and, as a result, adjustments of all kinds are constantly needed both in the United States and in the world economy. The long-run benefits are apparent; it is the day-to-day problems that are difficult.

"Economic development," strictly defined, means the development of the resources of a nation in a way that will contribute to a rising real income and expanding output and trade. For instance, in many countries, the first step should logically be the development of a more efficient agriculture. In the United States in 1978, only 3.4 per cent of the civilian labor force was engaged in agriculture; yet, because of the use of capital and scientific methods, this relatively small number of persons was able to produce more than enough

food and fiber for the entire population. In most under-developed countries, however, virtually the whole population labors on the land to try to keep itself alive. A more efficient agriculture would release labor for use in industrial and commercial pursuits.

In many countries, however, development is thought of primarily in terms of factories. They want to industrialize rapidly because they feel that industrialization will bring not merely more goods but also military power, an advanced urban society, modern technology, and social institutions in keeping with nationalistic desires for recognition and status in the world. The mixture of economic and noneconomic considerations results in economic programs that are not always in the best interests of greater productivity and trade. Nevertheless, nationalism and the desire for industrial development and military power are the major facts of life today in most of Asia, Latin America, and the Middle East and seemingly are considered more important objectives than the most efficient use of resources.

WORLD TRADE AND ECONOMIC STABILITY

Over the years, it has become clear that there is a close relationship between world trade and economic conditions within major countries. Inflation and recession can be transmitted from one country to another through the medium of international trade. In particular, the three economic giants—the United States, Japan, and West Germany—are often called the "locomotives" of the world economy. If they are prosperous, they import products from the rest of the world and pull other countries along into prosperity with them. If their economies are sluggish, however, then they import less and the economies of other countries, which now do not export so much, are likely to be sluggish too.

The United States exerts a greater influence on the world economy than any other country. American industries and households were responsible for the buying by the United States of $176 billion worth of imported goods during 1978—more than one eighth of total world imports. The United States is, in other words, the greatest market in the

world for exports of other countries. Indeed, Canada, Venezuela, the Philippines, and Brazil ship one quarter, one third,
and even one half of their total exports to the United States.
The prosperity of these and many other countries depends on
their ability to sell in the American market—and on our ability and willingness to buy. As prosperity and political stability go together in some underdeveloped countries, the
burden of responsibility resting on the United States is
particularly great.

*A decrease in national income and employment in the
United States is often transmitted quickly to other countries.*
Even relatively mild and brief recessions in the United
States, like that of 1970, can have a serious effect on the
economies of other countries, because the "income elasticity
of demand" for imports into the United States tends to be
fairly high. This means that a small change in the national
income will result in a rather large change in imports.

The countries that are most affected today by these declines in income and employment in the United States and
other industrial countries are the less developed ones which
sell raw materials. These countries suffer a decline in their
export earnings when they sell less to their industrial customers and when they are forced to sell at lower prices. This
was particularly evident during the severe recession of
1974–75, which affected all the industrial countries of the
world. World trade declined for the first time since World
War II. Particularly hard hit were the less developed exporters of minerals and raw materials.

On the other hand, the world-wide boom in 1972–73
caused an upsurge in demand for raw materials all over the
world. This demand forced up the prices of commodities and
generated inflationary pressures in many countries. Thus fluctuations in the level of income and employment in the industrial countries are a matter of world-wide concern. A program for stabilizing economic activity at a high and rising
level is therefore important to all of them and to the world
economy.

Let us now analyze a specific policy issue that has been of
great concern to the American people since World War II:
foreign aid. We shall once again use the procedure outlined

in Chapter 1 and seek in this way to gain skill in dealing with economic problems.

The Problem and the Issues

It is widely accepted today that the rich nations of the world have a collective responsibility to do what they can to help the poor countries develop and raise their living standards. In 1977, the group of seventeen rich countries constituting the Development Assistance Committee (DAC) of the Organization for Economic Cooperation and Development (OECD) provided $14.8 billion of what is called "Official Development Assistance" (ODA) or economic aid to the poor nations. The United States provided about 28 per cent of this amount.

What is loosely called "foreign aid" in the United States actually comprises a variety of different things. It includes loans and grants of money from the Agency for International Development (AID), our foreign-aid agency, to needy countries; shipments of food to hungry people under the "Food for Peace" program; the financing of technical-assistance programs in such fields as agriculture, education, and public health; contributions to such international organizations as the International Development Association (IDA), the Food and Agriculture Organization (FAO), and the World Health Organization (WHO); loans by the government's lending arm, the Export-Import Bank of the United States; and the Peace Corps. All these constitute ODA, or economic aid, by the United States. In addition, the United States has over the years provided a great deal of military aid to various allies and other countries whom we have wished to strengthen militarily.

Numerous issues arise when a nation commits itself to foreign aid, as the United States has since World War II. One is simply how much aid the nation can or should provide. The target agreed on by the DAC countries in OECD is for each country to provide ODA each year in an amount equal to 0.7 per cent of its GNP. The idea here is that, as the rich countries grow and their GNPs rise, they would automatically provide more to the poor nations. In 1977, only three of the seventeen countries—Sweden, the Netherlands, and Norway

—met this target. The United States ranked thirteenth, with an amount equal to 0.22 per cent of its GNP. In the 1978 federal budget, economic aid constituted about 1.2 per cent of total federal spending. These figures give some idea of the extent to which economic aid constitutes a burden on the United States. The question, of course, is whether or not such wealthy countries as the United States, Japan, and West Germany can or should do more.

A second issue concerns how much economic aid should be in the form of nonrepayable grants and how much in the form of loans. This should be decided primarily on the basis of the financial standing of the recipient and particularly its ability to repay the principal and interest over the years. Some very poor countries, such as Bangladesh and Chad, have big balance-of-payments deficits and simply do not have enough foreign exchange to service a debt over the years. For such countries, grants would seem to be in order. Other countries, further along the road of development, such as South Korea and Brazil, can afford to pay principal and interest. In between are countries that might be provided with "soft loans"—that is, loans carrying only a nominal rate of interest, rather than the market rate, and an extended maturity date.

A third issue is whether aid should be provided directly by the United States to a recipient nation (bilateral aid) or indirectly in the form of contributions to international organizations which then help those in need (multilateral aid). For example, the United States is one of more than 130 countries contributing to the World Bank, which makes development loans to poor countries.

There are two big advantages to the multilateral approach. One is that the burden of aid is shared by many countries instead of falling on one or a few. The other is that such aid can for the most part be kept nonpolitical and oriented solely toward the economic development of the borrower. When bilateral aid is provided, it is easy for political considerations to enter the picture and for the United States, for example, to use the aid as an instrument for furthering its foreign-policy objectives. The enormous amounts of aid channeled in past years to such small countries as South Vietnam, South

Korea, and Taiwan, as compared with smaller amounts to very large countries such as Bangladesh and India, can be explained only by foreign-policy considerations. On the other hand, one must recognize that foreign aid can be an important foreign-policy instrument and that the United States is going to use it as such—as do the Soviet Union, France, China, and Germany.

A fourth issue concerns the strings that should be attached to aid. On the one hand, the United States wants to be sure that the aid is used for intended purposes and does not finish up in the pockets of those who practice graft and corruption. To avoid this, a certain amount of supervision seems desirable. On the other hand, if the United States interferes too much in the internal affairs of another country, it can simply alienate the recipients.

Finally, there is the question of what kind of aid is most appropriate for a particular country. Aid should be tailored to the needs of the country. One country might have a rapidly growing population and inadequate food supplies, in which case technical assistance in the fields of family planning and agriculture might have top priority. Another country might be handicapped by a shortage of foreign exchange, preventing it from importing needed capital equipment, in which case a dollar loan might be helpful. In all cases, careful planning and the establishment of priorities are needed if aid is to be successful.

These are only some of the issues that need to be considered when implementing a foreign-aid program. Making decisions with respect to these issues requires that we carefully set forth our objectives.

The Objectives

At least three policy objectives may be identified as we consider foreign aid. One is political. Two are economic. The political objective is to help the less developed countries become stable societies that, if not democratic in the American sense, are at least friendly to the United States. The belief here is that, by providing aid, we can help some of these countries remain friendly to our political interests and encourage others to lean in our direction.

One of the economic objectives is to promote the growth of poor countries so that they will be good trading partners and provide profitable investment outlets. Poor countries are not good customers. As the leading trading and investing nation in the world, the United States has a self-interest in helping countries achieve rising incomes and higher living standards.

The other economic objective leads us in the opposite direction. Many Americans feel that we have plenty of economic problems here at home, including the need to rebuild our central cities, establish a national health program, improve our educational facilities, and reduce poverty. If we really want to strengthen our society, we should focus our resources on these pressing domestic needs and not divert our limited resources to the needs of other countries.

Americans also would like some relief from their tax burdens. Many people are disturbed by the succession of unbalanced federal budgets in prosperous times. One way to cut taxes is to reduce federal spending—and foreign aid is one area where some claim that cuts could be made.

The Alternatives

We shall explore only two of the alternative courses of action: (1) cut foreign aid and reduce taxes or (2) continue the program as it now exists. There are other alternatives, but these will illustrate some of the choices that must be made in international economic policy.

What are the probable consequences of reducing the aid program and cutting taxes? Let us assume that the tax cut is equal to the cut in federal expenditures. Those who would cut the aid program and reduce taxes argue that a tax cut will boost our domestic economy and might help us achieve our international objectives. They point out that a tax cut can stimulate private investment—a strong program of domestic investment will help us to grow and maintain our economic lead over the rapidly growing and competitive economies of Japan and Western Europe. Furthermore, a prosperous domestic economy will be a market for foreign goods, and therefore other nations can obtain capital equipment from us by selling us what we need. In a word, they can grow via trade—not aid. Lastly, it is argued that private investments are more likely to be made overseas if investment incentives are not harmed by continued high taxation. They argue, therefore, that it is possible that the tax reduction might contribute greatly to continued international economic growth.

Those who support the second alternative—continuing the foreign aid program—point out that the foreign aid program is actually a type of insurance policy. If it helps to prevent war or an intense arms race, it will, in the long run, save taxpayers' money. If we cease our aid program and lose some of our friends, the long-run costs of a direct defense system may be far more expensive.

Supporters of the foreign aid program point out that we cannot rely on tax cuts to provide domestic and international economic growth. It is true that tax cuts leave more funds in the hands of the public, but as this program also calls for a decline in federal spending, the level of national income may fall. Moreover, as some of our agricultural and manufacturing industries depend on foreign markets, they may have to curtail production. By cutting taxes and foreign aid, the problems of farm surpluses and unemployment may be aggravated.

The supporters of the present program note that if the government collects $5 billion in taxes for foreign aid and allows foreign governments to spend this on American goods and services, it is providing a full $5 billion of foreign assistance. But if taxes are cut, so that American citizens can spend the money, far less will be made available for other nations. American spending for foreign products will be a small part of the $5 billion. The supporters of foreign aid argue, therefore, that the tax cut might result in slower domestic economic growth and an inadequate flow of dollars for the use of other nations.

A continued foreign aid program can provide new skills and capital to the nations abroad. The supporters of the present program argue that under present conditions, it is more effective than relying on private investment abroad. They agree that lower taxes will provide *some* stimulation to private investment, but they argue that the effect will be slight. The main barriers to private investment abroad by American firms are foreign controls over profits, possible foreign government seizure, exchange controls, and many red tape problems. A domestic tax reduction will not eliminate these barriers, but they might be reduced by a foreign aid program that brought nations together in co-operative ventures.

As we noted earlier, taxation is but one of the issues in the foreign aid question. Other issues such as the various types of aid, the place of foreign assistance in our world-wide foreign policy, the timing of cuts in federal spending and taxing, or the military aspects of foreign assistance cannot be explored here. What we have shown is that the problem cannot be viewed merely as a "give-away" program which yields no benefits to the United States.

Appraising the Alternatives

As do other economic issues, the problem of foreign aid imposes on the American people the necessity for making decisions among alternatives. Such decisions can only be made within the framework of the goals the American people seek to achieve and with the recognition that not all goals can be fully achieved and that difficult trade-offs must be accepted.

The goals include promoting the economic and political interests of the United States in the world, resolving difficult domestic economic problems, and achieving some relief from high taxes and budget deficits. How many of our resources should be allocated directly to the less developed countries and how many of them to our domestic economy? Should foreign aid be increased, reduced, or left at the same level? What are likely to be the consequences of each of these courses of action and how are our various goals likely to be affected by them? Once the decision has been made on how much to allocate to foreign aid, further decisions, of the kind discussed earlier in this chapter, then must be made. Again, the consequences of each alternative must be evaluated and trade-offs determined in the light of our goals.

This chapter has stressed these basic ideas:

1. International trade is an extension of the principle of specialization that exists within national boundaries. Specialization permits resources to be used in the production of

goods and services where they will be comparatively most efficient. But specialization requires trade.

2. There are a number of political, economic, and social barriers to international trade. These barriers hamper the growth of the level of living for the world as a whole. They may, however, contribute to specific national objectives of military security or the development of desired industries. The arguments for higher barriers to international trade emphasize specialized, short-run, or noneconomic objectives; those favoring freer trade are more general, long-run, and stress economic issues.

3. Complex problems arise in the world economy because each country has its own money and its own monetary policy. Thus the world needs a smoothly functioning international monetary system that will permit us to overcome this obstacle and carry on our business around the world as though the problem did not exist. The international monetary system that served the world so well for a quarter of a century after World War II has now gone and the world faces the task of constructing a new one.

4. Our policy toward international trade has an effect on the economic growth and stability of nations abroad. Many of the conditions that have contributed to our economic development do not exist in other countries, but some of them can be transplanted. Because the economic development of other nations contributes to our own economic development, the measures we take to increase the technological equipment and skills of other peoples, are in the long run helping our own economic growth. Similarly, the efforts we make to stabilize our economy will help stabilize the economies of other nations.

Suggested Reading

Paul A. Samuelson, *Economics,* Chaps. 34 and 35, pp. 668–724. George L. Bach, *Economics: An Introduction to Analysis and Policy,* Chaps. 39–41. A simple review of the principal theories and problems related to international economics is to be found in James D. Calderwood, *The World Economy* (New York: Joint Council on Economic Education, 1972). At least one chapter in the annual *Economic Report of the Presi-*

dent is always devoted to world economic problems. Robert Z. Aliber, *The International Money Game,* 3rd ed. (New York: Basic Books, 1979), is a lively and readable introduction to international monetary relations.

Chapter 10

GOVERNMENT AND THE AMERICAN ECONOMY

Earlier chapters have shown that government has established such devices as money and the law of contracts to facilitate the free market exchange of goods and services, and that it has set up import duties and regulations to restrain or control free exchange.

We have seen that antimonopoly measures have been instituted to make competition more effective, and that other measures, such as labor laws and agricultural price supports, have been instituted to restrain or alleviate the effects of competition.

It was shown in Chapter 7 that taxes and credit controls may be used to help maintain the employment of our resources at a high level, and in Chapter 2 that taxes and public expenditures may be used to modify the pattern of income distribution. The purpose of this chapter is to describe the scope of governmental influences in the American economy and to assess some of the differences between the public and private sectors of the economy.

THE SCOPE OF THE PUBLIC ECONOMY

The public economy (the government share of economic activity) has grown at an accelerated rate since 1900. In 1900, the *percentage* of the labor force working for governments was much smaller than it is today. About one worker out of twenty-four was employed by federal, state, or local governments in 1900; by 1979, about one out of six workers was on a government payroll. Similarly, the share of the government in total production is estimated to be about four times as large today as it was in 1900. Total federal, state, and local government debts have grown even more rapidly in relation to private debts; in 1900, they were about 6 per cent of the total public and private debt, and in 1977, they were about one fourth of the total.

The increase in government expenditures shown in the accompanying chart is not a wholly accurate indication of the growth in governmental functions. Inflation accounts for part of the rise, because over the period since 1900 the price level has risen nearly eightfold. Moreover, spending does not indicate the significance of many governmental services. For example, the operation of the Federal Reserve Board involves

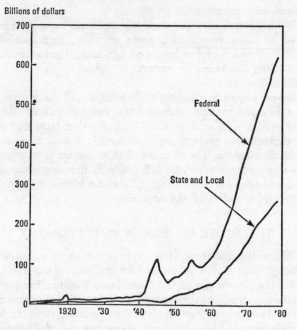

Government Expenditures, 1915- 78

Source: *Historical Statistics of the United States, Colonial Times to 1970*, and *Economic Report of the President*, 1979, p. 267.

very little spending yet has a great impact on the economy. With these limitations, however, we can get a general idea of the expanding role of government by looking at its spending. In 1949, government spending (federal, state, and local) totaled about 14 per cent of the gross national product. In 1960, it was nearly 20 per cent, and it has hovered around this figure since that time.

Government expenditures have not only increased; they have also been redirected. The change shows up dramatically in federal outlays since 1960. The proportion of the budget allocated to national defense has been cut in half, and the amount allocated to medical care, income security, and other domestic programs has doubled, as shown in the accompanying table.

CHANGES IN THE PATTERN OF FEDERAL EXPENDITURES, 1960–78
(PER CENT)

| Year | National defense | Nondefense | | | |
		Payments to individuals	Net interest	Aid to states and localities	Other
1960	49.0	24.8	7.5	7.6	11.1
1965	41.0	25.7	7.3	9.2	16.7
1970	40.3	30.4	7.3	12.2	9.8
1975	26.6	43.7	7.1	15.2	7.4
1978	25.5	43.6	7.1	17.1	6.7

Sources: Statistical Abstract of the United States, 1977, p. 248, and Budget of the United States, 1978.

The amount of federal government spending each year is determined by the budget and appropriation processes. Formulation of a budget begins about a year and a half before the fiscal year starts on October 1. (Thus work on the budget for fiscal 1980 began in the spring of 1978 for submission to Congress in January 1979.) The budget must be transmitted to the Congress within fifteen days after the start of each new session, and Congress is expected to complete action by the following September 25, a few days before the start of a new fiscal year.

Under the Congressional Budget Act of 1974, a schedule of steps to be taken by specified dates by the Congress was established to complement the work of the executive branch. For example, in the spring the Congress sets targets for budget receipts and outlays. After appropriation and tax bills have been enacted by the House and Senate, the Congress sets a floor on budget receipts and ceilings on budget outlays. These steps are part of an effort established by the 1974 act to encourage Congress to look at the entire budget and to keep these total income and spending targets in mind as it considers the desirability of the individual programs. Previously, individual appropriations were enacted without much explicit concern about the over-all level of spending and taxes and their impact on the level of income, employment, and prices. Revenues to finance federal expenditures are obtained primarily from taxes. The most important is the individual income tax, and the second most important are tax receipts from social insurance, as shown in the chart.

The major functions of the federal government identified

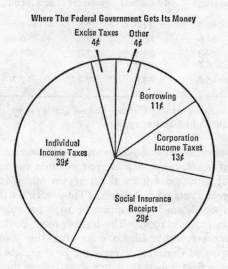

Where The Federal Government Gets Its Money

Excise Taxes 4¢
Other 4¢
Borrowing 11¢
Corporation Income Taxes 13¢
Individual Income Taxes 39¢
Social Insurance Receipts 29¢

Source: The Budget of the United States, 1978.

above only begin to suggest the scope of government activity. A complete list of government operations that affect the economic system would require more pages than this chapter offers. A broad listing prepared many years ago indicates the array of governmental services (federal, state, county, city, and special district) and classifies them under fifteen major headings:[1]

  I.   Overhead Activities
 II.   Protection to Persons and Property
III.   Highway Construction and Maintenance
 IV.   Development and Conservation of Natural Resources
  V.   Sanitation and Waste Removal
 VI.   Health
VII.   Hospital
VIII. Public Assistance and Social Services
 IX.   Corrections
  X.   Social Insurance
 XI.   Housing and Home Ownership
XII.   Educational Activities
XIII. Library Facilities
XIV.   Public Recreation and Cultural Facilities
 XV.   Public Service Industries

For the range of governmental activities, let us look at a breakdown of just one of these classifications as presented by this survey. Class II, "Protection to Persons and Property," is further divided into eight headings, as follows:

A. National Defense
B. Police Protection and Law Enforcement
C. Fire Protection and Fire Fighting
D. Protective Inspectors
E. Regulation of Business and Industry
F. Insurance of Life, Money and Property
G. Other Protection Activities
H. Protection of Industrial Workers

[1] C. H. Chatters and M. L. Hoover, *An Inventory of Governmental Activities in the United States,* Municipal Officers Finance Association (1947), pp. 5–15.

Each of these items, in turn, embraces a long list of subordinate activities. Under the heading "E. Regulation of Business and Industry" are listed, for example:

1. Prevention or elimination of monopolies or trusts
2. Regulation of competitive practice
3. Banks and Banking
   a. Granting bank charters
   b. Conducting bank examinations
4. Credit institutions
5. Securities
   a. Regulation of sale
   b. Regulation of security exchanges
   c. Licensing security dealers
6. Insurance
   a. Establishment of insurance rates
   b. Inspection of financial status
   c. Granting right to do business
   d. Licensing of insurance agents
7. Transportation
   a. Railroads
   b. Interurban railroads
   c. Street railways
   d. Motor bus and truck companies
   e. Water carriers
   f. Air carriers
8. Transmission and sale of electricity and gas
9. Communications
   a. Telephone, telegraph, cable companies
   b. Radio broadcasting
10. Petroleum industry
11. Employment bureaus—private
12. Agriculture
   a. Inspecting and regulating warehouses
   b. Regulating commodity exchanges and futures
   c. Regulating and inspecting commission merchants

Each of these classifications, of course, covers a governmental activity the cost and effect of which are not even remotely suggested by the modest listing in the survey. As we shall see, they all influence, directly or indirectly, the operation of the economy—whether these effects are intended or not.

Although the broad functions of government are well established and fairly constant, there are changes in specific tasks and responsibilities every year. The federal government in 1977, for example, created a new Department of Energy, the twelfth cabinet department; it revised its system for escalating social security benefits to offset the loss of purchasing power resulting from inflation; Congress enacted amendments to the Clean Air Act that allowed the auto industry more time to meet emission standards and gave more authority to the states and local governments; it enacted a "midcourse" correction in the Federal Water Pollution Control Act that provided more money for construction of sewage treatment plants and gave the Environmental Protection Agency authority to protect drinking water from toxic chemicals; the standard deduction for taxpayers was increased, along with other revisions in the individual income tax system; the food stamp program was extended for four years; the deregulation program of the Civil Aeronautics Board led to reductions in air fares and to greater competition among air lines. Federal legislation often leads directly to changes in state legislation, because states must act in order to become eligible for federal funds. States and localities independently also are continually revising specific programs and responsibilities.

WHY HAVE THE ACTIVITIES OF GOVERNMENT GROWN?

Population growth has led to a long-run expansion of governmental activities. The population of the United States in 1978 was about 50 per cent greater than it was in 1950. As a result, many areas that were formerly sparsely populated have been turned into urban and suburban communities that need all the services usually provided by government. This growth has required government to build more schools, roadways, and sewer lines, to dispose of more garbage, to put out more fires, and to build more jails and hospitals.

A rising level of living for consumers has prompted a ris-

ing level of governmental services. Bigger and faster automobiles required the replacement of two-lane highways by four- and six-lane freeways with cloverleaf intersections. As more people sent their children to college, larger and better-equipped state colleges and universities were required. As the well-being of the society grew, more attention was given to health, sanitation, libraries, and a host of other ingredients of a high level of living. As many of these services are best provided by government, its economic role expanded.

Defense needs and a variety of international commitments have greatly enlarged the economic impact of the federal government. When a society is confronted by the problem of national survival, its efforts turn to the production of the things needed to preserve the peace or to win a war—the services of soldiers for the battlefront must be supported by vast quantities of goods and services. Moreover, as weapons have become more technical, dependent on greater industrial resources and scientific research, the economic burden placed on society has increased. All this activity is funneled through the national government—the only instrument that society has for co-ordinating individual efforts in a major national emergency.

Governmental activities have expanded as a result of efforts to resolve group conflicts. As noted in earlier chapters, a breakdown in any part of a highly specialized economy may be of vital concern to the entire society. Conflicts between groups, such as the conflict between labor and management, between the agricultural and industrial sectors of the economy, and between consumers and producers, have led to broad governmental programs. These programs have attempted to settle disputes and also to change the relative economic power of the groups involved. Child labor laws, bankruptcy laws, factory inspection, workmen's compensation, and laws against discrimination because of race and sex are some of the ways that governments have attempted to protect the economically weak from the strong. Protection of society from the conflict of interests between society and particular groups has led to monopoly laws and the regulation of public utilities. As society has become more complex and more specialized, governmental intervention to resolve such conflicts has tended to grow.

The expansion of governmental functions has been furthered by a changing attitude of the public toward the use of government to provide security against many economic risks. One of these risks is the risk of depression and recession. Some reasons for the reaction of society to recessions have been suggested in earlier chapters and need only be mentioned here. Ours is a complex urban society. When people move to cities, they are dependent upon a vast system of production and exchange for the necessities of life. In earlier days, when a large share of the population lived on farms, most people could at least produce for themselves in a period of declining economic activity. The conveniences of life might not be forthcoming, but life could go on. In an urban, specialized, industrial society, a large part of the working population has no way to produce for itself—in a recession, an unemployed factory worker may be completely without means of livelihood. Thus economic decline is regarded as a social problem—a problem that the individual cannot, by himself, solve. The primary instrument we have today for dealing with this social problem is government.

Recession results in a contraction in the flow of income. Therefore, in order to offset the decline in private spending and to maintain the level of national income, the government now uses a variety of monetary and fiscal controls. But the flow of a worker's income can also be stopped by accident or old age. Therefore various levels of government attempt to diminish this personal risk by workmen's compensation, unemployment compensation, and old-age payments.

There is scarcely a group in the United States that has not shifted some of its economic risks to the government. Depositors in banks and savings associations have deposit insurance, farmers have crop insurance, lenders have housing mortgage insurance, veterans have life insurance, most older workers have medical insurance, some businesses have obtained subsidies, others have obtained tariffs, others have tax privileges that reduce the risks of investment, and so on. The very length of the list suggests that the American people as a whole place great value on economic security. In doing so, they have contributed to the growth in governmental activities.

As governmental activities expanded, there was also a shift of many state and local responsibilities to the national government. Most of what is called "social legislation"—care for the aged, unemployment relief, aids to agriculture, regulation of monopolies, regulation of financial institutions, and so on—first appeared at the state or local level of government. But as the country grew and became more closely knit, affairs in Kansas or Louisiana affected the welfare of the people of New Jersey or Oregon; hence, they were no longer left to the exclusive discretion of the states. Furthermore, some of the problems became too large for state or local resources—unemployment payments during the depression, for example. In many of these instances, the conflict between "states rights" and "federal power" was resolved in favor of the level of government that was willing and able to assume the economic costs of the program—the federal government.

Nevertheless, state and local governments still provide most of the funds for education and other nondefense purposes. The demand for these services has increased greatly in recent years, placing major stresses on the taxing systems of these governments. As a consequence, problems of tax reform and tax co-ordination are attracting increasing attention. Today, state and local governments spend about three times as much as the federal government for civilian services—education, roads, sanitation, police and fire protection, and welfare—and an increasing share of these expenditures are financed by the federal government. Many of the programs are financed by grants-in-aid, which totaled about $70 billion in 1977, compared with only $2 billion in 1950. During the 1966–76 decade they increased more rapidly than total federal outlays or GNP. These grants not only finance direct payments to individuals for medicaid, public-assistance cash payments, and housing payments, they also pay for such programs as highway construction, sewage and waste-treatment facilities, and general revenue sharing. In 1977, grants-in-aid financed about 25 per cent of state and local spending.

To summarize, the growth of governmental activities has been due to a variety of factors, but mainly to:

War and defense, which require a mobilization of an important part of the national economy, the continuation of services for veterans, and the maintenance of allied nations as strong political, military, and economic powers.

Economic fluctuations, which bring about the development of programs of unemployment relief and the use of governmental controls to limit the range of economic fluctuations.

Economic growth, which has led an expansion of governmental services and a demand for improvements in the quality and variety of governmental services to keep pace with the improvements in our over-all level of living.

Conflicts within the economy, which have resulted in the government influencing the economic power of conflicting groups and, in some instances, determining the characteristics of their operations.

The quest for economic security, which has led to the creation of a variety of programs designed to diminish many of the risks of economic activity in a modern industrial society.

HOW DOES THE GOVERNMENT INFLUENCE THE OPERATION OF THE ECONOMY?

Government provides the necessary framework for private economic activity. Without certain basic institutions and practices, an elaborate system of production and exchange like ours could not develop. Vital to our economy are the institution of private property, enforceable contracts, a regulated money system, individual rights, and a system of justice.

The institution of private property is established and maintained by government. Without government, personal property rights would generally be only as strong as people's ability to keep others from taking their possessions. Federal, state, and local governments enforce property rights (even against themselves and against each other) and, in doing so, they maintain a source of economic incentive for many of the productive activities of the people.

Government provides the economy with the legal basis for free contracts. This basic feature of the economy sanctions agreements among individuals, permitting them to join together for collective production and to enter into transactions with one another. They may, however, receive support from the law only if their contractual agreements do not harm the public interest (they cannot band together for the purpose of monopolizing the market, for instance). As co-operation among individuals is a necessary part of an economy based on the division of labor, the contract laws that facilitate co-operation are major requirements for our type of system. Together with governmental sanction for the corporate form of business, the law of contracts, which requires people to perform agreements they make, is a fundamental requirement for countless business transactions.

The federal government has established a monetary system. Money provides a standard unit by which individuals may compare the value of commodities. It is a medium of exchange that permits trading without the hindrances of bartering. To protect the usefulness of money, the government defines its characteristics and establishes the conditions under which it is issued. As the government has granted commercial banks the authority to create deposits, which constitute the major part of the nation's money supply, governmental control of commercial banks is essential for an orderly monetary system.

The freedoms enumerated in the Bill of Rights, a system of administering justice, equal protection under the law, "due process" (prohibiting government from depriving any person of "life, liberty, or property" without recourse to the standard protections of the legal system), have all helped to determine the basic characteristics of the American economic system. They have facilitated the growth of organized production and exchange in an environment of individual freedom.

Government promotes and aids various types of economic activities. Public policy is used regularly to encourage and discourage various lines of development. For years the federal government has used tariffs to encourage the production of certain goods that might be supplied by foreign competitors. Many state and local governments have used their powers and public monies to support the construction of roadways, canals, and railroads. The federal government also contributed, by its land grants, to the development of a railroad system. Governments have issued franchises, assuring freedom from competition to producers of various services. Loans and direct subsidies have been made to farmers, airlines, electric power companies, shipping companies, and metal producers. State governments, interested in economic development, have offered tax advantages and a variety of other benefits to new industries.

In addition to these promotional activities, governments also provide a vast number of continuing aids to the economy. The results of governmental research are made available to the public through publications provided by government. The commerce departments of the federal and state governments provide statistics on employment, prices, incomes, shipping, sales, and a variety of other data needed for business planning. Agriculture departments supply information on crops, insecticides, erosion control, farm management, and many other productive aids to farmers. Governments maintain port facilities and highways, provide weather bulletins, job training assistance, health information, education, and welfare; the list of such governmental aids to the economy seems almost inexhaustible. In supplying these aids, government not only influences the use of the nation's economic resources but it also contributes to the growth of the national income.

Control or regulation of certain economic activities is undertaken to foster social objectives. Government at times intervenes in behalf of the public to outlaw undesirable practices or to impose restrictions on private conduct. It regulates monopolies and establishes many of the standards for private economic operations. Producers may not advertise falsely, refuse to bargain with their employees' representatives, issue fraudulent securities, discriminate unfairly among their employees and customers, or produce certain products considered to be dangerous to the health, safety, or morals of the public. In recent years, environmental and occupational safety and health regulations have been especially prominent, as have programs to assure equal employment opportunities for women and minorities.

The government, through regulation, has established a

wide range of so-called "welfare activities." Inasmuch as the government establishes the conditions under which the economy will operate, those conditions must change as social objectives change. Thus employers may no longer hire child labor or pay wages below the minimum established by the government. Producers must pay some of the costs of protecting their workers from loss of income due to accidents, unemployment, or old age. Factories must be inspected for safety; doctors, pharmacists, and many other producers must be licensed by the state; and home construction must meet certain standards.

Regulation sometimes leads to detailed direction of economic activity. The Interstate Commerce Commission, the Civil Aeronautics Board, and state public utility commissions, to mention a few, have strong powers to determine the prices and service of the activities they control. As described in Chapter 3, these regulatory bodies are generally set up when the free market is unable to provide a check on the activities of the producers. Similarly, the Federal Trade Commission investigates and regulates for the purpose of maintaining a competitive economy.

Economy-wide regulation has also been applied from time to time—generally during emergencies. The National Recovery Administration of the 1930s, the Office of Price Administration of the 1940s, the Office of Price Stabilization of the 1950s, and the Federal Energy Administration of the 1970s are examples of governmental regulation of prices for the whole economy. Similarly, other controls, such as wage ceilings, output quotas for farmers, and regulations over bank loans, have been used by government to compel economic activity to meet certain social objectives.

Government takes over the ownership of some forms of economic activity. When private operation or regulated operation does not yield the results desired, government sometimes engages directly in the production of the needed goods and services.

There are many reasons for governmental enterprises such as municipal water systems, schools, transportation systems, state liquor monopolies, insurance programs, federal credit agencies and electric power installations. In some instances, these government-owned enterprises have involved activities that were provided by private enterprise until they became unprofitable. In others, the government has entered the field in order to regulate the consumption of the product or because it is a good source of revenue. Private producers have sometimes been displaced because it was felt that they were attempting to "gouge the public." On occasion, the government has undertaken such operations because the magnitude of the task to be performed was beyond the resources of private producers. And some governmental enterprises came into being partly to provide the government with a "yardstick" to measure the performance of private producers.

The lending activities of the federal government furnish a useful illustration of governmental operation to provide needed services and to facilitate economic development. By establishing a number of agencies or lending services within agencies, the government has entered the business of banking and finance. Principal lending agencies include:

Export-Import Bank
Federal National Mortgage Association
Federal Housing Authority
Government National Mortgage Association
Federal Home Loan Mortgage Corporation
Small Business Administration
Veterans Administration

Not all federal credit agencies lend money—some of them merely guarantee loans or deposits made by private lenders. Each is designed to reduce the difficulty of obtaining credit in a particular field by placing the credit of the federal government behind that of the borrower. Collectively, these federal programs are intended to encourage certain kinds of economic activity by providing individuals, businesses, and government agencies with credit at lower interest rates, with longer maturities, and so on, than are available in the private market.

The volume of federal credit activity has been expanding significantly—quadrupling in the decade 1967–77—but most of it does not show up in the budget. Thus the budget understates the full extent of the federal government's impact on the economy. Moreover, since they are not part of the budget, these credit programs escape the periodic scrutiny given to regular budget outlays.

Government also pursues policies intended to influence the over-all level of economic activity. The stabilization of the level of income and employment has become an accepted economic activity of the federal government. Its major tools for this purpose are the fiscal and monetary controls discussed in Chapter 7. During war, however, the government may expand its controls and adapt many of its existing regulations, aids, and other programs to the larger purposes of expanding and directing nation-wide production and to controlling prices. Price and wage controls, rationing, and priorities are frequently used to meet such emergencies. Furthermore, monopoly controls may be relaxed, credit regulations may be changed, taxes on investments may be reduced, and governmental operation of enterprises may be expanded to meet the immediate necessities of war. Over-all control of the economy in wartime generally results in setting aside temporarily many of the basic features of our economic system.

In summary, governmental activity affects the operation of the economy by:

Providing some of the necessary framework for private economy activity;

Promoting and aiding various kinds of private activity;

Controlling and regulating certain types of private economic activity;

Owning and operating some forms of economic activity;

Influencing the level of income, employment, and prices.

Whatever the government does will, directly or indirectly, affect national income and production. The following are some of the ways this influence might be felt if, for instance, the government should decide to spend an additional $10 billion for sewage treatment.

1. *The allocation of resources will be different from what it would have been without the governmental program.* Unless there are unemployed resources (natural resources, labor,

capital, and skills) available, there will first be a shift of resources into the production of sewage facilities. If the government obtains the $10 billion by taxing or borrowing from the public, resources will not go into producing those things that people would have bought if they had kept their money. The national income will be produced differently and will consist of different items.

2. *The program of the government will influence the way the national income is distributed.* This changed allocation of resources will probably occur as a result of changing prices (if all the resources are fully employed). For the government to get the materials for its building program, it will have to bid them away from present uses; it will have to pay enough to cause workers and other resources to shift into the production of different things. If the level of national income remains the same, those who receive incomes from producing pollution-control facilities will tend to receive a larger share, and those in some other industries a smaller share of the national income.

3. *The program could change the level of resource use and the level of national income.* If there are unemployed resources available, the government's decision may not only shift the *allocation* of resources, but it may also change the *amount* of resources used. This might happen if the program changed aggregate demand in the economy. If the additional taxes to pay for the program are paid without a corresponding drop in private spending, total spending will rise and the level of production and employment will tend to rise. In a period of rising prices, the rise in spending will contribute to inflationary pressures. On the other hand, if the taxes that are levied should cause a sharp cut in private spending by more than $10 billion, the governmental program could conceivably lead to a decline in the over-all level of national income and employment.

The taxes must be collected by some plan. They might be collected according to a "benefit principle" so that the people pay taxes in accordance with the benefit they would be expected to derive from environmental improvement; or they might be taxed according to their "ability to pay," so that those who were deemed least able to afford the tax would pay less and others would pay proportionately more. The tax might also be made an equal amount for everyone. Or it could be a sales tax so that the individual paid in relation to his purchases of taxable goods; it could be a progressive income tax or a proportional income tax; it could be a property tax (not for the federal government, however), or it could be a tax on corporation income, liquor, gasoline, or imported commodities. Whichever tax is used will have an influence on some people that it does not have on others. Whatever way the tax burden is distributed will influence the distribution of "after-tax income" and will therefore influence the way the nation's disposable income is spent. Moreover, if the tax reduces the rewards of some kinds of business, again, the allocation of resources and the composition of national income will be changed. If it seriously distorts the pattern of incentives for the whole society, it may lead to a decline in economic effort and a reduction in the level of resources used. If it increases the volume of total spending, it will raise the *level* of national income.

The indirect effects of governmental policy may be more significant than the observable direct results. In the above illustration, the direct effect may have been better pollution control and higher taxes, but, as we saw, the indirect effects on the level, composition, and distribution of national income would significantly influence the ultimate welfare of the public.

If the government supports subsidies for agriculture, municipal sewage plants, tariffs, or electric power plants, it will change the characteristics of the nation's income and production from what they would be if the forces of the market were allowed to operate without the additional influence of government. Moreover, even though the government does not spend any more than is required for administering the necessary agencies, such activities as anti-monopoly laws, deposit insurance, "fair labor standards," or security regulations will change the pattern of the economy. In other words by setting the "rules of the game" the government takes some decisions away from the area of individual discretion—in doing so, it modifies the performance of the economic system.

It is because *the government can change the operation of the economy that society uses governmental processes.* As many of the chapters in this book have shown, the public does not believe that the results obtained from the free market are always the most desirable. Through the government, the public has modified the operation of the economy by a variety of controls, aids, sanctions, regulations, and other activities. The result is a "mixed economy," in which government and the free market are combined to determine the level, composition, and distribution of the nation's production.

SOME PROBLEMS OF DETERMINING GOVERNMENTAL ECONOMIC POLICIES

One of the most important problems confronted by society is to decide what governmental policies should be. What exactly is it that the American people want their government to do? As noted earlier, the answers to this question are constantly changing. Moreover, it is not sufficient to say, for example, that "full employment" is an objective; as shown in Chapter 6, opinions differ over what constitutes "full" employment. Broad generalizations do not provide adequate guides for economic policy. Ultimately, governmental policy is determined on specific issues, and broad policies—such as "conservation of resources," "maintaining competition," "a fair distribution of income"—must constantly be interpreted or redefined to fit these specific issues.

Deciding what governmental policy will be is further complicated by the fact that the public has conflicting objectives. Some people want high interest rates, and others want a large volume of credit, some want a large defense program, and others want lower taxes—somehow, these conflicting objectives must be resolved. Governmental economic activity, therefore, is similar to private economic activity in that it involves "economizing." The government cannot do everything it may want to do (even if people are willing to have it do so), because whenever one thing is done, something else cannot be done. A basic task of government, then, is to decide which of a variety of alternative courses will yield the greatest social benefits in relation to the social costs.

Deciding between alternatives by measuring a benefit-cost relationship is not easy. Consumers in the market place can make such benefit-cost calculations when they are considering alternative purchases. They do so by comparing the benefits they expect to receive from a known purchase with those they expect to receive by spending their money for something else. But in contemplating a governmental program, the process is much more complicated. The cost of a price stabilization program, for instance, involves more than the money spent by the government; it may also involve the loss of a certain amount of economic freedom for producers, the use of some of the nation's resources in a seemingly wasteful manner, a tendency to create expectations that the government will solve economic problems, the erection of trade barriers between this and other nations, the actual destruction of some of the nation's production, or shifts in the balance of economic power among various groups in the society. How is the citizen to measure these costs to enable him to compare them with the benefits of the program? What are the benefits of the program? Precise measurement of the economic, political, and social consequences of governmental policy is virtually impossible.

Except in the very broadest terms, the citizen does not attempt to weigh costs versus benefits. When the voter is given an opportunity to vote directly on a given issue (such as a school bond issue), he can perform such a calculation. He can compare the monetary and other costs with the benefits— as he sees them from a personal or social point of view. On most issues, though, the citizen cannot do this. The costs may be unknown and the benefits highly uncertain. Moreover, he often must choose by voting for a representative who will vote on this and many other issues. The citizen, in other words, often casts his vote for a vast complex of decisions—he votes for "a package" and must take the bad with the good. It is not possible to say, therefore, that governmental policy is a reflection of the rational cost-benefit calculations of the people. The most that can be said is that governmental policy can represent, in a very general way, the broad consensus of desires of the people.

It is sometimes suggested that the problem would be simplified if the government would adopt a few basic "principles" and live by them. But government operates under constantly changing conditions, and principles that are broad enough to offer guidance for all conditions are usually too broad to offer a basis for choice in a particular situation. For example, considerable effort has been made to follow the principle of "maintaining a free competitive system." But it is sometimes argued that the way to preserve the system is to abandon the principle in particular instances. In the end, principles that cannot be uniformly followed become themselves matters of choice. No short cut to an estimate of benefits and costs exists for the public official, the legislator, or the citizen.

Public policy decisions are influenced by group or sectional pressures. The activities of lobbies in securing the passage of legislation favorable to the groups they represent have become a basic part of governmental processes in this country. By being on the scene when legislation is being considered, by providing details on the issues involved (details favorable to their position), and by developing "contacts" among the administrators of governmental programs, lobbies can influence the course of governmental activities. The growing number of lobbies in the federal and state capitals indicates the importance of this type of activity—it also indicates, perhaps, that the effectiveness of any given lobby can be offset by another. Thus some legislative proposals evolve into quarrels between representatives of opposing groups, for example, between the National Association of Manufacturers and the AFL-CIO, between environmentalists and advocates of nuclear power, and between the American Cancer Society and cigarette companies.

Additional influence on public policy comes from governmental officials. Administrative officials in government have ideas about how a program should be carried out; they are seldom mere automatons who carry out a definite program set down by the people. In fact, the range of discretion provided by legislation leaves a vast number of decisions to the administrative branch of government. The officials, therefore, argue for the kind of program that will, in their view, be better from the standpoint of society or from that of their own agency. Moreover, conflicts between agencies frequently arise. For instance, there is a long history of conflict between the Army Corps of Engineers and the Bureau of Reclamation of the Department of the Interior over the development of the nation's rivers. More recently, the conflict between the Department of Energy and the Environmental Protection Agency has illustrated the difficulty of reconciling programs with differing objectives.

These are but a few of the problems associated with attempts of society to accomplish social objectives through the instrument of government. Several points bear emphasizing. The government is more than a collection of individuals. Decisions regarding governmental action are not made in the same way that private decisions are made. The machinery of government becomes more complicated as the role played by the government becomes larger; it is frequently too complicated to understand, in all its minute details. Nevertheless, careful analysis of particular activities can yield greater understanding of the important consequences of governmental policy. And as careful and dispassionate economic analysis is more widely employed, public policies may be more rationally chosen to promote an effective economy and the general welfare.

The Problem and the Issues

The Social Security Act was passed in 1935 to help provide retirement income for the elderly and their dependents. Although about half the states had some form of old-age and survivors' protection at that time, coverage and benefits were spotty. The new law established for the first time a uniform system for the nation.

Originally, the coverage of the act was limited to about 60 per cent of the employed population. Agricultural workers were excluded, and so were domestic employees, governmental employees, employees of nonprofit agencies, and the self-employed.

Costs were initially modest as well. The program was

financed by contributions by employers and employees, and even twenty years after passage of the act the tax on each was only 2.25 per cent of the first $4,200 of the employee's salary. But a schedule of step increases was established that was intended to raise the rate for both employers and employees to 4.25 per cent by 1975 and then remain at this figure.

Over the years, the coverage of the program was expanded to about 90 per cent of the work force. Today, federal employees, some state and local employees, and some nonprofit employees are the major groups that do not participate. The scope of the program was expanded to include hospital insurance and medical care for the elderly. Benefits have been increased greatly too. Thus the costs of the social security system have increased enormously. The burden was made heavier by inflation, which reduced the value of earlier contributions and led to the need to escalate the pensions beyond the sums originally contemplated. The number of workers on disability also increased.

By the mid-1970s, annual social security payments were exceeding annual tax receipts, and the trust funds that had been set up to assure the permanence of the system were being dissipated. The fund's assets, which at one time had been equal to 100 per cent of annual outlays, had declined to 41 per cent by the end of 1977. Exhaustion of the old-age and survivors' insurance trust fund by the early 1980s was anticipated.

The need for remedial action was widely recognized, and in 1977, legislation was enacted that eased the immediate crisis by correcting a flaw in the system that had led to payment of excessive benefits to newly retired workers and by raising payroll taxes. Effective in 1979, the tax rate on both employers and employees was 6.13 per cent, and a schedule of future increases would raise the rate to 7.65 per cent in 1990, where it would remain. The biggest change was the increase in the wage base on which the tax was levied. It was scheduled to rise from $16,600 in 1977 to $22,900 in 1979 and to $34,800 in 1983. Workers would pay more money in taxes even without a change in the tax rate.

These emergency changes took care of the immediate

problem, but they left unsettled some basic issues that have been the subject of debate for many years: the impact of the rapid rise in payroll taxes on wage earners in the lower brackets and the capacity of the system to provide benefits when the postwar baby-boom generation reaches retirement age, in 2015 and after. At that time, the retirement population, which is now about nineteen persons per hundred aged 19–65, will rise to thirty-four persons—a virtual doubling.

The Objectives

The original objective of the social security legislation was to provide retirement income for workers and death benefits for their dependents. The program was later expanded to include disability insurance and medical and hospital care. With these goals now largely achieved, at least for the time being, the major objective of any reform of the law would be to put the financing of the program on a firm long-run basis. Financing should be flexible enough to cope with future changes in economic conditions and in the proportion of the population that is retired. The reform would have to be politically acceptable to the present generation and should not pass along an undue burden to the future.

The Alternatives

One alternative is to muddle through, making short-run adjustments as a financial crisis looms and modifying the scope of the program in line with changing political requirements. This approach runs the risk that the government may not be able to respond quickly enough on short notice, and it increases the danger that future generations may find the financial resources of the system utterly inadequate. If this inadequacy is perceived but ignored, confidence in the social security system would be undermined long before disaster overcomes it.

A second alternative is to abandon the contributory approach on which the system was founded. Since there is already a large gap between the pensions that retirees receive and what they would receive under a true insurance system set up in accord with actuarial practices, there is a logical case for divorcing benefits and contributions entirely. The proponents of this point of view state that benefits should be financed out of general revenues. The level of benefits could be flexible and could reflect economic and political realities on a current basis.

Another alternative is to divorce the retirement program and death benefits from the welfare payments that have been added in recent years. If this were done, the payroll tax rate could be reduced by about one third and the retirement and death benefits could be more reasonably related to contributions. The rest of the benefits—particularly medical care—are not related to earnings, working life, or retirement prospects. Rather, they are properly regarded as part of the welfare program and should be supported out of general revenues. The welfare portions of the program might be folded into the Supplemental Security Income program, administered by the Social Security Administration, for the elderly, the blind, and the disabled. It is financed from general revenues.

Appraising the Alternatives

Economic analysis of social security policy, as well as of other policy issues discussed in this book, deals with only one dimension of the decision. Economists can estimate tax receipts and payments under alternative proposals, the long-run financial viability of the system, the fairness of treatment of various groups of contributors and beneficiaries in this generation and from one generation to the next, and the impact of the system on economic growth and stability. Elected officials and government administrators, on the other hand, are concerned not only about these economic issues but also about the workability of the system and public support for it. The first alternative identified above thus represents a kind of fallback position indicating what will probably happen if neither of the alternative proposals wins widespread public support. The risks associated with muddling through are more of a long-run nature, whereas the advantages of postponement may have an immediate .attractiveness to elected officials who are uncertain about the merits and political acceptability of the alternatives. Government administrators may be split between those who are resistant to change and those who are preoccupied with the long view.

Abandoning the contributory approach has an advantage but it runs up against the uncertainty of public attachment to the principle that there should be a link between wages and retirement income. One advantage of the proposal to separate the welfare and retirement systems is that the financial base of the retirement system would thereby be protected from the drain of funds to provide welfare protection. Moreover, the regressive effects of the payroll taxes would be eliminated. The present system, they argue, places too heavy a burden on low-income groups.

These specific illustrations of alternatives are linked to broader concerns. The rapid pace of change has forced new responsibilities on government. New technology and the great increase in urbanization have made people more dependent on each other and on public services. Family life has changed. Young people have found it easy to move from one part of the country to another, and older people have preferred, when they could afford to do so, to live apart from their children and thereby reduce their feelings of dependency.

These changes have been reflected in all aspects of government operations, and they have been felt very acutely in the areas of welfare and retirement. The problem in this chapter is focused on one aspect of the effort to provide American families with security against poverty and protection against disability and illness in old age. In the mid-1930s, the proposal for a social security program, though highly controversial and possibly difficult to implement, seemed relatively straightforward. Today, coverage and benefits are far greater than they were envisioned when the program was started, though some inadequacies and inequities remain. Nevertheless, despite the progress, the policy problems posed by social security loom almost as large as they did then. They are different, but not less challenging. The focus has shifted from providing minimum protection, which has been largely achieved, to a more ambitious goal of providing coverage of income and health needs under a system for financing that will be able to maintain the integrity of a system linked to contributions and that is expected to fulfill its long-term obligations to future generations.

While many people applaud the changes that have been wrought by the extension of government services over the years, others worry about the weakening of social institutions that used to enable people to cope with problems of income and medical care with less reliance on government. To what extent, if any, is the gain in government services offset by a loss of services formerly provided by the family, friends, and voluntary institutions? Is too much being spent today on such governmental protections?

Expressions of satisfaction and dissatisfaction with what has been achieved and what needs to be done today partly reflect the fact that modern human societies tend to redefine problems, rather than to solve them. In part, we keep raising our sights; in part, we create new problems when we try to solve old ones; in part, some problems probably aren't solvable. Certainly we have raised our sights for the social security program; benefits that once seemed very generous look skimpy years later. New problems arise from unforeseen side effects, such as the rapid rise in the payroll taxes that finance social security and that place a disproportionate burden on low-wage groups. Probably there is no way to assure protection against the hazards of old age that will fully satisfy everyone. The purpose of economic analysis is to provide a systematic way of sorting out and assessing the alternatives for coping with a continually changing stream of problems.

As we have noted before, decisions on proposals must be made. And if we want to have a role in deciding the economic conditions under which we live, we must help make these decisions. If we do not, someone else will. All of us can do a better job of establishing such policy if we undertake a careful analysis of our goals and alternative methods of attaining them.

Suggested Reading

George L. Bach, *Economics: An Introduction to Analysis and Policy,* Chap. 37. Paul A. Samuelson, *Economics,* Chap. 8, pp. 147–62. These selections cover three major topics: (1) the expansion of the functions of government, (2) the economic problems of war mobilization, and (3) the similarities and differences between the American economy and those economic systems in which government plays a larger role. Most of the selections in *Readings in Economics* (Samuelson et al., eds.) are related in one way or another to the issues of the economic role of government. See especially "On Improving the Economic Status of the Black American," by James Tobin, pp. 265–69, and "Planning and the Market in the U.S.S.R.," by Abram Bergson, pp. 366–70.

INDEX

46A